Luca Patrizi

In the Presence of the King

Theology and Tradition in Islam: Studies on Prophecy, Transmission, and Spirituality

Edited by
Francesco Chiabotti, Luca Patrizi, and
Ruggero Vimercati Sanseverino

Volume 1

Luca Patrizi

In the Presence of the King

Intermediation and Intercession in Islam

DE GRUYTER

First published in Italian © Editrice Morcelliana srl, *Al cospetto del Re. Intermediazione e intercessione nell'Islam*, Brescia 2023.

ISBN 978-3-11-150087-4
e-ISBN (PDF) 978-3-11-150096-6
e-ISBN (EPUB) 978-3-11-150120-8
ISSN 2942-6499

Library of Congress Control Number: 2025931479

Bibliographic information published by the Deutsche Nationalbibliothek
The Deutsche Nationalbibliothek lists this publication in the Deutsche Nationalbibliografie; detailed bibliographic data are available on the Internet at http://dnb.dnb.de.

Cover image: Part of a Hadith transmitted on the authority of Abū Dardā', mentioned in the compilations of Ibn Ḥanbal, Tirmidhī, and Ibn Mājah. Calligraphy by Mohammed Serrhini. Translation: "Truly, the scholars are the heirs of the prophets, and truly, the prophets do not leave behind them gold or silver, they only leave knowledge as their heritage; so whosoever seizes it has acquired a bountiful fortune".
Printing and binding: CPI books GmbH, Leck

www.degruyter.com
Questions about General Product Safety Regulation:
productsafety@degruyterbrill.com

MIX
Papier | Fördert gute Waldnutzung
FSC www.fsc.org
FSC® C083411

The Prophet's proximity to God in Paradise
is like the position of the vizier in relation to the king

ʿAbd al-Jalīl ibn Mūsā al-Qaṣrī al-Anṣārī (d. 1211–12),
The Branches of Faith (*Shuʿab al-īmān*)

Contents

Transliteration table

ء	ʾ	ط	*ṭ*
ا	*a*	ظ	*ẓ*
ب	*b*	ع	ʿ
ت	*t*	غ	*gh*
ث	*th*	ف	*f*
ج	*j*	ق	*q*
ح	*ḥ*	ك	*k*
خ	*kh*	ل	*l*
د	*d*	م	*m*
ذ	*dh*	ن	*n*
ر	*r*	ه	*h*
ز	*z*	و	*ū*
س	*s*	ي	*ī*
ش	*sh*	آ	*ā*
ص	*ṣ*	ة	*a/t*
ض	*ḍ*	ى	*ā*

https://doi.org/10.1515/9783111500966-001

Translations

Quotations from the Bible are taken from:
NRSVCE translation.

Quotations from the Qur'ān, modified by the author where it was deemed necessary, are taken from:
The Qur'ān. Translated into English by Alan Jones. Cambridge: Gibb Memorial Trust, 2007.

https://doi.org/10.1515/9783111500966-002

Collections of sayings of the prophet Muḥammad (*ḥadīth*)

Abū Dāwūd, Sulaymān ibn al-Ash'ath al-Azdī al-Sijistānī. *Sunan Abī Dāwūd*, 7 vols. Bayrūt: Dār al-risāla al-'ālamiyya, 2009.

al-Ḥākim al-Nīsābūrī, Abū 'Abd Allāh Muḥammad ibn 'Abd Allāh. *al-Mustadrak 'alā al-ṣaḥīḥayn.* Bayrūt: Dār al-kutub al-'ilmiyya, 2002.

Bukhārī (al-), Muḥammad. *al-Adab al-mufrad.* al-Qāhira: al-Matba'a al-salafiyya, 1955.

Bukhārī (al-), Muḥammad. *Ṣaḥīḥ al-Bukhārī*, 8 vols., ed. Markaz al-buḥūth wa taqniyyat al-ma'lūmāt, al-Qāhira/Bayrūt: Dār al-tāṣīl, 2012.

Dārimī (al-), 'Uthmān ibn Sa'īd. *Sunan.* Bayrūt: Dār al-kitāb al-'arabī, 1986.

Ibn Ḥanbal, Aḥmad. *Musnad al-imām Aḥmad ibn Ḥanbal*, 50 vols. Bayrūt: Mu'assasat al-risāla, 1997.

Ibn Mājah, Abū 'Abd Allāh Muḥammad ibn Yazīd. *Sunan ibn Mājah.* Bayrūt: Mu'assasat al-risāla nāshirūn, 2009.

Muslim ibn al-Ḥajjāj. *Ṣaḥīḥ Muslim*, 8 vols., ed. Markaz al-buḥūth wa taqniyyat al-ma'lūmāt. al-Qāhira/Bayrūt: Dār al-tāṣīl, 2014.

Nasā'ī (al-), Abū 'Abd al-Raḥmān Aḥmad ibn Shu'ayb. *Sunan al-Nasā'ī.* Bayrūt: Mu'assasat al-risāla nāshirūn, 2014.

Ṣan'ānī (al-), 'Abd al-Razzāq, ibn Hammām. *al-Muṣannaf*, 12 vols. Bayrūt: al-Maktaba al-Islāmī, 1973.

Suyūṭī (al-), Jalāl al-Dīn. *al-Jāmi' al-ṣaghīr fī aḥādīth al-bashīr al-nadhīr*, 2 vols. Bayrūt: Dār al-kutub al-'ilmiyya, 2004.

Ṭabarānī (al-), Abū al-Qāsim Sulaymān ibn Aḥmad ibn Ayyūb al-Lakhmī. *al-Mu'jam al-ṣaghīr li-l-Ṭabarānī*, 2 vols. Bayrūt: Dār al-kutub al-'ilmiyya, 1973.

Tirmidhī (al-), Abū 'Īsā Muḥammad ibn Sawra. *Sunan al-Tirmidhī.* Bayrūt: Mu'assasat al-risāla nāshirūn, 2011.

https://doi.org/10.1515/9783111500966-003

Abbreviations

EI²: *Encyclopaedia of Islam, Second Edition*, edited by Peri Bearman, Thierry Bianquis, Clifford Edmund Bosworth, Emeri van Donzel, Wolfhart Peter Heinrichs, 1954–2005. (online, https://referenceworks.brillonline.com/browse/encyclopaedia-of-islam-2)

EI³: *Encyclopaedia of Islam, THREE*, Kate Fleet, Gudrun Krämer, Denis Matringe, John Nawas and Devin J. Stewart (eds.), 2007–. (online, https://referenceworks.brillonline.com/browse/encyclopaedia-of-islam-3)

EQ: *Encyclopaedia of the Qurʾān*, Jane Dammen McAuliffe, Johanna Pink (eds.), 2001–. (online, https://referenceworks.brillonline.com/browse/encyclopaedia-of-the-quran)

EIr: *Encyclopaedia Iranica*, Ehsan Yarshater and Encyclopædia Iranica Foundation (eds.), 1985–. (online, https://www.iranicaonline.org/)

EJ: *Encyclopaedia Judaica, 2nd ed.*, 22 vols., edited by Michael Berenbaum and Fred Skolnik (Detroit: Macmillan Reference USA, 2007).

https://doi.org/10.1515/9783111500966-004

Introduction

Within the field of Islamic studies, there has long been a tendency to view the Islamic religion as essentially oriented towards orthopraxis and jurisprudence, with an absolutely marginal role reserved for theology. This view has spread even among the general public, and it still represents one of the main components of the unchanging projection of the Islamic religious world in the modern and contemporary Western world. According to this view, after the formative phase of Islam, between the eighth and tenth centuries, when the main theological doctrines were elaborated, and clashes, even violent ones, took place between the various factions, the development of theology in the Sunnite context came to a halt and underwent a progressive fossilisation that relegated it to the rear of jurisprudence. This position is certainly reductive and does not do justice to the importance of theology in the religious and political history of Islam. A number of studies show how such an essentialist and monolithic view of Islam developed in the milieu of the first Western specialists in Islamic studies from the eighteenth and nineteenth centuries onwards, and how their culture, mostly coming from a Protestant background, exerted a substantial influence on the conclusions they arrived at.[1] On the other hand, as we shall see, the study of Judaism also fell victim to similar prejudices for a long time, which did not do full justice to the complex theological elaboration within the Jewish religion.

It was precisely between the eighteenth and nineteenth centuries, in the context of Islamic societies, that the literature produced by these scholars of Islam began to spread among and exert a profound influence on reformist Muslim intellectuals. This, added to the religious reformist tendency already present in the Islamic world in this period and the great influence that these Muslim intellectuals have in turn exerted on the culture of Islamic countries up to the present day, resulted in the spread of an image of the relationship between theology and jurisprudence in Islam that does not correspond, as we shall see, to the empirically observable reality. Another consequence is that academic studies on Islamic theology have always been scarce compared to the research available on other areas of Islamic knowledge, such as history, orthopraxy, jurisprudence, philosophy or esoteric and mystical doctrines.[2]

1 Carl William Ernst, *Following Muhammad: Rethinking Islam in the Contemporary World* (Chapel Hill & London: The University of North Carolina Press, 2003), 47–69.

2 Tim Winter, "Introduction," in *The Cambridge Companion to Classical Islamic Theology*, edited by Tim Winter (Cambridge: Cambridge University Press, 2008) 1–2; S. Schmidtke, *Introduction*, in

https://doi.org/10.1515/9783111500966-005

The aim of this study is therefore to enrich our knowledge of Islamic theology by analysing two specific and closely interconnected notions: intermediation and intercession. As we shall see, these two concepts occupy a very important place in the Islamic theological and eschatological framework, but despite this, they have not enjoyed much attention in Islamic studies so far.

Theology in Islam

Islam is a religion that originated and developed in close contact with two other religions in particular, Judaism and Christianity. It very quickly supplanted the polytheistic – or rather henotheistic – cults prevalent in the environment in which it was born and developed, namely in Mecca, in the Ḥijāz region of the Arabian Peninsula, during the seventh century. Although many ritual characteristics of pre-Islamic cults will be preserved in the context of Islamic religious practices, from a theological point of view, the doctrine of the Unity of God, in Arabic *tawḥīd*, asserts itself overwhelmingly.

When one thinks of theology, reference is usually made to the elaboration, by a class of religious scholars, of the doctrines and beliefs of a particular religion, through reasoning and language and the use of specific technical terminology. The Greek term *theologia* itself means, as is well known, "discourse about God", and the corresponding Islamic term, *ʿilm al-kalām*, "science of speech (or discourse)" – implied, "about God" – possesses the same meaning, having been formed in a context of Muslim scholars who possessed extensive knowledge of Greek theology and philosophy, and often also of Christian theology. However, this is the scientific point of view, which presupposes a study and systematisation of material drawn from primary sources, thus the basis on which theology is built as a science. From the point of view of religion, on the other hand, the main doctrines, such as the Unity of God and, for example, the doctrine of intermediation and intercession, emerge clearly already from the Qurʾān and the sayings of the prophet Muḥammad (*ḥadīth*) and are only later studied and systematised by Muslim specialists in theology. These same specialists are at the beginning scholars of various Islamic sciences, and not only of theology, as is the case with Abū Ḥanīfa al-Nuʿmān (d. 767), the famous founder of the eponymous legal school (*al-madhhab al-ḥanafī*) but whose teaching is, at the same time, at the origin of the first theological treatise to have come down to us, "The Greatest Understanding" (*al-Fiqh*

Schmidtke, S. (ed.), *The Oxford Handbook of Islamic Theology*, (Oxford: Oxford University Press, 2016), 5–7.

al-akbar). This indicates that, within Islam, the boundary between theology and jurisprudence is much less marked than one might think.

What are the fundamental principles that emerge from the primary sources? These are six principles, the most important of which is, of course, the doctrine of the Unity of God, on which all the main subdivisions that constitute the Islamic religious landscape agree, in particular Sunnism, Twelver and Ismaili Shiʿism and the Islamic Reformation movements.[3] The belief in angels (*malāʾika*), in holy books sent by God (*kutub*), in prophets (*rusul*) and the Day of Resurrection (*yawm al-qiyāma*) also finds agreement among the main movements within Islam. On the other hand, the sixth principle, predestination (*al-qaḍāʾ wa al-qadar*), is the one that gave rise to the first theological disputes within Islam, particularly between Sunni ashʿarites and muʿtazilites.

This is the case if one considers God's point of view, whereas if one considers man's point of view, the main theological issue is that of the relationship between faith and deeds, an issue well known also in other religious contexts, where it has historically been at the centre of theological controversies. In the Islamic context, the relationship between faith and deeds has generated much controversy and has characterised the thought of various schools.

Another theological notion that emerges from the primary sources and finds a place in the creeds is the notion of intercession, namely the possibility of an angel or a human being, such as a prophet or even a devout believer, to act as an intermediary vis-à-vis God on behalf of other human beings, in order to obtain the salvation of the soul or the elevation of spiritual degrees. Again, this is not a theological novelty but a well-established notion in the history of religions, as we shall see particularly in Judaism and Christianity. In Christianity, for example, intercession is such a central theological issue that it was one of the main points of disagreement in the schism between the Catholic Church and the Reformed churches. This is also one of the most relevant theological issues in Islam and is undoubtedly one of the main sources of conflict between the different movements that constitute the religious landscape of modern and contemporary Islam. This is because in

3 I will use the formula "Islamic Reformation" to refer to various movements within the world of Islam, which have emerged since the eighteenth century and which propose: a return to the primary sources (Qur'ān and Sunna); a direct reference to the first generations of believers (*al-salaf al-ṣāliḥ*); a partial or total overcoming of the classical Sunnite theological and juridical system and its spiritual and esoteric component (Sufism). These movements are mainly Wahhabism, Salafism and the Society of Muslim Brothers. The use of this formula is justified by the obvious similarities between these movements and certain movements that developed in other religious contexts, and particularly in Christianity during the Protestant Reformation of the fifteenth and sixteenth centuries.

the doctrines of the Islamic Reformation movements, as we shall see, there is a strong opposition to the notion of intercession, and this rejection has often led the reformists, particularly of radical Wahhabi and Salafist affiliation, to enact the systematic destruction of the tombs of the prophets and saints, which are the places where intercession is put into practice. The destruction of holy places, often accompanied by the indiscriminate slaughter of those who frequent them, is one of the most obvious and painful outward signs of the many internal rifts characterising the contemporary Islamic world.

This research was perfected through a number of lectures, seminars, and teaching two master's degree courses. The first at the University of Turin during the 2020/2021 academic year and the second at the Almo Collegio Borromeo (University of Pavia, 2021/2022). I thank the colleagues and students with whom I have established fruitful exchanges concerning the topics addressed in this study. I thank in particular Giovanni Maria Martini, Alessandro Cancian, Sophie Tyser and Matteo Suardi for their re-reading, revision and advice. I would also like to thank the Chair for Hadith Studies and Prophetic Tradition of the Center for Islamic Theology (ZITh) at the University of Tübingen for supporting the translation and Muhammad Babar Arshad for the revision of the English text. Finally, I would like to thank Torsten Wollina and the De Gruyter staff for their full support.

After this brief introduction, I will now begin to present the main characteristics of the notions of intermediation and intercession in the Jewish and Christian contexts, thus laying the groundwork, thanks to the obvious similarities between these different contexts, for the understanding of these notions also in the Islamic context.

Chapter 1
Intermediation and Intercession in the History of Religions

1 The theological notion of intermediation

The notion of intercession proceeds from a primary theological notion that is sometimes called intermediation, particularly in Jewish theology studies.[4] This term derives from the Latin *intermèdius*, composed of *inter* (between) and *medius* (middle), meaning "to stand in the middle", and indicates a state that stands between two realities and, at the same time, represents a link between them. This notion is expressed through a geometric and spatial metaphor, indicating at the same time an intermediate state and a connection between the divine and human worlds. Ancient literature was produced almost exclusively in a religious and cultic context and used a large and ancient reservoir of metaphorical images, which are often still part of the culture of various peoples today. In religious literature, one often finds the idea that the human intellect has limits, and that recourse to metaphor and allegory is necessary to grasp certain theological and metaphysical realities. The main example is that relating to the idea of divine Unity, to express which some theological systems resort to a numerical metaphor, which assumes that the number one is an odd number that cannot be divided and indicates the unity of the divine Principle, which is thus defined as "One", from Plotinus to the so-called "monotheistic" religions. In other contexts, such as some doctrines belonging to Hinduism, a "non-dualistic" formulation is preferred instead.

In addition to the numerical model, the theological discourse often employs another widely used model known as the geometric and spatial model. A metaphor facilitates the transition from the concept of unity to that of multiplicity by positing two distinct realms: a divine realm associated with unity and one or more realms associated with multiplicity. The divine place is metaphorically located at the top, while the place or places connected to multiplicity are located at the bottom. The connection between these two places is properly the theological realm of intermediation, a realm we will explore in the following chapters.

---

4 George Herbert Box, "The Idea of Intermediation in Jewish Theology. A Note on Memra and Shekinah," *The Jewish Quarterly Review* 23, 2 (1932), 103–119.

https://doi.org/10.1515/9783111500966-006

2 Etymology of the term intercession

The notion of intercession in the religious sphere also originates from a metaphor. It derives from the Latin legal term *intercessio*, from *intercedo*, from *inter* (between) and *cedo* (to go, to pass), with the meaning, similar to that of intermediation, of "being in the middle". This term was used to denote a Roman Tribune's right of veto over another magistrate of equal or lesser authority, thus preserving a Plebeian from incurring a definite sanction.[5] Thanks to the process of metaphorical integration of ancient Roman terminology into Christianity, of which the case of the term pontiff (*pontifex*, "bridge-builder") represents one of the most relevant and pertinent examples relating to the symbolism analysed here, the term "intercession" has become part of Christian theological terminology. In this new meaning, it indicates the action of "placing oneself in the middle" by a mediator to "preserve" a person from "eternal punishment". Since its use in Christianity, this term has been employed in major Western languages to refer to a similar theological notion found in other religious contexts.[6]

3 Intermediation and intercession in Judaism

As we have already stated, despite prejudices by modern Western scholars, who have long described it as a tradition tending to be flattened by the legal dimension, Judaism possesses an ancient and complex theological tradition.[7] In a context such as that of Jewish theological studies, which is already poorly endowed with specific research, contemporary specialists in Judaism complain about a lack of monographic studies devoted to intercession and a few studies that underestimate its importance and wide dissemination.[8] These same scholars show, on the contrary,

5 Renzo Lambertini, "Sull'origine e la natura dell'intercessio tribunizia," in *Tradizione romanistica e Costituzione*, ed. Luigi Labruna (Naples: Edizioni Scientifiche Italiane, 2006), 613–632.

6 Jon Balserak et al, "Intercession, Intercessory Prayer," in *Encyclopedia of the Bible and its Reception (EBR)*, Vol. 13, Integrity – Jesuit Order, edited by Dale Clifford Allison et al (Berlin: De Gruyter, 2016), 2–32.

7 Steven Kepnes, ed., *The Cambridge Companion to Jewish Theology* (Cambridge: Cambridge University Press), 2020.

8 François Rossier, *L'intercession entre les hommes dans la Bible hébraïque : l'intercession entre les hommes aux origines de l'intercession auprès des Dieu* (Göttingen: Universitätsverlag Freiburg Schweiz/Vandenhoeck & Ruprecht, 1996), 1–4; Maria Brutti, "The Topic of Intercession in Second Temple Judaism: Between 2 Maccabees and 4 Ezra," in *Understanding Texts in Early Judaism. Studies on Biblical, Qumranic, Deuterocanonical and Cognate Literature in Memory of Géza Xeravits*, edited by Jozsef Zsengellér (Berlin: De Gruyter, 2022), 189–192.

how intercession, in the Jewish tradition, is strongly present in everyday religious practice rather than in theological literature.[9] This is due, in their opinion, to a certain caution against some theological implications underlying it on the part of some Jewish religious authorities, namely the fear that the presence of overly powerful intermediaries could undermine Divine Sovereignty and Justice and even Unity,[10] arguments that we also find in Islamic sources.[11]

Indeed, within medieval Judaism, there is a fear that the request for intercession might turn into an invocation to other entities besides God, even in the case of angels and prophets. We can notice that in the canonical creed attributed to Moses Maimonides (d. 1204), the fifth point states that prayer should be addressed solely and exclusively to God, and that other elements such as the stars, planets and angels should not be used as intermediaries to reach Him.[12]

A further fear that transpires from the ancient Hebrew sources is that of affirming the possibility for the "righteous" (*tzadik*, pl. *tzadikim*) to intervene after death in favour of the living.[13] The general tendency of these sources, therefore, is to state that, in any case, no intercession will retain its validity on the Day of Judgement, a tendency that is also found in some passages of the Qur'ān, which we will analyse below.[14]

The idea of intermediation and intercession is strongly present in Jewish tradition through angelic creatures and certain categories of men, such as prophets, kings, "righteous" and martyrs.[15] Angels and prophets share the intermediary function between the divine and human worlds. The ascension of prophets is also a modality of intermediation, as it brings them closer to the divine world. In the Hebrew exegetical tradition, the ascent to the mountain is, indeed, interpreted as an actual ascension towards God,[16] and non-canonical traditions also de-

9 Roger Le Déaut, "Aspects de l'intercession dans le Judaïsme ancient," in *Journal for the study of Judaism* 1, 1 (1970), 57.

10 Ibid., 51.

11 John Westerdale Bowker, "Intercession in The Qur'an and the Jewish Tradition," *Journal of Semitic Studies* XI, 1 (1966), 81.

12 Marc B. Shapiro, "Maimonides' Thirteen Principles: The Last Word in Jewish Theology?" *The Torah U-Madda Journal* 4 (1993), 187–242.

13 Roger Le Déaut, "Aspects de l'intercession dans le Judaïsme ancient," *Journal for the study of Judaism* 1, 1 (1970), 44.

14 Ibid., 45; John Westerdale Bowker, "Intercession in The Qur'an and the Jewish Tradition," *Journal of Semitic Studies* XI, 1 (1966), 69–82.

15 Roger Le Déaut, "Aspects de l'intercession dans le Judaïsme ancient," *Journal for the study of Judaism* 1, 1 (1970), 40–41; Josef W. Meri, *The Cult of Saints among Muslims and Jews in Medieval Syria* (Oxford-New York: Oxford University Press, 2002), 63.

16 Kaufmann Kohler and Louis Ginzberg, "Ascension," in *Jewish Encyclopedia* 2:164–165.

scribe the seven heavens traversed by Moses until his encounter with God.[17] This ascension allows the prophet to rise to the role of mediator between God and man.[18]

Regarding intercession, specialists in Jewish studies state that there is no specific term to refer to in the Old Testament but a series of formulas.[19] In the book of Job, we find a passage in which ancient exegetes and contemporary specialists discern the earliest biblical reference to angelic intercession. This passage is found in the context of a dialogue between an angel sent by God and Job, in which the angel suggests him a precise intercessory invocation that should enable him to avert the moment of his departure.[20] Another example of angelic intercessory prayer in the Old Testament concerns the prophet Zechariah.[21]

As far as the intercession of prophets is concerned, the oldest biblical reference is the dialogue between God and Abraham, who attempts to intercede to prevent the destruction of Sodom.[22]

The mediator and intercessor prophet par excellence in the Jewish tradition is certainly Moses, given the direct manner of his relationship with God. When his people worship the golden calf, he intercedes with God to prevent the sending of collective punishment.[23] In another passage, after prostrating himself on the ground, he asks for forgiveness for his people[24] and then successfully intercedes to prevent divine punishment from falling upon his people in the form of the plague.[25]

Another central character of the Old Testament, Solomon, goes before the altar when the Ark of the Covenant is introduced into the temple in Jerusalem and, before the assembled congregation, kneels down with his hands outstretched to-

17 Louis Ginzberg, *Legends of The Jews, Translated from the German Manuscript by Henrietta Szold and Paul Radin* (Philadelphia: The Jewish Publication Society, 2003), 1:502–505.

18 Frank H. Polak, "Theophany and Mediator: The Unfolding of a Theme in the Book of Exodus," in *The Book of Exodus*, ed. Marc Vervenne (Leuven: Leuven University Press and Peeters, 1996), 113–147.

19 Jon Balserak et al, "Intercession, Intercessory Prayer," in *Encyclopedia of the Bible and its Reception (EBR)*, Vol. 13, Integrity – Jesuit Order, edited by Dale Clifford Allison et al (Berlin: De Gruyter, 2016), 2–3.

20 *Job* 33:23–34; Dariusz Iwanski, *The Dynamics Of Job's Intercession* (Rome: Pontifical Biblical Institute, 2006).

21 *Zechariah*, 1:12.

22 *Genesis* 18: 23–33.

23 *Exodus* 32:11–14.

24 *Exodus* 34:8.

25 *Numbers* 14:13–20; Michael Widmer, *Moses, God, and the Dynamics of Intercessory Prayer: A Study of Exodus 32–34 and Numbers 13–14* (Tübingen: Mohr Siebeck, 2004).

wards heaven. At this point, he recites an invocation to intercede for his people, to ask God for forgiveness for their sins and mitigate the divine punishment that may descend in the form of drought, famine and disease, war and captivity.[26]

As far as the possibility of the intercession of the "righteous" is concerned, it is attested in various Old Testament passages.[27] The sacrificial function of the Temple priest is also interpreted as a form of intercession, as can be seen, for example, from the passage in which the High Priest Onias offers a sacrifice for the salvation of Heliodorus, and his action achieves the desired result.[28] This idea of sacrifice as intercession will emerge particularly, as we shall see, in Christianity.

Despite the theological precautions mentioned above, in Talmudic and post-Talmudic Judaism, the custom of asking the "righteous" to intercede with God, and visiting their graves after their death to ask for their intercession, was widespread.[29] In the Talmud, we can find some passages that seem to encourage these practices. In one, we find a commentary on the passage in which Moses, during the Exodus, sends the leaders of the Twelve Tribes, the so-called "spies", to explore the Promised Land in order to understand its geography and obtain information on the peoples who inhabit it.[30] The biblical text adds a detail about a stop in Hebron (*Numbers* 13:22). However, according to Talmud exegetes, this passage uses a verb in the singular and thus does not refer to all the envoys but only to Caleb. The visit to the Cave of Machpelah prompted him to make this deviation, where he prostrated himself and asked the Patriarchs buried there to pray for divine Mercy on him.[31]

In another passage of the Talmud, one who has a sick person at home is advised to go to a "righteous one" to ask for mercy for him.[32] A third passage states that devotees visit graves to ask for the intercession of ancestors on their behalf.[33]

---

26 *1Kings*, 22–54.

27 Jon Balserak et al, "Intercession, Intercessory Prayer," in *Encyclopedia of the Bible and its Reception (EBR)*, Vol. 13, Integrity – Jesuit Order, edited by Dale Clifford Allison et al (Berlin: De Gruyter, 2016), 3.

28 *2 Maccabees* 3–40; Maria Brutti, "The Topic of Intercession in Second Temple Judaism: Between 2 Maccabees and 4 Ezra," in *Understanding Texts in Early Judaism. Studies on Biblical, Qumranic, Deuterocanonical and Cognate Literature in Memory of Géza Xeravits*, edited by Jozsef Zsengellér (Berlin: De Gruyter, 2022), 193.

29 Josef W. Meri, *The Cult of Saints among Muslims and Jews in Medieval Syria* (Oxford-New York: Oxford University Press, 2002), 64, 229.

30 *Numbers*, 13.

31 *Sotah*, 34b.

32 *Bava Batra*, 116a.

33 *Ta'anit*, 16a; Josef W. Meri, *The Cult of Saints among Muslims and Jews in Medieval Syria* (Oxford-New York: Oxford University Press, 2002), 215.

Within the Ashkenazi mystical tradition, in the Rhine Valley, the practice of praying to a "special cherub" as an intercessor before the divine Throne became widespread in the Middle Ages. In some sources, this role is directly impersonated by the Shekhinah, the divine Presence.[34]

Some studies also highlight the similarities between this intermediary and intercessory role of the Shekhinah in Judaism and the similar role of Mary in Christianity.[35]

4 Intermediation and *logos* in Judaism

According to the interpretation of the Hellenistic Jewish priest and philosopher Philo of Alexandria (c. 50 AD), God created and governed the world through mediators. The *logos* is the main one, the closest to God. It is immaterial and a faithful image of God, his shadow, specifically defined as 'the firstborn of God'. It is neither uncreated like God nor created like men but occupies an intermediate position. For Philo, *logos* is the bond that holds all things together, binds all parts, and prevents them from dissolving and separating. It is the divine Light offered to men, the source of the world's archetypes, and the synthesis of all intermediate realities: Ideas, Wisdom, angels, Spirit and powers. As far as intercession is concerned, the *Logos* has the function of patron on behalf of humanity and also that of God's envoy to the world.[36] Philo considers the earthly image of the *logos to* be embodied in the priestly function, whose representative par excellence is Moses.[37] He thus takes the notion of *logos* from ancient Greek philosophy but develops it in the Jewish context. This conception of *logos* as an intermediary between the divine and human worlds and as an archetype of the figure of the earthly mediator will return in later centuries, as we shall see, in both the Christian and Islamic contexts.

34 Daniel Abrams, "The Evolution of the Intention of Prayer to the 'Special Cherub': From the Earliest Works to a Late Unknown Treatise," *Frankfurter Judaistische Beiträge* 22 (1995), 1–26.
35 Arthur Green, "Shekhinah, the Virgin Mary, and the Song of Songs: Reflections on a Kabbalistic Symbol in Its Historical Context," *Association for Jewish Studies Review* 26:1 (2002), 1–52.
36 Harry Austryn Wolfson, *Philo: Foundations of Religious Philosophy in Judaism, Christianity, and Islam* (Cambridge, Massachusetts: Harvard University Press, 1962), 1:226–294; Marian Hillar, *From Logos to Trinity: The Evolution of Religious Beliefs from Pythagoras to Tertullian* (Cambridge: Cambridge University Press, 2012), 36–70.
37 John Dillon, "Ganymede as the Logos: Traces of a Forgotten Allegorization in Philo?" *The Classical Quarterly*, New Series, 31, 1 (1981), 184.

5 Intermediation and intercession in Christianity

The notion of intermediation and intercession is deeply rooted in the doctrine and practices of Christianity, starting from the first centuries. The Holy Spirit exercises one mode of intercession that emerges from the sources, interceding for believers.[38] Similarly, the prophecy of Jesus in John's Gospel concerning the *parakletos*, the "comforter" or "advocate" whom God will send after him,[39] is also assimilated to the function of intercession towards believers, and Jesus himself is referred to as *parakletos* in the New Testament, "advocate" for believers vis-à-vis God.[40]

In the New Testament, Jesus already exercised the function of intercessor during his lifetime, as appears from the passage in which he prays for the apostle Simon, thus avoiding a diabolic attack on him.[41] In another passage, he exhorts the devout to ask for what they need in his name.[42] Finally, his long invocation during the Farewell Discourse in John's Gospel is an intercessory prayer before God on behalf of his disciples.[43]

In Christian interpretations, however, the fundamental intercessory function is that exercised by Jesus through his death and after his Resurrection and Ascension into heaven. His death represents a sacrifice for believers with intercessory value, following the tradition of the Jewish atoning sacrifice mentioned above. The Christian sources propose a very complex eschatological metaphor, deeply rooted in Old Testament symbolism and, at the same time, original.[44]

As we have seen, one of the main figures to whom Jewish tradition attributes the intercessory function is the High Priest of the Temple, who intercedes precisely through animal sacrifice, particularly on Yom Kippur, the Day of Atonement. Thanks to the metaphorical and spiritual relationship between the Temple's animal sacrifice and the sacrifice on the cross, Jesus is assimilated to the High Priest of the Hereafter.[45] Jesus' priesthood, unlike the earthly one, is eternal; he is con-

---

38 *Romans*, 8:26–27.
39 *John*, 14:16–17, 26; 15:26; 16:7–8.
40 *1John*, 1–2.
41 *Luke*, 22:31–32; David Crump, *Jesus the Intercessor: Prayer and Christology in Luke-Acts* (Tübingen J.C.B. Mohr – Paul Siebeck, 1992).
42 *John*, 14:13–14; 15:7.
43 *John*, 17:1–26.
44 Lawrence Harvey Schiffman, "Temple, Sacrifice and Priesthood in the Epistle to the Hebrews and the Dead Sea Scrolls" In *Echoes from the Caves: Qumran and the New Testament*, ed. Florentino García Martínez (Leiden: Brill, 2009), 165–176.
45 *Hebrews* 4:14–16; David M. Moffitt, "Jesus as Interceding High Priest and Sacrifice in Hebrews: A Response to Nicholas Moore," *Journal for the Study of the New Testament* 42, 4 (2020), 542–552.

stantly present to intercede for believers.[46] Moreover, unlike the earthly priests, he does not need to offer frequent sacrifices since he has already definitively offered himself as the perfect and final sacrifice.[47] He, who possesses a "greater and more perfect" Temple, does not use in his sacrifice the blood of the victims, but his own blood, which procures purification and eternal redemption for believers.[48] As High Priest, Moses inaugurates the "first covenant" with the blood of the sacrifice, sprinkling the book, the people, the Tent as the prototype of the Temple, and all the furnishings of worship.[49] According to the divine Law transmitted by Moses, the shedding of the blood of the sacrificial victim is necessary to atone for sins and obtain forgiveness. The heavenly realities, on the other hand, had to be atoned for with an even greater sacrifice, and so Jesus appeared in the heavenly Temple before God, offering a single sacrifice and not many as in the earthly Temple, nullifying with the sacrifice of Himself all sins ever committed by men up to that time. He is therefore defined in Christian ancient sources as the "mediator" (*mesitēs*) of a "new covenant", just as Moses was the mediator of the "first covenant".[50] Jesus will reappear at the End of Times to intercede for future sins.[51] The same formulation also appears in *1 Timothy:* "For there is one God; there is also one mediator between God and humankind, Christ Jesus".[52]

The image of Jesus in the writings of the Apostles as a heavenly intercessor is consistent, according to some specialists in Christianity, with many Jewish works from the intertestamental period, which present human beings, particularly prophets, who exercised intercession while on earth and now continue to intercede in heaven.[53]

Another metaphorical dimension related to Jesus' intercessory role is his royal consecration in heaven. The following passage is found in the Psalms:

> The Lord says to my lord, 'Sit at my right hand until I make your enemies your footstool'.[54]

---

46 *Hebrews*, 7:23–25.
47 *Hebrews*, 7:26–28.
48 *Hebrews*, 9:11–14.
49 *Hebrews*, 9:18–21.
50 *Hebrews*, 9:15. D.R. de Lacey, "Jesus as Mediator," *Journal for the Study of the New Testament* 29 (1987), 101–121.
51 *Hebrews*, 9:22–28.
52 *1Timothy*, 2:5.
53 David Crump, *Jesus the Intercessor: Prayer and Christology in Luke-Acts* (Tübingen J.C.B. Mohr – Paul Siebeck, 1992), 154–236.
54 *Psalms*, 110:1.

In the Gospel of Matthew, we find the interpretation of this passage proposed by Jesus himself:

> Now while the Pharisees were gathered together, Jesus asked them this question: "What do you think of the Messiah? Whose son is he?" They said to him, "The son of David." He said to them, "How is it then that David by the Spirit calls him Lord", saying,
>
> "The Lord said to my lord, 'Sit at my right hand, until I put your enemies under your feet'"?
>
> "If David thus calls him lord, how can he be his son?" No one was able to give him an answer, nor from that day did anyone dare to ask him any more questions.[55]

This interpretation is reiterated in the Acts of the Apostles, where Jesus appears seated at the right hand of God,[56] and also in Romans, where it is stated that he "is at the right hand of God, who indeed intercedes for us".[57]

Starting from this conception, from the early Christian period, it is common to define Christ, to use the formula *Pantokrator*, "Almighty", which traces the divine attribute of God's Omnipotence and Sovereignty in Judaism.[58] This assumption is at the origin of the famous depiction of Christ *Pantokrator* in glory, typical of Byzantine art, found especially in apsidal mosaics and frescoes. In it, Jesus is depicted, at the End of Times, dressed in purple, wearing a crown, sitting like an emperor with his sceptre on the throne, and both his robes and the throne and furnishings are studded with precious stones.[59]

As far as the official position of the Catholic Church is concerned, it is useful to refer to the opinion of St. Thomas Aquinas (d. 1274), who, in the *Summa Theologica*, summarises and completes the doctrines of the Church Fathers preceding him, in particular St. Augustine (d. 430). In a question entitled "Of Christ as called the mediator of God and man", he argues that the Pauline statement that "there is also one mediator between God and humankind" indicates that Christ is the perfect mediator, but the Scriptures show that there are also other mediators: the Holy Spirit, angels, prophets, priests, and even, in a negative way, demons.[60] Regarding priests, Thomas states:

---

55 *Matthew*, 22:41–46.
56 *Acts*, 2:33–36.
57 *Romans*, 8:31–34.
58 Jean-Pierre Batut, *Pantocrator: « Dieu le Père tout-puissant » dans la théologie prénicéenne* (Paris: Institut des Études Augustiniennes, 2009).
59 Marina Copsidas, *Le Christ Pantocrator. Présence et rencontre* (Paris: Cerf, 2009).
60 Thomas Aquinas, *The Summa Theologica* (Chicago: William Benton Publisher, 1923), 2:845–846.

> The prophets and priests of the Old Law were called mediators between God and man, dispositively and ministerially, in so far as they foretold and foreshadowed the true and perfect Mediator of God and men. As to the priests of the New Law, they may be called mediators of God and men in so far as they are the ministers of the true Mediator by administering, in His stead, the saving sacraments to men.[61]

Regarding the mediation of Christ, he adds:

> Christ, as God, is in all things equal to the Father. But even in the human nature He is above al men. Therefore, as man, He can be Mediator, but not as God.[62]

Regarding his power of intercession, however, Thomas adds further details:

> Wherefore every absolute will of Christ, even human, was fulfilled, because it was in conformity with God; and consequently His every prayer was fulfilled. For in this respect also is it that other men's prayers are fulfilled, in that their will is in conformity with God, according to *Romans* 8:27: "And He that searcheth the hearts knoweth," that is, approves of, "what the Spirit desireth," that is, what the Spirit makes the saints to desire: "because He asketh for the saints according to God," that is, in conformity with the Divine will.[63]

According to Christian tradition, on the other hand, Mary exercised her intercession even before her Assumption into heaven, but this power was later strengthened.[64] The earliest evidence of the belief in Mary's intercession is very old and is found in the Gnostic text known as the "Apocrypha of the Dormition", and in particular in the Syriac manuscript entitled *Liber Requiei Mariae.* Scholars date this text to the early 5th century, but according to them it would show the development of this idea as early as the 3rd century. These traditions then emerged strongly in Constantinople precisely during the 5th century.[65]

Like Jesus, Mary's Assumption gradually took the form of an ascent to the throne, culminating in her coronation as the "Queen of Heaven". In the case of Mary, the appearance of an iconography associated with this epithet is late, start-

---

61 Ibid., 2:845.

62 Ibid., 2:846.

63 Ibid., 2:826.

64 Michael O'Carroll, "Intercession, Mary's" In *Theotokos. A Theological Encyclopedia of the Blessed Virgin Mary*, ed. Michael O'Carroll (Eugene – Oregon: Wipf and Stock Publishers, 2000), 186–189.

65 Stephen J. Shoemaker, "The Ancient Dormition Apocrypha and the Origins of Marian Piety. Early Evidence of Marian Intercession from Late Ancient Palestine" In *Presbeia Theotokou: The Intercessory Role of Mary across Times and Places in Byzantium (4th-9th Century)*, ed. Leena Mari Peltomaa, Andreas Külzer and Pauline Allen (Wien: Verlag der Österreichische Akademie der Wissenschaften, 2015), 23–39.

ing in the Gothic Middle Ages. In it, she is depicted dressed in royal robes and with a crown on her head. However, according to specialists, the frequency of this iconography in the Christian architecture of the following centuries is sufficient to attest to the widespread diffusion of this belief in the Christian world.[66] Over the centuries, Mary's intercessory function has gradually taken on a central role in Christian religious life, giving rise, for instance, to the practice of the Hail Mary. This prayer incorporates passages from the New Testament and which, at least in the Catholic context, concludes with the intercessory formula "Pray for us sinners, now and at the hour of our death. Amen"[67].

Specialists in Byzantine art have come to isolate three main categories related to Mary: the Virgin of Majesty, the Virgin of Tenderness and the Virgin Protector. We have already observed the first category. The third category originates in Byzantium, and describes the Virgin as protector and mediatrix, interceding for the salvation of humankind, through the Greek term *skepe*, the etymology of which refers to the flesh covering the bones, but also to a garment. According to legend, the Virgin appeared in Constantinople in the Church of the Blacherne, built by Empress Aelia Pulcheria around 450 AD. In the vision, the Virgin appeared surrounded by angels and saints and spread her protective veil or cloak over the population. From this moment on, this term has become synonymous with the Virgin's protection and mediation of believers.[68]

As far as the intercession of saints is concerned, it developed in parallel with the cult of saints, which originated from the cult of martyrs in early Christian epoch. According to the doctrines and practices of Christianity, martyrs, as well as saints, can exercise intercession because of their proximity to Jesus Christ. This concept survives to this day in both Catholic and Orthodox circles[69].

---

66 Philippe Verdier, *Le Couronnement de la Vierge. Les origines et les premiers développements d'un thème iconographique* (Paris: Librarie Philosophique J. Vrin, 1980); Jon Balserak et al, "Intercession, Intercessory Prayer," in *Encyclopedia of the Bible and its Reception (EBR)*, Vol. 13, Integrity – Jesuit Order, edited by Dale Clifford Allison et al (Berlin: De Gruyter, 2016), 23–27.

67 Michael O'Carroll, "Intercession, Mary's" In *Theotokos: A Theological Encyclopedia of the Blessed Virgin Mary*, ed. Michael O'Carroll (Eugene – Oregon: Wipf and Stock Publishers, 2000), 165–166.

68 Philippe Dujardin, "Du rapport aux images religieuses à l'époque moderne: images, médiateurs et médiations," in *Bulletin du Centre de recherche du château de Versailles, Le promeneur de Versailles* (2018).

69 Thomas Scannell, "Intercession (Mediation)," In *The Catholic Encyclopedia*, Vol. 8. (New York: Robert Appleton Company, 1910); Margaret E. Kenna, "Icons in Theory and Practice: An Orthodox Christian Example," *History of Religions* 24, 4 (1985), 345–368.

6 Intermediation and *logos* in Christianity

The ancient Greek idea of *logos* also exerted an undeniable influence on some early Christian circles, to the extent that it appears in the famous *incipit* of the Gospel of John, which reads:

> In the beginning was the Word [*logos*], and the Word was with God, and the Word was God. He was in the beginning with God. All things came into being through him, and without him not one thing came into being. What has come into being in him was life, and the life was the light of all people.[70].

As we noted earlier, in Philo, we find the idea of *logos* as a mediator, embodied from the human point of view by the prophetic figure of Moses. Considering, on the other hand, the complex metaphysical dimension accorded to Jesus in Christianity, it is more complicated here to show the interconnection between divinity and intermediary humanity. For this reason, specialists in Christianity tend instead to emphasise the differences between Philo's conception and the Christian conception.[71] However, it is difficult to deny that more than one analogy can be found between Philo's conception of the *logos* as a mediator between the divine world and the human world and that of Jesus as the image of the *logos* and "perfect mediator" of Christianity.

7 Intermediation and intercession according to the Christian Reformation

The Christian Reformation, from its beginnings in the sixteenth century, strongly opposed the cult of saints approved by the Roman Catholic Church, as well as the notion of the intercession of saints. The conception of the Christian Reformation is that the intercession of Jesus is sufficient for the forgiveness of sins and the obtaining of grace and that this role was not shared with any other creature, as the passage in *1 Timothy* 2:5 about the one mediator indicates. This is also clear in the Protestant creed, which reiterates that Christ is the only mediator between God and man, and the glory belongs to God alone.[72] For this reason, a strong opposition

70 *John*, 1–4.

71 Jules Lebreton, "The Logos," In *The Catholic Encyclopedia*, Vol. 9 (New York: Robert Appleton Company, 1910).

72 Philip Schaff, *The Creeds of Christendom, with a History and Critical Notes: Volume III, The Evangelical Protestant Creeds, with Translations* (New York: Harper & Brothers, 1919), 26.

to the idea of the intercession of angels, Mary and the saints gradually developed within the Christian Reformation.[73] Calvin, for example, in his *Institution of the Christian Religion*, accepts only the intercession of Christ and rejects any other intercession, especially that of the saints.[74] On the other hand, the Council of Trent (1545–1563), which was convened by the Catholic world precisely to counter the criticism brought forward by the Christian Reformation, reaffirmed the value of intercession, not limiting it to Jesus Christ but condemning the excesses to which some of these practices had reached.[75]

This concise analysis of the main features of intermediation and intercession in Judaism and Christianity can undoubtedly serve as a valuable preface to the in-depth analysis of the analogous notion in the Islamic sphere carried on in the following chapters.

73 Paul F. Palmer, "Mary in Protestant Theology and Worship," *Theological Studies* 15, 4 (1954), 519–540; Marc E. Chapman, "A Lutheran Response to the Theme of the Virgin Mary as Mother of God, Icon of the Church and Spiritual Mother of Intercession," *Marian Studies* 48 (1997), 124–125.

74 Jean Calvin, *Institutes of the Christian Religion*, ed. John T. McNeil (Louisville: Westminster John Knox Press, 2006). 2:874–887.

75 Jon Balserak et al, "Intercession, Intercessory Prayer," In *Encyclopedia of the Bible and its Reception (EBR)*, Vol. 13, Integrity – Jesuit Order, edited by Dale Clifford Allison et al (Berlin: De Gruyter, 2016), 19.

Chapter 2
Academic Studies on the Notion of Intermediation and Intercession in Islam

Even in the field of Islamic theology, as we have observed about Jewish theology, there has so far been a substantial lack of scholarly interest in the notion of intermediation and intercession. What follows is an analysis of references to this notion in the main handbooks on Islamic theology and studies on devotion to the prophet Muḥammad. Finally, the scant research devoted entirely to this notion will be analysed.

1 Theology handbooks

In the few studies that attempt a synthesis of Islamic theology in the main European languages, the notion of intermediation and intercession plays an absolutely marginal role.

The famous pioneer of Islamic studies, Ignaz (Ignác) Goldziher, merely mentions the notion of intercession in a few passages both in his *Muhammedanische Studien* (1889–1890)[76] and in his *Vorlesungen über den Islam* ("Lectures on Islam", 1st ed. 1910, 2nd ed. 1925).[77] We will have to wait until the publication of his last work, dedicated to Qur'anic commentaries and entitled *Die Richtungen der islamischen Koranauslegung* ("The Guidelines of the Islamic Interpretation of the Qur'ān", 1920),[78] to find a brief discussion on the notion of intercession. In this passage, Goldziher expounds his view that this notion was gradually formed under the impetus of popular beliefs until it was canonised within Sunnism. Despite this, he argues, as the polemic with the Muʿtazilite rationalists shows, this notion is not consistent with Islamic Qur'anic theology, and for this reason, it was undoubtedly fully derived by Muḥammad from his knowledge of Jewish tradition.[79]

76 Ignaz Goldziher, *Muhammedanische Studien*, 2 vols (Halle: M. Niemeyer, 1889–1890); engl. tr. *Muslim Studies*, 2 vols. (Chicago: Aldine Publishing Company, 1966–1971).
77 Ignaz Goldziher, *Vorlesungen über den Islam. Von Dr. Ignaz Goldziher. Zweite, umgearbeitete Auflage von Dr. Franz Babinger* (Heidelberg: Carl Winter's Universitätsbuchhandlung, 1925); engl. tr. *Introduction to Islamic Theology and Law* (Princeton: Princeton University Press, 1981).
78 Ignaz Goldziher, *Die Richtungen der islamischen Koranauslegung, An der Universität Uppsala gehaltene Olaus-Petri-Vorlesungen.* (Leiden: Brill, 1920).
79 Ibid., 169–172.

https://doi.org/10.1515/9783111500966-007

In Arent Jan Wensinck's *The Muslim Creed,* first published in 1932, we find sporadic references to intercession, especially with reference to the *Waṣiyya* by Abū Ḥanīfa al-Nuʿmān (d. 767). Wensinck suggests that the Sunnis' adoption of the doctrine of intercession originated from the need to counterbalance the rigid Islamic notion of predestination. He also notes that the categories of intercessors are very similar to those of Christianity thus hypothesising the influence of Christian doctrine on Islamic doctrine[80].

In another famous handbook, the *Introduction à la théologie musulmane* by Louis Gardet and M. –M. Anawati, published in 1948, there is no mention of this notion.[81] Later, in 1967, Gardet devoted a few pages to intercession in his *Dieu et la destinée de l'homme,* commenting briefly on some of Wensinck's considerations.[82]

In his *The Formative Period of Islamic Thought,* published in 1973, William Montgomery Watt briefly comments on Wensinck's considerations, adding that, in his view, the Sunni doctrine of intercession arose from an attempt to alleviate the despair that could arise from excessively rigid moral positions such as those of the Kharijites and Muʿtazilites.[83]

In his book *The Theology of al-Shaikh al-Mufid,* published in 1978, Martin J. McDermott develops an intriguing discussion on the notion of intercession, which serves as a focal point of dissonance between Muʿtazilite theology and Twelver Shiʿa theology.[84]

Robert Caspar, in his *Traité de théologie musulmane,* published in 1987, does not mention the notion of intercession at all.[85]

In his voluminous study on the emergence and development of theology in Islam, originally published in German between 1991 and 1995 and then translated into English between 2017 and 2019, Josef van Ess devotes a few pages to interces-

---

80 Arent Jan Wensinck, *The Muslim Creed. Its Genesis and Historical Development* (New York: Barnes & Noble, 1932), 180–183.

81 Louis Gardet et Marie-Marcel Anawati, *Introduction à la théologie musulmane: Essai de théologie comparée* (Paris: Librarie Philosophique J. Vrin, 1948).

82 Louis Gardet. *Dieu et la destinée de l'homme* (Paris: Librairie Philosophique J. Vrin, 1967), 154–156, 311–314.

83 William Montgomery Watt, *The Formative Period of Islamic Thought* (Edinburgh: Edinburgh University Press, 1973), 138.

84 Martin J. McDermott, *The Theology of al-Shaikh al-Mufid (d. 413–1022)* (Beirut: Dar al-Mashreq, 1978), 254–256.

85 Robert Caspar, *Traité de théologie musulmane, t. I, Histoire de la pensée religieuse musulmane* (Rome: Pontificio Istituto di Studi Arabi e d'Islamistica, 1987).

sion,[86] showing how the idea of intercession originates both from pre-Islamic conventions and resorts to the metaphor of divine kingship common to the three Abrahamic religions:

> The *shafāʿa* [intercession] represented a share in the power; one might imagine that Muḥammad did not even prostrate himself but actually sat next to God on the throne. It was thus the Islamic counterpart to Christian redemption; the concept is yet another piece of evidence that God was imagined as a terrestrial monarch.[87]

He then briefly analyses some Qur'anic references to intercession, then summarises some articles on intercession in Islam, and finally focuses on the opinions of prominent theologians of various affiliations.[88]

In Tilman Nagel's The *History of Islamic Theology* published in 2000, there are only a few references to the theological controversy concerning the Prophet's intercession.[89]

In more recent collective volumes devoted to Islamic theology, the notion of intercession is treated, likewise, in a very marginal manner. In *The Cambridge Companion to Classical Islamic Theology*, published in 2008, we find only a few sporadic references to it,[90] while in *The Oxford Handbook of Islamic Theology*, published in 2016, we find a few mentions and no specific treatment of the notion.[91]

2 Studies on devotion to the Prophet

In studies on the figure of the prophet Muḥammad and Muslims' devotion to him, however, the notion of intermediation and intercession is often addressed. The first of these studies, the pioneering *Die person Muhammeds in lehre und glauben seiner gemeinde* (The person of Muḥammad in the teachings and beliefs of his community, 1917), was written by the Swedish theologian, a specialist in the history of religions and Islam in particular, Tor Andræ. Since he perceives in the Qur'ān, which

86 Josef van Ess, *Theology and Society in the Second and Third Centuries of the Hijra, Tr. from German by John O'Kane* (Leiden-Boston: Brill, 2019), 4:606–610.
87 Ibid., 607.
88 Ibid., 608–610.
89 Tilman Nagel, *The History of Islamic Theology From Muhammad to the Present* (Princeton: Markus Wiener Publishers, 2000).
90 Tim Winter, ed., *The Cambridge Companion to Classical Islamic Theology* (Cambridge: Cambridge University Press, 2008).
91 Sabine Schmidtke, ed., *The Oxford Handbook of Islamic Theology* (Oxford: Oxford University Press, 2016).

he considers to be the work of Muḥammad, a certain hesitancy regarding intercession, he concludes by stating that the idea of intercession in Islam derives rather from Judaism than Christianity. His analysis is punctuated with many quotations from the Qur'ān, the *ḥadīth,* and the work of Muslim authors such as Abū Ḥāmid al-Ghazālī (d. 1111) and al-Qāḍī ʿIyāḍ (d. 1149), and he shows good knowledge of the different views of the various theological movements in formative Islam.[92] He also shows a profound understanding of the metaphor of kingship connected to the notion of intermediation and intercession, as we will see later.

In the same year, Max Horten published an essay entitled *Die religiöse Gedankenwelt des Volkes im heutigen Islam* (The Religious Universe of the Peoples in Today's Islam, 1917), in which he dedicates several passages to intercession. He titles one section "Muḥammad as saviour and mediator of grace," and concludes it this way:

> Muḥammad is thus the cardinal point around which the whole of human salvation history and creation in general revolves, the centre of the world in this world and in the Hereafter.[93]

In another section, he briefly introduces the characteristics of the Prophet's intercession, also listing the other categories of intercessors: the angels, the Prophet's Companions, the martyrs, the learned and the saints.[94]

In her pioneering study on manuals related to spiritual practices in Islam, entitled *Muslim Devotions* and published in 1961, Constance Padwick devotes a chapter to the issue of intermediation and intercession, entitled "The Prayer of Mediation: *wasīla, shafāʿa*". Padwick travelled extensively in different areas of the Islamic world as an Anglican evangelical missionary and therefore showed a good understanding of the value of religious practices and devotion of Muslim peoples to the prophet Muḥammad, which is generally underestimated in Islamic studies. His analysis opens with a quotation from Tor Andræ's passage on the metaphor of kingship and continues with a careful analysis, at once linguistic and theological, of the terms *wasīla* and *shafāʿa.* However, the limited number of texts at her disposal does not allow her to appreciate the importance of the notion of general intercession in Islam, which is not strictly related to the Prophet. After examining the idea of intercession in some passages of the Qur'ān, Padwick attempts to show the similarities between the doctrine of intercession in Islam

92 Tor Andræ, *Die person Muhammeds in lehre und glauben seiner gemeinde* (Stockholm: Norstedt & Toner, 1917), 234–244.

93 Max Horten, *Die religiöse Gedankenwelt des Volkes im heutigen Islam* (Halle: Verlag Von Max Niemeyer, 1917), 137 (tr. by the author).

94 Ibid., 333.

and redemption in Christianity. The author then analyses several formulas for requesting intercession with the Prophet, taken from various manuals from different centuries, from which the importance and centrality of this practice clearly emerge. Padwick shows a certain perplexity, because she believes that this practice is not based on the primary sources of Islam but rather on the development of the devotion of Muslim peoples. However, she excludes from her analysis the study of the Prophet's sayings, which would undoubtedly have allowed her to reach less clear-cut conclusions on this question. Finally, the chapter ends with a brief analysis of the Twelver Shiʿite context, where the intermediation and intercession of the Imāms occupy a preponderant space.[95]

In 1981, Annemarie Schimmel published a book on devotion to Muḥammad, entitled *Und Muḥammad Ist Sein Prophet* (And Muḥammad is His Prophet).[96] One of the chapters is entitled "Muḥammad the Intercessor and Blessings Be Upon Him," in which she rightly emphasises a direct relationship between the request for intercession and the prayer of blessing upon the Prophet (*al-ṣalā ʿalā al-nabī*).[97] Thanks to his extensive knowledge of poetic materials in various Islamic languages, Schimmel highlights the transversality of Muslim peoples' recourse to intercession. Islamic devotional literature, particularly poetry, is rich in references to the Prophet's role as mediator and intercessor. The author gives numerous examples from different poems used in devotional songs from various historical periods and geographical areas of the Islamic world, concluding with this sentence, which perfectly summarises the issue:

> There is scarcely any author, be he poet or scholar, 'heretic (*bidʿatī*), drug-addict (*bhāngī*), or wine-bibber', who has not entreated the Prophet's intercession and, to use Jāmī's poetical term, did not 'sow the seed of blessing for the Prophet in the soil of asking for forgiveness.'[98]

3 Studies on intermediation and intercession

The only monograph devoted entirely to the notion of intercession in Islam is a doctoral thesis discussed at the University of Leiden by Taede Huitema in 1936

95 Constance E. Padwick, *Muslim Devotions: A Study of Prayer-Manuals in Common Use* (London: S.P.C.K, 1961), 37–47.

96 Annemarie Schimmel, *Und Muḥammad Ist Sein Prophet* (Dusseldorf/Koln: Eugen Diederichs Verlag, 1981); eng. tr. *And Muhammad Is His Messenger. The Veneration of the Prophet in Islamic Piety* (Chapel Hill and London: The University of North Carolina Press, 1985).

97 Ibid., 92–104.

98 Ibid., 87.

and published the same year under the title *De voorspraak (Shafāʿa) in den Islam* (Intercession (*Shafāʿa*) in Islam).[99] The author's starting point is the considerations introduced earlier on this topic by Tor Andræ and Wensinck.

The first chapter lays the groundwork for understanding the Islamic vision of the Hereafter to set the context for the eschatological promise of intercession. The second chapter gets to the heart of the matter, analysing the Qur'anic occurrences of the notion of intercession and the interpretations of exegetes. Huitema argues, following Wensinck, that the position that emerges from the Qur'ān is not at all favourable towards intercession. He then concludes his argument with this synthesis:

> All these different statements and the vague indications as to who, if any, can act as intercessor, for whom intercession is intended and what its utility is, offer ample scope for speculation and elaboration in different and contradictory directions; although, with the exceptionally great emphasis placed on Allah's permission (*idhn*), it is still surprising that the doctrine of intercession has developed as it has.[100]

Huitema, therefore, considers that, in a context such as Islam, characterised, according to the author, by "an arid formalism and legalism", the formation of the notion of intercession proceeds from the Muslim peoples' precise need, as Wensinck first stated, to "counterbalance the rigid Islamic notion of predestination".[101] Moreover, he considers that this very formation is strongly influenced by Judaism and Christianity. Notwithstanding this premise, he also considers it necessary to highlight some substantial differences. In his opinion, Judaism and Christianity emphasize intercession in life and for the dead, but they do not consider intercession on the Day of Resurrection. In particular, Christianity postulates that Jesus will not be an intercessor on that day, but a judge. Instead, the emphasis of Islamic sources is precisely on the Prophet's role as intercessor in the Last Judgement.[102]

After noting that the Qur'ān does not grant an explicit role to the Prophet in relation to intercession, Huitema considers instead that, in the *ḥadīth*, there are many references to Muḥammad's intercession, both in life and after death, and particularly in an eschatological key. These traditions particularly highlight Muḥammad's pre-eminence over the other prophets on the Day of Judgement.

Huitema then goes on to study different creeds belonging to various subdivisions of Islam. However, he does not seem to appreciate the difference between these various movements, mixing up the information in his possession so that,

99 Taede Huitema, *De voorspraak (*Shafāʿa*) in den Islam* (Leiden: Brill, 1936).
100 Ibid., 16 (author's tr.).
101 Ibid., 62.
102 Ibid., 18–20.

for example, an eighth-century Sunni creed such as that of Abū Ḥanīfa al-Nuʿmān (d. 767) is put on the same context as an eighteenth-century reformist creed such as that of Muḥammad ibn ʿAbd al-Wahhāb (d. 1792). However, he reports in another passage Louis Massignon's opinion: "The neo-hanbalites [Salafists] and Wahhabis declare that the majority of Muslims are polytheists because of their great faith in the intercession of Muḥammad and the saints."[103]

Huitema also devotes a few lines to the practice of the "prayer of blessing on the Prophet" (*al-ṣalā ʿalā al-nabī*), well highlighting its connection with the intercessory request to the Prophet himself. He then dwells on the view of certain authors of Islamic esotericism, in particular Ibn al-ʿArabī (d. 1240) and his school, in relation to intercession,[104] finally concluding with an analysis of Fakr al-Dīn al-Rāzī's (d. 1210) Qur'anic commentary, which he rightly presents as the primary source for appreciating the respective Sunni and Muʿtazilite views on this notion.[105]

The same year (1936), volume IV of the First Edition of the *Encyclopaedia of Islam* was published, where an entry entitled *Shafāʿa*, written by Wensinck, appears. The definition of this term is, in addition to "intercession," also "mediation," and the political and legal meanings of the term are also briefly addressed. Wensinck then returns to his belief that Muḥammad introduced the notion of intercession into the Islamic theological system due to his knowledge of Judaism and Christianity since the categories of intercessors in these different contexts appear similar. He introduces a summary of the Qur'anic passages and *ḥadīth* that deal with intercession, concluding that, as a result of analysing these recurrences, Muslim scholars arrived at the canonisation of the Prophet's intercession through the *ijmāʿ*, the majority consensus of the scholars. The article ends with a brief analysis of the positions of the different theological schools and movements in relation to intercession.[106] In the Second Edition of the *Encyclopaedia of Islam*, Wensinck's entry is almost entirely preserved, reworked by Daniel Gimaret only minimally, and with an updated bibliography. In it, however, a section entitled "[the *shafāʿa*] in popular piety" is added, drafted by Annemarie Schimmel, which is a summary of what she expounded in the chapter on intercession in her text on devotion to the prophet Muḥammad.[107]

---

103 Ibid., 121.

104 Ibid., 115.

105 Ibid., 122–123.

106 Arent Jan Wensinck, "Shafāʿa," In *The Encyclopaedia of Islam. A Dictionary of the Geography, Ethnography and Biography of the Muhammadan Peoples, edited by M. Th. Houtsma, A. J. Wensinck, H.A.R. Gibb, W. Heffening and Lévi-Provençal* (Leiden – London: E.J. Brill, Luzac & Co, 1934), Vol. IV (S-Z), 250–251.

107 Arent Jan Wensinck; Daniel Gimaret and Annemarie Schimmel, "SHAFĀʿA," in *EI*^{2}.

In 1966, in a pioneering albeit incomplete study, John Westerdale Bowker attempted to analyse the similarities between the notion of intercession in Judaism and Islam, mentioned by some scholars before him. Following an analysis of the Qur'ān and canonical and apocryphal Hebrew sources, devoted in particular to Abraham's intercession, Bowker concludes by stating, less peremptorily than his predecessors, that the uncertainty and ambiguity of the sources in both religious contexts could prove that Muḥammad used Jewish materials on this issue to confirm and complete his own conception of intercession.[108]

In 1981, Eva Riad proposed an in-depth analysis of the notion of *shafāʿa*, considering both ancient Arabic literature and Qur'anic occurrences.[109] The first part of the article opens with an original and detailed linguistic and etymological introduction that dwells on the meaning of the root *sh-f-ʿ* as "even" and as "association with something or someone" and then moves on to the social and legal meaning of the term. The author then expresses an interesting insight: just as membership of a tribe in pre-Islamic times was a guarantee of being able to obtain intercession from its members in cases of need and danger, in the same way belonging to the *umma* of Muḥammad guarantees religious intercession. To further clarify this passage, Riad reports some verses by poets of the Prophet's epoch that mention Muḥammad's intercession, among which one in particular is attributed to the famous Companion Ḥassān ibn Thābit (d. 674).[110]

Riad then investigates the presence of the notion of intercession in the Qur'ān from the perspective of some scholars before her, among whom she cites Tor Andrae and Huitema, a perspective according to which Muḥammad is the author of the Qur'ān, and it is, therefore, possible to deduce his personal opinion on *shafāʿa* from the sacred Islamic text. It is precisely because of this perspective, which ultimately denies the relationship between intercession and the person of the prophet Muḥammad, that it also shows great perplexity with regard to the widespread use of this notion in medieval Islam and up to the present day. Riad states that the Qur'ān shows the Prophet's strongly negative view of *shafāʿa*, while after his death, progressively, in an attempt to "fill the need to bridge the great distance that separates God from mankind" shared by the Abrahamic communities, Muslim peoples would develop the notion of intercession to include further categories, under the influence of Judaism and Christianity. The generations of Muslims following Muḥammad felt the need to express a mediating figure between God and mankind, and for this reason, as in the Jewish and Christian contexts, neo-platonic influen-

---

108 John Westerdale Bowker, "Intercession in The Qur'an and the Jewish Tradition," *Journal of Semitic Studies* XI, 1 (1966), 69–82.

109 Eva Riad, "Šafāʿa dans le Coran," *Orientalia Suecana* XXX (1981), 37–62.

110 Ibid., 54–55.

ces can be found in this doctrine. According to the author, Muḥammad, in his time, would instead have undoubtedly rejected this doctrine, as it would have represented a threat to monotheism.[111]

In 2002, Feras Hamza devoted sections of his doctoral thesis to intercession.[112] He returns to the theories of various specialists in Islamic studies before him, starting with Goldizher, centred on the exogenous origin of this notion, arguing on the contrary that the eschatological doctrine of intercession was able to develop precisely because the doctrine of intercession specific to the Prophet was already established during his lifetime and in the early Islamic era.[113] Hamza then argues that some historical evidence of the antiquity of this doctrine is clearly attestable. Among these, he mentions the quotations of intercession within one of the inscriptions on the Dome of the Rock in Jerusalem and the presence of this term with this precise meaning in ancient Arabic poetry, already from the time of the Prophet. He quotes the verses attributed to Ḥassān ibn Thābit mentioned above and explores the question of their authenticity.[114] In Appendix 5 of the thesis, he deepens this question by analysing some passages from ancient Islamic historiographical literature.[115] During his discussion, he also argues that, although the Qur'ān does not explicitly grant Muḥammad intercession, Muslim exegetes refer to several verses related to *shafā'a to* the Prophet. This is also the case in the earliest Qur'anic commentaries, such as that of Muqātil ibn Sulaymān (d. 767), as well as later in the seminal commentary of Muḥammad ibn Jarīr al-Ṭabarī (d. 923), both commentaries reporting interpretations on intercession by relevant personalities from an even earlier era, such as Mujāhid ibn Jabr (d. 722).[116] Hamza concludes this argument with the following remark:

> As we have seen, the Qur'ān says nothing explicitly about the role of Muḥammad as an intercessor. But it seems logical to suppose that the Qur'ān was not about to make an explicit reference to the Prophet having *shafā'a*, and that sat comfortably with the generally modest portrayal of Muhammad in the Qur'ān. And yet the Qur'ān was hardly discouraging a conception of Muhammad as *shafī'* [intercessor] when it made statements to the effect that he had been sent as a "mercy" (*raḥmatan li'l-'ālamīn*) to the world. In addition, the Prophet is on frequent occasions enjoined to ask forgiveness for others so that God may forgive them: *istighfār* may be taken as synonymous with *shafā'a.*[117]

111 Ibid., 55.
112 Feras Hamza, *To Hell and back: a study of the concepts of Hell and intercession in early Islam, PhD Thesis* (Oxford: Wolfson College, University of Oxford, 2002).
113 Ibid., 124.
114 Ibid., 124–131.
115 Ibid., 195–198.
116 Ibid., 132.
117 Ibid., 133.

Hamza then focuses on analysing ancient Shiʿa-inspired poetry, showing the antiquity of the Prophet's notion of intercession appearing against the backdrop of the controversy between Sunnis and Shiʿs in the formative phase of Islam.[118] Similarly, in the next section, he uses studies on the political and religious context related to the Dome of the Rock to deepen the understanding of the inscription on the Prophet's *shafāʿa* contained therein.[119] At the end of his analysis, Hamza proposes a more nuanced theory than the exogenous one mentioned above, according to which the doctrine of Muḥammad's intercession originated in the Arabic and Islamic context of origin, only to be "coloured" with Abrahamic overtones as it spread to the Near East, coming into constant contact with similar doctrines of Judaism and Christianity.[120] This theory is finally explored further in Appendix 6 of his thesis.[121]

In 2004, Valerie Hoffman published an entry entitled *Intercession* in the *Encyclopaedia of the Qur'ān*, in which she summarised the main features of the notion of intercession, concluding with a section on the intercession of saints and the opposition to intercession by Islamic Reformation movements.[122]

In 2010, a very important article by Carl William Ernst was published, entitled *Muhammad as the Pole of Existence*, which introduces concisely and clearly the cosmological and metaphysical dimension of the Prophet, which, as we shall see, is closely related to his function as mediator and intercessor.[123]

At the end of this analysis of academic studies on the notion of intercession, a number of entries in encyclopaedias and dictionaries, as well as a few articles dealing with specific issues related to this notion, are proposed.

Encyclopaedia entries and dictionaries

Javier Albarrán Iruela, "Intercession," in *Islam. A Worldwide Encyclopedia*, ed. Cenap Cakmak (Santa Barbara: ABC-CLIO, 2017), 725–728.

Asma Afsaruddin, "Shafāʿa," in *The Qur'an: An Encyclopaedia*, ed. Oliver Leaman (London: Routledge, 2006), 582–583.

Mohammed Hocine Benkheira, "Intercession," in *Dictionnaire du Quran*, ed. Mohammad Ali Amir-Moezzi (Paris: Robert Laffont, 2007).

118 Ibid., 137–145.

119 Ibid., 145–149.

120 Ibid., 149–152.

121 Ibid., 199–204.

122 Valerie J. Hoffman, "Intercession," in *EQ*.

123 Carl William Ernst, "Muhammad as the pole of existence," in *The Cambridge Companion to Muhammad*, ed. Jonathan E. Brockopp (New York: Cambridge University Press, 2010), 123–138.

Francesco Chiabotti, "Intercession," in *Muhammad in History, Thought, and Culture: An Encyclopedia of the Prophet of God*, edited by Coeli Fitzpatrick, Adam Walker. Santa Barbara: ABC-CLIO, 2014, 299 – 302.

Articles on specific intercession-related topics

Feras Hamza, "Temporary Hellfire Punishment and the Making of Sunni Orthodoxy," in *Roads to Paradise: Eschatology and Concepts of the Hereafter in Islam*, ed. Sebastian Günther and Todd Lawson (Leiden: Brill, 2017), 1:371 – 406.

Paul L. Heck, "An Early Response to Wahhabism from Morocco: The Politics of Intercession," in *Studia Islamica* 107, 2 (2012): 235 – 254.

Tehnyat Majeed, "The Chār Muḥammad Inscription, *Shafāʿa*, and the Mamluk Qubbat al-Manṣūriyya," in *Roads to Paradise: Eschatology and Concepts of the Hereafter in Islam*, ed. Sebastian Günther and Todd Lawson (Leiden: Brill, 2017), 1:1010 – 1032.

Shaun E. Marmon, "The Quality of Mercy: Intercession in Mamluk Society," *Studia Islamica* 87 (1998): 125 – 139.

Catherine Mayeur-Jaouen, "L'intercession des saints en Islam égyptien: autour de Sayyid al-Badawī," *Annales Islamologiques* 25 (1991): 363 – 388.

Emilio Tornero, "Šafā'a. La cohesión de una sociedad," *Al-Qanṭara* XI 2 (2019): 431 – 454.

Chapter 3
The Theological Notion of Intermediation in Islam

1 Intermediation and intercession in the Qur'ān and the sayings of the Prophet

The theological notion of intermediation appears in the primary sources of Islam in various forms. The main one is that of the metaphorical descent from the higher divine place to the lower places, a descent that involves, at the same time, an ascent. Various designations in the primary sources and religious literature indicate these places, which are related to specific names of God.

One of these names is Lord of the worlds (*Rabb al-ʿālamīn*), which is very frequent in the Qur'ān. The term *rabb* was already used in pre-Islamic terminology to denote the relationship between master (*rabb*) and servant (*ʿabd*). In Islamic times, this relationship will provide the framework for the main theological metaphor of Islam, hence the Arabic term *Islām* itself to indicate the submission of the manservant (*ʿabd*) to the God-Lord (*Rabb*). According to Islamic religious literature, the Lord exercises his authority over three worlds: the world of the visible (*ʿālam al-shahāda*), the world of the invisible (*ʿālam al-ghayb*),[124] and the world of the intermediary (*al-barzakh*). The world of the intermediary is usually described as the place of the souls of the dead awaiting the Day of Judgement.[125] Various interpretations of this notion can be found in Islamic literature, some of which are of an esoteric nature.[126]

Another name of God in relation to places in Islamic cosmology is *al-Malik*, the King, who also, in this respect, exercises his authority over three worlds: the world of the visible realm (*ʿālam al-mulk*, comparable to *ʿālam al-shahāda*), the world of the invisible realm (*ʿālam al-malakūt*, comparable to *ʿālam al-ghayb*), and the world of divine omnipotence (*ʿālam al-jabarūt*, sometimes assimilated to *barzakh* but more difficult to locate from secondary sources, not least because it is mentioned only in the *ḥadīth*).[127]

---

124 Duncan Black MacDonald and Louis Gardet, "al-G̲h̲ayb," in *EI*².

125 Christian Lange, "Barzakh," in *EI*³.

126 Salman H. Bashier, *Ibn al-'Arabi's Barzakh: The Concept of the Limit and the Relationship between God and the World* (Albany: SUNY Press).

127 Louis Gardet, "2. *ʿālam al-d̲jabarūt, ʿālam al-malakūt, ʿālam al-mit̲h̲āl*," in Tjitze de Boer and Louis Gardet, *ʿĀlam, EI*².

https://doi.org/10.1515/9783111500966-008

Other widely used designations for the relationship between the human and divine worlds are *al-dunyā*, this world, and *al-ākhira*, the Hereafter. To begin with, I will analyse the main features of the theological notion of descent from the divine world to the human world and then move on to the notion of ascent.

2 The Descent

In Islamic terminology, the notion of descent is mainly expressed through the Arabic root *n-z-l*, which holds the fundamental sense of "to descend" through various forms. Most recurrences are through verbal forms, such as *nazzala* or *anzala*, which express the related meaning of "to cause to descend, to send down". In addition to indicating the divine Action of sending down angels, Revelation and certain holy books, these forms are also used, as we shall see, to indicate the divine Action of sending down water in the form of rain or other sustenance such as manna and quails on Moses and his people.[128] One of the main forms of this root is the verbal noun *tanzīl*, which recurs in numerous Qur'anic verses to indicate the descent of divine Revelation, eventually identifying Revelation itself. From the same root comes the term *manzil* (pl. *manāzil*), which means "the place where one descends" or "station", and which has also taken on the meaning of "dwelling", as well as the term *nuzul*, which has the similar meaning of "dwelling" and is used in some verses of the Qur'ān[129].

Ancient Arabic dictionaries report a very interesting meaning of the root *n-z-l*, according to which it indicated, in the context of the pre-Islamic Bedouin lexicon, the descent of the milk of the cow and other dairy animals into the udder, which is a natural receptacle.[130] It is interesting to note a possible metaphorical value behind the use of this root to indicate the descent of Revelation, given the value of the milk element in Islam as a symbol of knowledge. This is evident from some of the Prophet's sayings, such as the following, in which he recounts to his famous Companion ʿUmar ibn al-Khaṭṭāb (d. 644) a dream in which the Prophet is brought a cup of milk from which he drinks until the milk begins to leak from his nails, and then he hands the cup to ʿUmar himself. When asked by the latter about the meaning of this dream, he replied that milk is a symbol of knowledge (*ʿilm*).[131] However,

---

128 Q 2:57; 7:160; 20:80.

129 Simon P. Loynes, *Revelation in the Qur'an. A Semantic Study of the Roots n-z-l and w-ḥ-y* (Leiden: Brill, 2021).

130 Edward William Lane, "*n-z-l*," in *An Arabic-English Lexicon* (Williams and Norgate, London 1863–93).

131 Bukhārī, *Ṣaḥīḥ al-Bukhārī*, 1:255.

who and what descends during this descent and which entities are involved in this process?

3 The Spirit

The main entity to descend, in the Qur'ān, is the Spirit (*al-rūḥ*), which appears as an emanation proceeding from God in different ways. It can be breathed (*nafakha*) directly into creatures, as is the case with Adam, about whom God says: "And I breathed into him some of My spirit,"[132] and Mary: "And then We breathed some of Our Spirit into her."[133] It can be revealed (*awḥā*): "And thus We have inspired you with a Spirit of Our command,"[134] and in this case, the term *rūḥ* is usually identified by exegetes as a reference to the Qur'ān itself.[135] Alternatively, it can be sent (*arsala*), as is the case with the angel sent to Mary in human form: "And We sent to her Our Spirit."[136] Similarly, the fruit of the divine breath in Mary's womb, Jesus, also takes the name of the Spirit proceeding from God in another passage and the Word of God placed in Mary.[137] Jesus, in his mission, is assisted (*ayyada*) by the Holy Spirit (*rūḥ al-quds*), a denomination that appears in the Qur'ān in three similar passages,[138] while in a fourth passage, it appears in relation to Muḥammad's mission, where it would seem to be the Holy Spirit himself who makes the Qur'ān descend (*nazzala*).[139] This is the only verse in which the action of making the Qur'ān descend, which is usually reserved for God, seems to be attributed to another entity, in this case, the Holy Spirit, who "accompanies" the Qur'ān sent by God in its descent. Both ancient Muslim exegetes and contemporary Qur'anic specialists are not unanimous in identifying the Holy Spirit as it appears in the sacred text of Islam with the analogous person of the Christian Trinity due to obvious differences in theological perspective.[140] At the same time, they disagree on the identity between the Holy Spirit and the Faithful Spirit (*rūḥ al-amīn*), who in another passage of the Qur'ān descends "upon the heart" of Muḥammad with the Revelation (*tanzīl*): "This is a Revelation from the Lord of the worlds,

132 *"wa nafakhtu fīhi min rūḥī,"* Q 15:29; cf. also Q 32:9, 38:72.

133 *"fa-nafakhnā fīhā min rūḥinā"*, Q 21:91; cf. also Q 66:12.

134 *"wa-kadhālika awḥaynā ilayka rūḥan"*, Q 42:52.

135 Jalāl al-Dīn al-Suyūṭī, Jalāl al-Dīn al-Maḥallī, *Tafsīr al-Jalālayn* (al-Qāhira: Dār al-ḥadīth, 2001), 642.

136 *"fa-arsalnā ilayhā rūhanā"*, Q 19:17.

137 *"ʿIsā ibn Maryam rasūl Allāh wa-kalimatuhu alqāhā ilā Maryam wa-rūḥ minhu"*, Q 4:171.

138 Q 2:87, 2:253, 5:110.

139 *"nazzalahu rūḥ al-quds min rabbika bi-l-ḥaqq"*, Q 16:102.

140 Sidney H. Griffith, *Holy Spirit*, in *EQ*.

which the Faithful Spirit has brought down upon your heart."[141] At the same time, Revelation (*tanzīl*) and the Faithful Spirit descend. The identity of the latter is revealed by another verse, where it is stated that Gabriel (*Jibrīl*) was made to descend (*nazzala ʿalā*) on Muḥammad's heart with God's permission (*bi-idhn Allāh*).[142] From these analogies derives the syllogism, expressed by ancient Muslim exegetes, according to which there is identity between the Holy Spirit and Gabriel, who is never referred to as an angel in the Qurʾān, and who therefore seems to possess a higher degree than angels.[143] This superiority is described in Christian terminology by the term "archangel", which is taken from the New Testament,[144] but which finds no counterpart in the Islamic lexicon, with the possible exception of the formula "the close angels" (*al-malāʾika al-muqarrabūn*),[145] which can be related instead to the term "cherubim", itself derived from the Hebrew language by a root analogous to the Arabic one (*q-r-b*).

Finally, a verse in the Qurʾān states that Muḥammad received the Revelation of the Spirit directly from God: "And thus We have inspired you with a Spirit of Our command."[146] He also witnesses, first-hand, the descent of Gabriel. The first descent takes place during his Ascension (*miʿrāj*), when Muḥammad reaches the apex of the human possibility of ascent and therefore, Gabriel, who was seated as if on a throne (*fa-stawā*) at the highest point of the horizon, begins to descend, coming very close to Muḥammad, at the metaphorical distance of two arches (*qāb qawsayn*), and revealing to him some divine secrets.[147] A second descent (*nazla*) then takes place close to the "Lotus of the Limit" (*sidrat al-muntahā*), near the level of Paradise defined as "the Refuge" (*al-Maʾwā*), and in this passage, the Qurʾān alludes to the fact that the veil covering the Lotus was lifted, and he saw "the greatest signs of his Lord".[148]

4 The Angels

Along with the Spirit, angels also descend (*malāʾika*), particularly during the "Night of Measure" (*laylat al-qadr*), with permission (*idhn*) by God and according to divine

141 "*wa-innahu la-tanzīl rabb al-ʿālamīn nazala bihi al-rūh al-amīn ʿalā qalbika*", Q 26:192–194.
142 Q 2:97.
143 Michael Sells, *Spirit*, in *EQ*.
144 *1Thessalonians* 4:16, *Jude* 9.
145 Q 4:172.
146 "*awḥaynā ilayka rūḥan min amrinā*," Q 42:52; cf. also Q 17:85, 40:15.
147 Q 53:2–11
148 Q 53:13–19.

Order (*amr*).[149] In an earlier verse, it is stated that God possesses reserves (*khazā'in*), which descend in measured quantity (*bi-qadr ma'lūm*).[150] On the other hand, during this night descends the entire divine Measure (*al-qadr*) until dawn (*ḥattā maṭla' al-fajr*), and for this reason, it is better than a thousand months (*khayr min alf shahr*).[151]

In another verse, however, it is specified that they descend together with the Spirit according to divine Order and only on God's servants whom He has chosen,[152] or they descend with the Truth (*bi-l-ḥaqq*).[153] Angels also descend on those who attest to the divine Lordship and set themselves on the right path.[154]

The descent of a messenger is indicated as necessary in the Qur'ān: if even on earth, God had replaced humans with angels, He would, in any case, have an angel descend among them as His envoy (*malak rasūl*).[155]

God can also make angels descend to aid believers in the form of armies (*junūd*) not visible to ordinary mortal eyes, as in the case of the famous battle of Badr (624), recounted in the Prophet's canonical biography, when the fate of the battle was decided precisely by the descent of angels.[156]

Moreover, it is precisely the invisibility of angels that is at the centre of some controversy among Muḥammad's contemporaries, who, according to the Qur'ān, do not trust his mission precisely because God does not send an angel in the form of a man,[157] or a group of angels,[158] to the Prophet.

In any case, on the Day of Judgement, the heavens will open and the angels will descend visibly, one by one.[159]

5 The devils

While angels can descend with a sacred text, this is precluded to devils (*shayāṭīn*), who are even prevented from listening to their recitation.[160] They can, however,

149 "*tanazzalu al-malā'ika wa al-rūḥ fīhā bi-idhn rabbihim min kull amr*", Q 97:4.
150 Q 15:21.
151 Q 97:4.
152 "*yunazzilu al-malā'ika bi-l-rūḥ min amrihi 'alā man yashā' min 'ibādihi*", Q 16:2.
153 Q 15:8.
154 Q 41:30.
155 Q 17:95.
156 Q 9.26, 9:40.
157 Q 6:8–9; cf. also 25:7.
158 Q 6:111, 23:24, 25:21, 41:14.
159 "*nuzzila al-malā'ikatu tanzīlan*", Q 25:25.
160 Q 26:210.

descend (*tanazzala*) on sinners to try to seize what is hidden to them about divine things.[161]

6 The Book

The most frequent descent mentioned in the Qur'ān relates to the Book (*al-kitāb*), which represents the earthly image of the prototype of the Celestial Book, referred to instead as the "Guarded Book" (*kitāb maknūn*)[162] or the "Clear Prototype" (*imām mubīn*).[163] The Celestial Book is contained in the "Preserved Tablet" (*al-lawḥ al-maḥfūẓ*),[164] also referred to as the "Mother of the Book" (*umm al-kitāb*).[165] It is interesting to note a relationship between these terms: the Guarded Book is in a clear semantic relationship with the Preserved Tablet, while the Clear Prototype is in a clear semantic relationship with the Mother of the Book since the respective terms *imām* and *umm* share the same root (*'-m-m*).

The term Book (*al-kitāb*), therefore, indicates in the Qur'ān both the sacred books revealed before Muḥammad's mission – which is why the communities that received them take the collective name of People of the Book (*ahl al-kitāb*)[166] – and the Qur'ān itself, the last among the books revealed by God.

From a Qur'anic perspective, the Book is one of the forms taken by the Spirit in its descent, as is evident from the verse already cited, where exegetes identify the term *rūḥ* as a reference to the Qur'ān.[167]

The book can be "inspired" (*waḥā*)[168] by the prophets, or it is "given" (*atā*) by God to them, in particular, on several occasions, to the prophet Moses,[169] but in most instances, it is "made to descend" (*anzala*). In the Qur'ān, this formula recurs several times: "God has sent down the Scripture with the Truth (*bi-l-ḥaqq*)",[170] while in various passages, it is specified that the Book descended on various proph-

161 Q 26:221–223.
162 Q 56:78.
163 Q 36:12.
164 Q 85:22.
165 Q 13:39, 43:4. Also in Q 3:7 reference is made to the Mother of the Book, but according to Muslim exegetes in this context the meaning is "the fundamental part" of the earthly Book and not the heavenly one.
166 See e.g. Q 2:105.
167 "*wa-kadhālika awḥaynā ilayka rūḥan*", Q 42:52.
168 Q 29:45, 35:31. In Q 12:3 and 42:7 it is instead the Qur'ān that is revealed (*awḥā*) to Muḥammad.
169 Q 2:53, 6:154, 11:110, 23:49, 25:35, 28:43, 32:23, 41:45, 45:16.
170 "*Allāh nazzala al-kitāb bi-l-ḥaqq,*" Q 2:176; see also 2:231, 4:105, 4:113, 4:140, 6:114, 6:155–157, 7:196, 42:15, 42:17, 5:48, 7:2, 16:64, 16:89, 18:1, 29:51, 38:29, 39:2, 39:41.

ets preceding Muḥammad,[171] and it also descends in the same way on the Prophet: "Those who believe that what has descended on Muḥammad is the Truth."[172] However, Muḥammad is the only prophet for whom the Qur'ān expressly uses the verb "to descend" (*anzala*) for the Book, while for the other prophets, other verbs among those mentioned above are used, in particular the verb "to give" (*atā*). In some verses, it is specified that the Book descended on Muḥammad is the same as that which descended on the prophets preceding him,[173] and it descended with the Truth (*bi-l-ḥaqq*) and through the Knowledge of God (*bi-ʿilmihi*).[174] In other verses, it is specified that the Book descended upon Muḥammad, verse by verse, is the Qur'ān: "Truly We have sent down to you the Recitation gradually (*tanzīlan*)."[175] In another verse, Muḥammad is accused, precisely for this reason, of not being a true prophet since the Qur'ān did not descend all at once (*jumla wāḥida*).[176]

In other passages, the descending Book takes the name "Descent, Revelation" (*tanzīl*),[177] "Descent, Revelation of the Book" (*tanzīl al-kitāb*),[178] "Discrimination" (*furqān*),[179] "Torah" (*tawrā*),[180] or "Remembrance" (*dhikr*),[181] while in some verses we find mention of the descent of a single "chapter" (*sūra*).[182]

The Qur'ān derides the claim by Jews and Christians (*ahl al-kitāb*) that God should materially cause a Book to descend from the sky in order to induce them to believe in Muḥammad's mission[183] and adds: "Had We sent down to yous a Scripture on parchment and they could have felt it with their hands, those who disbelieve would have said,'This is merely persuasive magic.'"[184] Another passage states that even the descent of a "treasure" (*kanz*) would not convince disbelievers.[185]

---

171 Q 2:213, 3:84, 6:91.
172 Q 47:2, see also 3:3, 3:7, 4:105, 4:113, 4:136, 5:48, 7:2, 13:1, 13:19, 16:64, 16:89, 18:1, 29:51, 38:29, 39:2, 39:41.
173 Q 4:60, 4:136, 4:162, 29:46.
174 Q 4:166, 11:14.
175 *"innā naḥnu nazzalnā al-qur'ān tanzīlan"*, Q 76:23, cf. also Q 2:185, 5:101, 17:105–106.
176 Q 25:32.
177 Q 20:4, 26:192, 36:5, 41:2, 41:42, 56:80, 69:43.
178 Q 32:2, 39:1, 40:2, 45:2, 46:2.
179 Q 3:4, 25:1.
180 Q 3:93, 5:44.
181 Q *15*:6, 15:9, 16:44, 38:8, 65:10.
182 Q 24:1, 47:20.
183 Q 4:153.
184 Q 6:7.
185 Q 11:12.

7 The wisdom

With the Book, "wisdom" (*ḥikma)* also descends: "Remember the benefits that God has bestowed upon you and what He has revealed of the Book and wisdom."[186] Wisdom is "given" (*atā*) to the prophets,[187] "taught" (*ʿallama*) to Jesus,[188] while, as for the Book, it is "made to descend" (*anzala*) only upon Muḥammad: "God has sent down to you the Scripture and the Wisdom, and He has taught you what you did not know."[189] The Prophet subsequently "teaches" (*ʿallama*) the Book and wisdom to the believers.[190]

8 The Spirit of Tranquility

Another form of the Spirit that descends on believers to assist and strengthen them in difficult circumstances is the "Spirit of tranquillity" (*sakīna*).[191] The root of this term (*s-k-n*) carries two primary meanings in Arabic: "to be calm, quiet" or "to dwell, reside in a place."[192]

This term has an equivalent in other Semitic languages, such as Akkadian and Aramaic, and in particular shows similarities with the Hebrew term *shekhinah*, which is also feminine like *sakīna.* This term does not appear in the Old Testament but only in rabbinic literature, with the meaning of "dwelling, residing in a place" and refers in particular to the divine Presence in the human world. According to these sources, the *shekhinah* resided specifically in the Ark of the Covenant, which at the end of the Exodus was kept in the Tabernacle of the Temple in Jerusalem (*mishkan*, from the same root as *shekhinah*). On this occasion, a miraculous cloud filled the entire Temple. After the destruction of the Temple, the *shekhinah* is present at specific moments, linked to prayer and recitation of the Torah.[193]

In the Qurʾān, we find six occurrences of the term *sakīna,* and, among them, in one in particular, we note more than one analogy with the Jewish notion of *shek-*

186 Q 2:231.
187 Q 3:81, 4:54, 31:12, 38:20.
188 Q 3:48, 5:110, 43:63.
189 Q 4:113.
190 Q *2*:129, 2:151, 3:164, 62:2.
191 Reuven Firestone, *Shekhinah,* in *EQ*; Emilio Tornero, "Sakina: contribución a su estudio," *Al-Qanṭara* XXXIV 1 (2013), 65–87.
192 Edward William Lane, "*s-k-n*", in *An Arabic-English Lexicon* (London: Williams and Norgate, 1863–93).
193 Alan Unterman et al, "Shekhinah," In *EJ*, 18:440–444.

hinah, in the passage narrating the events of King *Ṭālūt*, generally identified by Muslim exegetes with King Saul.[194] God grants Saul to inherit the Ark of the Covenant (*tābūt*), in which is the "Spirit of tranquillity that comes from your Lord (*sakīna min rabbikum*)."[195] In commentaries, Muslim exegetes claim that the Ark is a "chest" (*ṣundūq*) that God descended (*anzala*) upon Adam, and in which are found the images of all the prophets up to Muḥammad, as well as some relics of Moses and Aaron and fragments of the broken Tablets of the Law. At a later stage, the Ark was suspended between heaven and earth, guarded by angels, and God sent it to Saul to legitimise his authority over his people and to use it as divine help during the battle.[196]

This term appears in five other verses of the Qur'ān, which refer to specific moments in the life of the Prophet Muḥammad and the first community of believers. The first event takes place during the emigration (*hijra*) from Mecca to Medina, during which the Prophet hides together with his trusted Companion Abū Bakr al-Siddīq (d. 634) in a cave on Mount Thawr, located south near Mecca, to escape capture by the Meccans, who were on their trail. Here, among other miracles, the descent of the Spirit of Tranquility upon the Prophet and help from invisible hosts of angels takes place.[197]

In the *sūra* of Victory (*al-Fatḥ*) three verses mention the descent of the Spirit of Tranquility, and according to Muslim exegetes, they refer to a specific event that took place in 628, known as the "Treaty (*ṣulḥ*) of Ḥudaybiyya", a location near Mecca. This is the phase in which, after the great battles that had greatly exacerbated the clash between Mecca and Medina, Muḥammad decides, following a truthful dream (*ru'yā*),[198] to leave Medina with a group of about 1400 Muslims to undertake a pilgrimage to the Ka'ba in Mecca. For this reason, the group leaves with seventy dromedaries to be sacrificed at the end of the pilgrimage. After escaping an interception attempt by a group of Meccans, Muḥammad and the group of Muslims arrive at the gates of the sacred area around Mecca (*ḥaram*). Here begins a long negotiation that will lead to a ten-year truce agreement and the possibility for the Medinans to return to perform the pilgrimage the following year. During the negotiations, when an unfounded rumour spreads that 'Uthmān ibn 'Affān (d. 656), sent to Mecca as ambassador, had been detained and killed, Muḥammad

---

194 Liyakat Takim, *Saul*, in *EQ*.

195 Q 2:248.

196 Jalāl al-Dīn al-Suyūṭī, Jalāl al-Dīn al-Maḥallī, *Tafsīr al-Jalālayn* (al-Qāhira: Dār al-ḥadīth, 2001), 54.

197 *"fa-anzala Allāh sakīna 'alayhi"*, Q 9:40, cf. Jalāl al-Dīn al-Suyūṭī, Jalāl al-Dīn al-Maḥallī, *Tafsīr al-Jalālayn*, Dār al-ḥadīth, al-Qāhira, 2001, pp. 246–247.

198 Referred to, according to exegetes, Q 48:27.

begins to prepare for battle.[199] This is when the "Covenant of Satisfaction" (*baʿyat al-riḍwān*), or "Covenant of the Tree" (*baʿyat al-shajara*) takes place. Gabriel descends upon the Prophet as on the occasion of the Revelation of the Qur'ān, but instead of the usual transmission of the divine Word, Muḥammad is ordered to make a covenant with the group of Muslims who have come with him to that place. The Prophet announces: "Verily, God has ordered me to make a pact,"[200] and one of his Companions begins to call aloud to the others with these words: "Verily, the Holy Spirit has descended (*nazala rūḥ al-qudus*) upon the Messenger and has ordered him to make a pact."[201] The Prophet then places himself under a tree, at which point all those present take a covenant with him one by one. In the Prophet's eyes, this pact must have been of paramount importance, for although ʿUthmān was not present, he took the pact on his behalf by clasping his right hand with his left.[202]

Qur'anic exegetes relate this episode with certain verses of the Qur'ān, in particular with a passage referring to the descent of the Spirit of tranquillity:

> God was pleased with the believers when they made a covenant with you under the tree. He knew what was in their hearts and sent down upon them the Spirit of tranquillity: he rewarded them with imminent victory.[203]

This covenant, according to the Qur'ān, is made directly with God:

> Verily those who make a covenant with you, make a covenant with God: the hand of God is upon their hands.[204]

Another verse in the same *sūra* refers to the same event, recounting the negotiation with the Meccans, which increased the Medinans' anger towards them, but at that point, God sent the Spirit of tranquillity upon the believers:

> God was pleased with the believers when they swore allegiance to you under the tree, and He knew what was in their hearts. And so He sent down the Spirit of tranquillity [*sakīna*] upon

---

199 Ibn Isḥāq, *The Life of Muhammad, A Translation of Ibn Isḥāq's Sīrat rasūl Allāḥ, with introduction and notes by A. Guillaume* (Oxford: Oxford University Press, 1955), 499–504.
200 "*inna Allāh amaranī bi-l-bayʿa*", al-Wāqidī, *Kitāb al-maghāzī*, ed. Marsden Jones (London: Oxford University Press, 1966), 2:603.
201 "*innā rūḥ al-qudus qad nazala ʿalā al-rasūl wa amara bi-l-bayʿa*", *ibid*, 2:604.
202 Ibid., 2:605.
203 Q 48:18.
204 Q 48:10.

> them and rewarded them with a victory near at hand, and numerous spoils to take. God is Mighty and Wise.[205]

This descent is reiterated in another verse of the same *sūra:*

> It is He who sent down the Spirit of tranquillity [*sakīna*] into the hearts of the believers, that they might add faith to their faith.[206]

Finally, another episode mentioned in the Qurʾān, during which the descent of the Spirit of tranquillity took place, is the battle of Ḥunayn, which was fought in 630:

> God has helped you on many fields and at the battle of Ḥunayn, when your multitude pleased you but it availed you nothing. The land, wide as it was, was too narrow for you, and you turned your backs in retreat. Then God sent His Spirit of tranquillity [*sakīna*] down to His messenger and to the believers and sent down hosts whom you could not see and punished those who did not believe. That is the recompense of the unbelievers.[207]

Some sayings of the Prophet mention the descent of the Spirit of tranquillity, allowing a better understanding of this notion. In the first, during the preparation for the Battle of the Trench (627), at the moment when the people of Medina await the arrival of the Meccan army with great fear, Muḥammad makes an invocation to God asking for the descent of the Spirit of tranquillity upon the Muslims.[208]

In the second, the Prophet states:

> People will not sit and mention the name of God (*yadhkurūn Allāh*), without being surrounded by angels and covered by Mercy, and without the Spirit of Tranquility descending upon them, and without God mentioning them to those who are close to Him [the close angels].[209]

The third saying is very interesting because it brings us back to the dimension of the descent of the Spirit of tranquillity as divine Presence. This tradition relates that a Companion of the Prophet was reciting the *sūra* of the Cave (*al-Kahf*) as part of his ritual prayer, and at that moment, an animal of burden in his house began to jump in terror. When the man finished his prayer, he saw a cloud hovering around him. When he informed the Prophet, he stated that the cloud was the

205 Q 48:26.
206 Q 48:4.
207 Q 9:25–26.
208 Bukhārī, *Ṣaḥīḥ al-Bukhārī*, 5:281.
209 Muslim, *Ṣaḥīḥ Muslim*, 7:74–75.

Spirit of tranquillity descending during the recitation of the Qur'ān.[210] In this episode, there is an obvious analogy between the Spirit of Tranquility and the *shekhinah*, which according to rabbinic sources, descends during prayer and recitation of the Torah and takes the form of a cloud, as at the placement of the Ark of the Covenant in the Temple of Jerusalem.[211]

Ancient historiographical sources also report interesting details about the Spirit of tranquillity. The historian al-Azraqī (d. 865), in his *Akhbār Makka* (Histories of Mecca), relates some traditions according to which the Spirit of Tranquility accompanied Abraham when he reached the holy city of Islam. His appearance was precisely that of "a cloud or mist with a head like that of a cat and equipped with two wings."[212] The Spirit of tranquillity was also with Abraham when he returned from Armenia on a celestial mount (*burāq*), and on this occasion, too, the *sakīna* was endowed with a face with which it could speak, "whistling like a gentle breeze."[213] When Abraham undertook the construction of the Kaʿba, the *sakīna* coiled around the foundations like a serpent, enjoining him to build on her, thus allowing the divine Spirit to dwell permanently at the House of God.[214]

The Spirit of tranquillity thus appears, starting from the Qur'ān and the *ḥadīth*, as one of the forms of the Spirit, capable of descending not only on prophets but also on men.

9 The signs

Divine signs (*āyāt*), too, can descend upon prophets. One of these signs, in the Qur'ān, is, for instance, an earthly object of divine origin, the "station of Abraham" (*maqām Ibrāhīm*), which still stands in front of the Kaʿba.[215] Another example of a divine sign is the miracles that God sends to assist the prophets, as is the case with the nine signs (*tisʿ āyāt*) received by Moses to confront Pharaoh's magicians.[216] The Qur'ān was also descended by God upon the Prophet as one of the clear divine

210 Bukhārī, *Ṣaḥīḥ al-Bukhārī*, 4:529.
211 *1 Kings*, 8:10–12.
212 al-Azraqī, *Akhbār Makka wa-mā jā' fīhā min al-āthār*, (Makkat al-mukarrama: Maktabat al-asadī, 2003), 109, 112, 117.
213 Ibid., 110, 112.
214 Ibid., 114.
215 Q 3:97, cf. Meir Jacob Kister, "Maqām Ibrāhīm: A Stone with an Inscription," *Le Muséon* 84 (1971), 477–491.
216 Q 17:101, cf. also Q 58:5.

signs (*āyāt bayyināt*),[217] and at the same time, it contains within it clear divine signs, which are the verses of the Qur'ān, named *āyāt, āya* in the singular.[218] The disbelievers finally ask the Prophet to descend divine signs (*āyāt*), but he must reply that they are in the Invisible (*ghayb*),[219] with God (*'inda Allāh*), and that they can only descend by divine Will.[220] For if God willed, He would descend a sign directly from heaven.[221]

10 The Balance

In some verses, along with the Book, God also brings down the Balance (*al-mīzān*).[222] Most Muslim exegetes interpret this term as a metaphor for justice (*al-'adl*),[223] which has its divine archetype in the celestial Balance placed in the heavens.[224]

11 The Divine Order

We have already observed that in the Qur'ān, the Book descends by divine order (*bi-l-amr*). In one verse, however, God makes the divine Order itself descend, among the seven earths and the seven heavens, to teach creatures that God knows the measure of all things and that His knowledge embraces all that exists.[225]

12 The Light

In the *sūra* of the Women (*al-Nisā'*), it is stated that God has sent down (*anzala*) upon men a clear light (*nūr mubīn*),[226] usually identified by exegetes with the Qur'ān, and men must follow it if they wish to prosper.[227]

---

217 Q 2:99.
218 Q 22:16, 24:1.
219 Q 10:20.
220 Q 29:50, cf. also 6:37, 13:07, 13:27,
221 Q 26:4.
222 Q 42:17, 57:25.
223 Jalāl al-Dīn al-Suyūṭī, Jalāl al-Dīn al-Maḥallī, *Tafsīr al-Jalālayn* (Dār al-ḥadīth, al-Qāhira, 2001), 241.
224 Q 55:7.
225 Q 65:12.
226 Q 4:174.
227 Q 7:157.

13 The authority

Authority (*sulṭān*) over creatures comes from God, who grants it to whomever He wills. God granted it to Moses,[228] and he also granted it to Satan, but only over those who are misled,[229] while he has no power over believers.[230] God can bring down (*nazzala*) authority, but in the Qur'ān, this action is always indicated in a negative sense in relation to the deities who are associated with God:

> We shall cast terror into the hearts of those who disbelieve because they associate with God that with which He has not sent down any authority.[231]

14 The good

In a passage from the sūra of the Cow (*al-Baqara*), there is mention of the good that God brings down upon believers (*yunazzala ʿalaykum min al-khayr*), and how this displeases the unbelievers, whether they are part of the People of the Book or polytheists.[232]

15 The sciences of Hārūt and Mārūt

Another interesting reference is to "that which was made to descend (*mā unzila*) on the two angels Hārūt and Mārūt,"[233] the sciences taught to them by God, which they transmitted to the devils (*shayāṭīn*), and which the latter transmitted to men in the form of magical arts.[234]

16 Distress, safety and punishment

On the occasion of the wars fought at the time of the Prophet, God also causes feelings such as distress (*ghamm*) to descend upon the believers, followed by safety

228 Q 11:96; 23:45, 40:23, 51:38.
229 Q 15:42.
230 Q 16:99–100; 17:65.
231 Q 3:151; cf. also 6:81, 7:33, 7:71, 12:40, 22:71, 53:23.
232 Q 2:105.
233 Q 2:102.
234 Stephen R. Burge, *Angels in Islam: Jalāl al-Dīn al-Suyūṭī's* al-Habā'ik fī akhbār al-malā'ik (Abingdon, Oxon: Routledge, 2012), 154–159.

(*amāna*).[235] In other passages, God causes chastisement from heaven (*rijz min al-samā'*) to descend (*anzala*) upon the ungodly,[236] punishment (*'adhāb*) descending upon their land (*nazala bi-sāḥatihim*).[237]

17 The sustenance

The root *n-z-l* is used in the Qur'ān not only for the descent of spiritual and moral notions, as we have seen so far, but also for the descent of sustenance from the material point of view (*rizq*).[238] In this context, the most singular descent is mentioned in the *sūra* of the Banquet (*al-Mā'ida*), so called because it narrates that the Apostles asked Jesus to bring down a banquet from heaven. In response to this, he recited the following invocation:

> O God, our Lord, send a table down to us from heaven (*mā'ida min al-samā'*) to be a festival for us, the first of us and the last of us, and to be a sign from You. Give us sustenance. You are the best of providers (*arzaq al-rāziqīn*).[239]

In most occurrences, however, sustenance is brought down (*nazzala*) from God in the form of water (*mā'*),[240] and in some passages, it is specified that it is rain (*wadq*,[241] *ghayth*[242]) or hail (*barad*).[243]

Livestock (*an'ām*) were also "brought down" (*anzala*) by God for humankind in eight pairs,[244] and in the Exodus of Moses and the Children of Israel in the wilderness, God brought down (*anzala*) manna and quails (*al-manna wa-l-salwā*) on them.[245]

---

235 Q 3:154.
236 Q 2:59.
237 Q 37:176–177.
238 Q 10:59, 40:13, 45:5.
239 Q 5:112–115.
240 Q 2:22, 2:164, 6:99, 7:57, 8:11, 13:17, 14:32, 15:22, 16:10, 16:65, 20:53, 23:18, 25:48, 27:60, 29:63, 30:24, 31:10, 35:27, 39:21, 43:11, 50:9, 78:14.
241 Q 30:48–49.
242 Q 31:34, 42:28.
243 Q 24:43.
244 Q 39:6.
245 Q 2:57, 7:160, 20:80, 22:63.

18 The Blessing

In the Qur'ān, one of the dimensions of the Spirit that God can bring down is the blessing (*baraka*). This term derives from an ancient Semitic root, from which the Hebrew term *berakhah* is also derived, with a similar meaning.[246]

In the Qur'ān, this root appears only in the plural form *barakāt*, and under the form *mubārak*, blessed, referring to the Qur'ān or more generally to the Book, and in one instance to the olive tree, as well as in the formula "blessed be God" (*tabāraka-Llāh*). In the plural form *barakāt*, at least in one instance, blessings are opened (*la-fataḥnā*) from heaven and earth.[247] In one passage, however, the root appears in a verbal form:

> And We blessed him [Abraham] and Isaac.[248]

In a saying of the prophet Muḥammad, we observe the descent of the blessing instead through the use of the root *n-z-l:*

> Verily, blessing (*baraka*) descends (*tanzilu*) in the middle of the food. So eat from the sides, and do not eat from the middle.[249]

From these scriptural data, it is possible to identify the blessing (*baraka*) with one of the forms of the Spirit that can descend upon men and things, a less elevated and more accessible form than the Spirit of tranquillity (*sakīna*).

19 The saying of descent

To conclude this analysis of occurrences concerning the forms of the descent of the Spirit and sustenance in the primary sources of Islam, I will quote a saying of the Prophet that is very relevant to the present analysis:

---

246 Josef W. Meri, "Aspects of *Baraka* (Blessings) and Ritual Devotion among Medieval Muslims and Jews," *Medieval Encounters* 5 (1999), 46–69.

247 Q 7:96.

248 "*wa-bāraknā ʿalayhi wa ʿalā Isḥāq*", Q 37:113.

249 "*inna al-baraka tanzilu wasaṭa al-ṭaʿām fa-kulū min ḥāfatayhi wa-lā taʾkulū min wasaṭihi*", Tirmidhī, *Sunan*, 724. The custom among the Arabs when eating together with others is to use the same large plate, and since the blessing descends in the middle, it is necessary to share it with others by approaching it gradually from all sides, without eating immediately in the middle.

> Our Lord (*Rabbunā*), blessed and exalted be He, descends (*yanzilu*) every night into the lowest heaven when a third of the second part of the night remains, and says: 'Is there anyone who calls upon Me, that I may answer his call? Is there anyone who asks Me, that I may grant his request? Is there anyone who seeks My forgiveness, that I may forgive him?'[250]

Over the centuries, numerous Muslim religious scholars have debated and polemised over the meaning of this saying, given the theological issues it discloses. Briefly, the central issue concerns the correct interpretation of this "descent", so that it does not undermine divine transcendence (*tanzīh*). The wise men of the first generations (*salaf*) showed extreme reluctance in interpreting the "allegorical" Qur'anic verses (*mutashābiha*), while the wise men of later ages (*khalaf*) were more accepting of the allegorical interpretation (*ta'wīl*) of these same verses. For the latter, therefore, there was nothing wrong with considering this divine descent as a metaphor, which did not imply an actual descent, as was the case with the literal interpretation offered by some important ḥanbalite scholars, in particular Aḥmad Ibn Taymiyya (d. 1328), strongly opposed by most Sunnite scholars.[251] In any case, the interpretation of this ambiguous saying, which nevertheless lends itself well to mystical and esoteric interpretation, is still a source of disagreement among scholars of the various subdivisions of Islam.

20 The ascent

In addition to the notion of descent observed so far, it is possible to identify a complementary notion of ascent in the Qur'ān, which concerns the Spirit, angels and also men, particularly prophets.

The *sūra* of Ascensions (*al-Maʿārij*) is so called because two verses refer to God as Lord of Ascensions (*Dhū-l-maʿārij*):

> To Him the angels and the Spirit ascend (*taʿruju al-malā'ika wa-l-rūḥ ilayhi*), in a Day whereof the measure is fifty thousand years. [252]

According to the Qur'ān, therefore, the Spirit – who, as we have seen, is interpreted by Muslim exegetes in its highest dimension as identical to Gabriel – and the an-

---

250 Bukhārī, *Ṣaḥīḥ al-Bukhārī*, 2:157–158.

251 Khaled El-Rouayheb, "From Ibn Hajar al-Haytami (d. 1566) to Khayr al-Din al-Alusi (d. 1899), Changing Views of Ibn Taymiyya Amongst Non-Hanbali Sunni Scholars," in *Ibn Taymiyya and His Times*, ed. Yossef Rapoport and Shahab Ahmed (Oxford: Oxford University Press, 2010), 278–279.

252 Q 70:3–4.

gels, after having descended, undergo a process of ascent in the context of sacred time, identified in the "divine Day", which lasts "fifty thousand years".

The root used in these verses, *ʿ-r-j*, properly embodies the meaning of ascent, and *maʿārij* is the plural of *miʿrāj*, "ascension", a notion we will discuss shortly.

From the point of view of the Spirit and the angels, movement occurs in both directions since, as we have seen, according to the Qur'ān, these two entities descend and ascend with continuity in the context of cyclical sacred time, " divine Day" after "divine Day".

As for the descent that takes place in the context of divine Revelation (*tanzīl*), to every descent corresponds an ascent, and this function is ensured by the notion of prophetic ascension, which in Islamic tradition is precisely called *miʿrāj*, "ascension". In the Qur'ān, there is a relationship between the function of angels and prophets, since the same term, *mursal* (pl. *mursalūn*), "messenger", is used indistinctly to refer to both.

The process of the prophets' ascent proceeds by degrees or spiritual levels (*darajāt*):

> Those messengers – We have preferred some of them to others. There are some of them to whom God has spoken, and some of them He has raised in rank (*rafaʿa baʿdahum darajāt*).[253]

These two terms are found in various Qur'anic verses, with the same meaning; the verb *rafaʿa* means "to elevate, to make rise", and is thus analogous to the verb *rajaʿa*, while the term *darajāt*, "spiritual levels", refers to the level that each believer can reach in relation to God.[254] However, in the case of the prophets, as in the verse just mentioned, it refers metaphorically to the elevation stage of the ascent process. For this reason, God is defined in the Qur'ān as "He who elevates to the spiritual levels" (*Rāfiʿ al-darajāt*), followed by the attribute 'Possessor of the Throne' (*Dhū-l-ʿarsh*), which seems to metaphorically suggest the cosmological limit of the possibility of ascent precisely to the level of the divine Throne.[255]

Some verses seem to refer to a structure of the universe constituted through different degrees arranged on top of each other:

> And your Lord and the angels come rank on rank (*ṣaffan ṣaffan*).[256]

---

253 Q 2:253; cf. also 6:83, 12:76.
254 Q 3:163, 4:96, 6:165, 8:4, 17:21, 20:75, 43:32, 46:19, 58:11.
255 Q 4:15.
256 Q 89:22.

> But those who fear their Lord will have chambers [or levels] (*ghuraf*), with chambers built over them [or levels] (*ghuraf*).[257]

The Qur'ān then mentions a number of prophetic ascensions, of which the most archaic is considered to be that of the prophet Idrīs, as is evident from this verse:

> Mention Idrīs in the Scripture. He was a true friend of God, a prophet. We raised him to a high position.[258]

Most commentators identify Idrīs with the biblical prophet Enoch, who also performs a heavenly ascension in the Old Testament:

> Enoch walked with God; then he was no more, because God took him."[259]; "Enoch pleased the Lord and was taken up, an example of repentance to all generations.[260]

Another ascension mentioned in the Qur'ān is that of Jesus:

> Certainly, they did not kill him. No. God raised him to Himself.[261]

Since in a number of sayings, the Prophet declares that one of the signs of the End Times will be precisely the descent of Jesus, Islamic tradition takes Muḥammad's Ascension as a paradigm, which, as we shall see, also involves a descent, perceives his Ascension as still taking place, and therefore awaits his descent. The New Testament also describes Jesus' Ascension: "While he was blessing them, he withdrew from them and was carried up into heaven",[262] and also mentions his descent:

> When he had said this, as they were watching, he was lifted up, and a cloud took him out of their sight. While he was going and they were gazing up toward heaven, suddenly two men in white robes stood by them. They said, 'Men of Galilee, why do you stand looking up toward heaven? This Jesus, who has been taken up from you into heaven, will come in the same way as you saw him go into heaven.'[263]

Muḥammad's Ascension thus stands in continuity with the ascensions of Idrīs/ Enoch and Jesus, mentioned in the Qur'ān. This is not the occasion to go into detail

257 Q 39:20.
258 "*wa-rafaʿnāhu makānan ʿaliyyan*", Q 19:56–57.
259 Genesis, 5:24.
260 *Sirach*, 44:16; cf. also New Testament, *Hebrews*, 11:5.
261 "*rafaʿahu Allāh ilayhi*", Q 4:157–158.
262 *Luke*, 24:51.
263 *Acts*, 1:9–11; cf. also *Acts*, 1:2.

about this ascension, and I will limit myself to a few considerations, especially concerning the night on which it took place according to Islamic traditions, the Night of Ascension (*laylat al-miʿrāj*).[264] Most Sunni and some Shiʿa scholars place this night on the twenty-seventh day of the month of Rajab.[265] This night is complementary to the aforementioned Night of Measure (*laylat al-qadr*), which is generally placed by them on the twenty-seventh night of the month of Ramaḍān.[266] In the context of the Islamic sacred calendar, the Night of Measure represents, as we have seen, the moment in which the descent of the Spirit, of the angels and the Qurʾān upon the Prophet takes place. The ascension of the Spirit and the angels takes place instead, from a cosmological point of view, on the "divine Day" that lasts "fifty thousand years", mentioned in the *sūra* of the Ascensions, connected to the Night of Ascension, the night in which the Ascension of the Prophet Muḥammad took place.

Getting back to the main topic of this research, it can be observed that Muḥammad's Ascension is explicitly related in Islamic sources to God's bestowal of intercession on the Prophet. In one saying, for example, we observe the Prophet at the most crucial stage of the Ascension, when he is at the closest point to God, and he is granted three things: the five ritual prayers, the seals (*khawātim*) of the *sūra* of the Cow (*al-baqara*), and the forgiveness of the errors of the one who dies as a member of his community without associating anything with God.[267] In another saying, at this same time, God directly instructs the Prophet to exercise his intercession:

> Then it will be said to me: 'O Muḥammad! Lift up your head, intercede, for your intercession will be accepted (*irfaʿ raʾsaka wa-shfaʿ tushaffaʿ*), and ask, for it will be given to you.'[268]

21 The theological notion of intermediation in Islam

The respective metaphorical notions of descent and ascent imply a continuous connection, a constant flow, that somehow unites the divine and human worlds. What imagery transpires from the Islamic primary sources about this theological notion?

---

264 For an introduction to Muḥammad's Ascension, see Frederick S. Colby, *Narrating Muḥammad's Night Journey. Tracing the Development of the Ibn ʿAbbās Ascension Discourse* (Albany: State University of New York Press, 2008).

265 Bertram Schrieke et al, *Miʿrādj*, in *EI²*.

266 Roxanne D. Marcotte, *Night of Power*, in *EQ*.

267 Muslim, *Ṣaḥīḥ Muslim*, 1:522.

268 Bukhārī, *Ṣaḥīḥ al-Bukhārī*, 4:353–354.

22 The Rope of God

In the Qur'ān, we find a passage that seems to refer to the notion of intermediation:

> Hold fast to God's rope (*ḥabl Allāh*), all together, and do not split up.[269]

Muslim commentators of the classical era appear hesitant about the interpretation of this verse, with the majority of them stating that it is a metaphor for the Qur'ān, based on this saying of the Prophet:

> The book of God is a rope stretching from heaven to earth [...].[270]

As we have seen, the sacred text of Islam is indeed part of the descending entities and can involve a connection to the divine world, given its uncreated nature according to Sunni theology.[271] However, this spatial metaphor also seems very appropriate to describe the general intermediation process between the divine and human worlds since the rope, if placed vertically, can allow both descent and ascent. We will return later to the metaphysical dimension of the metaphor of the rope of God, through Islamic esoteric literature.

23 The ladder in the sky

Another Qur'anic passage mentions a further metaphor of intermediation:

> If their aversion lies heavy on yous, if you can seek a hole into the earth or a ladder into the sky (*sullam fī al-samā'*), and bring them a sign (*āya*).[272]

Among the divine signs brought by a prophet could, therefore, also be that of showing, to those who do not believe, a ladder in the sky, an image reminiscent of Jacob's dream in the Old Testament:

> He came to a certain place and stayed there for the night, because the sun had set. Taking one of the stones of the place, he put it under his head and lay down in that place. And he

---

269 Q 3:103.

270 *"Kitāb Allāh ḥabl mamdūd min al-samā' ilā al-arḍ," Tirmidhī, Sunan,* 1241–1242.

271 On the complex theological question concerning the uncreated or created Qur'ān, see Richard C. Martin, *Createdness of the Qur'ān*, in *EQ*.

272 Q 6:35.

> dreamed that there was a ladder set up on the earth, the top of it reaching to heaven; and the angels of God were ascending and descending on it.[273]

A very similar image also appears in the Qur'ān, in the *sūra* of the Ascensions (*al-maʿārij*), where, as we have seen, God is referred to as Lord of Ascensions (*Dhū-l-maʿārij*), with a root, *ʿ-r-j*, which can also indicate the notion of a ladder, and it is stated that:

> The angels and the Spirit ascend to Him (*taʿruju al-malāʾika wa al-rūḥ ilayhi*), on a day the measure of which is fifty thousand years.[274]

The image of the ladder in the sky in the above verse, besides showing an interesting example of intertextuality between the Old Testament and the Qur'ān, could refer precisely to this supernatural ladder that joins earth to heaven, on which the Spirit and the angels ascend, and on which the prophets also ascend, particularly Muḥammad during his ascension (*miʿrāj*). This ladder is not visible to the human eye because it is part of the invisible world (*ʿālam al-ghayb*), but if God willed, it could be made visible as a sign for the unbelievers so they would believe in the Prophet's mission.

24 Sacrifice (*qurbān*) as mediation and intercession

Among the forms of intermediation and intercession, in Judaism and Christianity, we also mentioned the notion of sacrifice. In Judaism, the sacrifice is performed by the High Priest in the Temple, while in Christianity through the self-sacrifice of Christ. As for Islam, one of the terms used in the Qur'ān for sacrifice, *qurbān*, seems to have a close relationship with the notion of intermediation and intercession. In fact, the primary meaning of the Semitic root *q-r-b* is "to bring near" or "to approach", originate the two meanings that interest us here. The first is related to the notion of *qurbān* as sacrifice, which is said to derive from the widespread custom, in the context of the ancient world – not only Semitic – of performing a sacrifice after which the sacrificial beast is incinerated on the altar. In Hebrew, the term used is *qorbān*, which in the Syriac and Arabic Christian lexicon takes on the metaphorical meaning of "Eucharist". As a result of the incineration, the smoke of the sacrifice rises to heaven, or the sacrifice itself metaphorically rises to heaven, thus drawing closer to God and placing itself in a position of interme-

273 *Genesis* 28:11–12.
274 Q 70:3–4.

diary vis-à-vis the person who performed or for whom the sacrifice was performed.

We can observe that also in Islam, the function of the ritual animal sacrifice, which is performed at the end of the pilgrimage to Mecca, as well as any other non-compulsory sacrifice, represents a request to God for atonement for sins, thus fulfilling an intercessory function.

From the perspective of the political lexicon, on the other hand, *qurbān* is the figure of the mediator towards the king, who possesses the rank defined as *qurba*, proximity to the king. It is precisely this proximity that allows him to fully exercise his intercessory function.[275]

25 The *wasīla*

Another Qur'anic notion precisely reflects the theological notion of intermediation: the *wasīla*. We find a reference to this notion in the *sūra* of the Banquet (*al-Mā'ida*):

> O you who believe, fear God and seek the means to approach Him (*wa-btaghū ilayhi-l-wasīla*).[276]

In the major Qur'anic commentaries of the classical period, the proposed meaning of *wasīla* is "closeness to God" (*al-qurba ilā Allāh*),[277] an exhortation to get as close as possible to God in a metaphorical and spiritual sense. From a linguistic point of view, the term *wasīla* means "trying to get close to something", and the etymological value offered by ancient lexicographical dictionaries is that of drawing water from the well employing a bucket, usually attached to a rope, a value that brings us back to the metaphor of the "rope of God" mentioned above.[278]

Another verse also states that even beings that humans sometimes mistake for gods, such as angels or some prophets, even those closest to God, are also forced to seek an intermediary to reach him (*yabtaghūna ilā rabbihim al-wasīla*).[279]

One thus finds in the Qur'ān an allusion to the idea of intermediation between the divine and human worlds, particularly through the notion of *wasīla*. It would

275 Arent Jan Wensinck, "Ḳurbān," in *EI²*.

276 Q 5:35.

277 Muḥammad Ibn Jarīr Ṭabarī, *Tafsir Ṭabarī: Jāmi' al-bayān 'an ta'wīl āyy al-Qur'ān* (Jīza: Hajr li-l-ṭibā'a wa-l-nashr, 2008), 8:403–404.

278 Edward William Lane, "*w-s-l*," in *An Arabic-English Lexicon* (Williams and Norgate, London 1863–93).

279 Q 17:56–57.

seem that the latter notion cannot be traced back to a specific entity, such as the Qurʾān, but rather to an extended notion of intermediation.

However, as we shall see below, in Islamic religious thought, the *wasīla* also represents a specific spiritual station, a cosmological place between the divine and human worlds. In this station, God allows the prophet Muḥammad to install himself in an undefined sacred time to enable him to exercise the intermediation and intercession reserved for him.

26 The *tawassul*

From the same root as *wasīla* comes the term *tawassul*, one of the terms in the Islamic technical lexicon used to indicate intermediation and intercession. This term does not appear in the Qurʾān but instead, we find it in the sayings of the Prophet, particularly in a saying attributed to ʿUmar that we will examine later, as it is related to the specific form of intercession for the evocation of rain (*istisqāʾ*). We shall also return to the notion of *tawassul* after dealing with *shafāʿa*, a term that, as we shall see, appears instead in the Qurʾān.

Chapter 4
The Theological Notion of Intercession in Islam

The main technical terms for intercession in Islam are *shafāʿa, tashaffuʿ* and *tawassul.* In addition, as we shall see, there are other terms in religious literature relating to intercession, notably *istighfār, istisqāʾ, istiʿāna, istighātha* and *tajawwuh.*[280]

1 The term *shafāʿa*

With regard to the root *sh-f-ʿ,* from which the term *shafāʿa* derives, ancient lexicographical dictionaries propose a very interesting etymology, according to which the form *shafʿ* indicates a single entity that becomes a pair (*zawj*), moving from unity to duality. In classical Arabic, *shafʿ* conveys the sense of "even", paired with *witr/watr* meaning "odd", as is evident from this verse of the Qurʾān:

> By the dawn, by ten nights, by the even and the odd (*wa-l-shafʿ wa-l-watr*), by the night when it travels[281]

Other meanings are inherent in the same semantic field, such as "doubling" and "duplicating".[282] The underlying idea seems to be that, in order to exercise intermediation, an other entity is required from a metaphysical point of view than the First Entity. Therefore only the transition from unity to duality, and subsequently to multiplicity, can imply the possibility of intermediation and intercession.

Another meaning in ancient dictionaries, again in connection with the first, is to add oneself to a person to help him, becoming his mediator and intercessor for a given matter.[283] This meaning is applied in particular with regard to intercession with a sovereign, especially when it is performed by a person with a higher rank than the one for whom it is intended. Other meanings are "to recommend someone", "to protect", and "to patronise".[284] These latter meanings do not refer, in their more external meaning, to a religious type of intercession. However,

280 Taqī al-Dīn al-Subkī, *Shifāʾ al siqām fī ziyārat khayr al-anām* (Dār al-kutub al-ʿilmiyya, Bayrūt 2008), 383.
281 Q 89:1–4.
282 Eva Riad, "Šafāʿa dans le Coran," in *Orientalia Suecana* XXX (1981), 37.
283 Ibid., 38.
284 Ibid., 39–44.

https://doi.org/10.1515/9783111500966-009

they are interesting from a linguistic and historical point of view as they show similarities with the type of non-religious intercession observed in the context of the ancient world, which, as we have seen, gave rise to the very term *intercessio* in Latin. This kind of intercession appears in ancient Islamic literature, for instance in the following sayings of the Prophet:

> The Messenger of God stated: 'One of the best intercessions is to intercede between two persons concerning marriage.'[285]

> If someone intercedes for one of his brothers (*man shafaʿa li-akhīhi bi-shafāʿa*) and he gives him a gift which he accepts, he has been guilty of a severe form of usury (*al-ribā*).[286]

A verse from the Qur'ān intervenes precisely to warn Muslim believers about the ethical issues underlying this kind of "social" intercession:

> Those who make fair intercession (*man yashfaʿ shafāʿa ḥasana*) will have a share of it; whilst those who make evil intercession (*man yashfaʿ shafāʿa sayyiʿa*) will bear the responsibility for it. God has power over everything.[287]

Finally, another non-religious meaning of this root, through the term *shufʿa* in the context of Islamic commercial law, refers to the idea of "granting the right of preemption" to someone.[288]

2 The *shafāʿa* in the Qur'ān, between negation and possibility

The root *sh-f-ʿ* appears in the Qur'ān on several occasions, through various forms, including the main form *shafāʿa*. The peculiarity of this term in the Qur'ān is that it appears there with a defective calligraphy, which does not show the long vowel after the letter *fāʾ*, but merely bears a small vertical miniature alif (*alif khanjariyya*) between the *fāʾ* and the *ʿayn*. This denotes that *shafāʿa* is one of the ancient terms that were written in this way in the earliest versions of the Qur'anic materials, the so-called sheets (*ṣuḥuf*), which only contained a few verses. These verses were written using only the simplified consonantal *ductus*, without the long ones, to serve as a mnemonic aid and not as a complete phonetic transcription. The first generations of Muslim philologists, out of conservatism, did not dare to "correct"

285 *"Min afḍal al-shafāʿa an yushaffaʿa bayna al-ithnayn fī al-nikāḥ,"* Ibn Mājah, *Sunan,* 352.
286 Abū Dāwūd, *Sunan,* 5:399.
287 Q 4:85. On the various interpretations of this verse by both Muslim exegetes and contemporary scholars, see Eva Riad, "Šafāʿa dans le Coran," in *Orientalia Suecana* XXX (1981), 50–51.
288 Bukhārī, *Ṣaḥīḥ al-Bukhārī,* 3:255.

the writing of these terms – to which the divine name *al-Raḥmān*, "the Merciful", for instance, also belongs – but transcribed them exactly as they had found them, in all subsequent versions of the Qurʾān, up to the present day, daring only to add a miniature *alif* to indicate their correct reading.[289] That this term is part of the most ancestral stratum of the Qurʾanic lexicon denotes its antiquity and highlight its importance in the eyes of the first generation of Muslims.

The notion of *shafāʿa* in the Qurʾān is expressed through a style characteristic of this sacred text. Some verses of the Qurʾān seem to absolutely deny the possibility of intercession on the Day of Judgement, while others seem to allow it, albeit under certain conditions.

Some passages are peremptory in indicating a suspension of intercession on the Day of Judgement:

> Protect yourselves against a day when no soul will give any satisfaction for any other, nor will any intercession be accepted from it (*wa-lā yuqbalu minha shafāʿa*) nor any equivalent be taken from it, and they will not be helped.[290]

"O you who believe, spend some of that which We have given you as provision before a day comes on which there will be neither bargain nor friendship nor intercession (*shafāʿa*). The unbelievers are the wrong-doers."[291]

> Do they expect anything but its interpretation? On the day when its interpretation comes, those who previously forgot it will say,'The messengers of our Lord brought the truth. Have we any intercessors to intercede for us (*fa-hal lanā min shufaʿāʾ fa-yashfaʿū lanā*), or shall we be returned to do other than what we were doing?'[292]
>
> The intercession of intercessors will be of no use to them.[293]

Other passages, however, seem to reserve intercession only for certain categories of people, as in the following verse:

> They will have no power of intercession, except those who have acquired a covenant with the Merciful.[294]

---

289 William Wright, *A Grammar of the Arabic Language, translated from the German of Caspari and edited with numerous additions and corrections by W. Wright* (Cambridge: Cambridge University Press, 2009), 9.

290 Q 2:48.

291 Q 2:254.

292 Q 7:53.

293 *"fa-mā tanfaʿuhum shafāʿat al-shāfiʿīn"*, Q 74:48.

294 *"lā yamlikūn al-shafāʿa illā man ittakhadha ʿinda al-Raḥmān ʿahdan"*, Q 19:87.

> Those [the deities] to whom they [the unbelievers] call apart from Him have no power of intercession, except in the case of those who bear witness to the truth and who have knowledge.[295]

Other verses, finally, seem to indicate that the exercise of intercession depends on divine permission granted to an angel or human being for this purpose. The most significant example can be observed within what is considered by Muslim scholars to be one of the most important verses of the Qurʾān, if not the most important, the verse of the Pedestal (*āyat al-kursī*), which has strong apotropaic significance:

> God. There is no god but Him, the Living, the Eternal. Neither slumber nor sleep seize Him. To Him belongs all that is in the heavens and all that is on earth. Who is there who intercedes with Him, save by His permission (*man dhā-l-ladhī yashfaʿu ʿindahu illā bi-idhnihi*)? He knows what is before them and what is after them, while they encompass none of His knowledge apart from that which He wishes. His Pedestal (*kursī*) comprises the heavens and earth, and He is not tired by guarding them. He is the Exalted and the Mighty.[296]

The Qurʾān thus asserts that no being can intercede with God without His permission, and this is also reiterated in another verse, which shows a semantic relationship with the verse already quoted, since the divine Throne (*al-ʿarsh*) is mentioned in it:

> Your Lord is God, who created the heavens and the earth in six days, then set Himself on the Throne, directing the affair. There is no intercessor unless He has given His permission (*mā min shafīʿ illā min baʿd idhnihi*].[297]

The same concept is repeated even more peremptorily in another verse, in which God invites the Prophet, and with him all believers, to make a statement:

> Say: 'To God belongs all intercession (*qul li-Llāh al-shafāʿa jamīʿan*).'[298]

Because of this ambiguity, throughout the history of Islam, various religious scholars have legitimised their own and sometimes opposing positions on intercession from the same verses. A thorough work of exegesis on these verses, as we shall see, is invariably provided in the opening chapters of the works that accept or reject inter-

---

295 *'wa-lā yamliku-l-ladhīna yadʿūn min dūnihi al-shafāʿa illā man shahida bi-l-ḥaqq wa-hum yaʿlamūn'*, Q 43:86.
296 Q 2:255.
297 Q 10:3.
298 Q 39:44.

cession and its various modalities, within the framework of Islamic religious literature.

3 The intercession of the Qur'ān

In addition to being the primary source for the doctrine of intercession in Islam, the Qur'ān itself appears to be a veritable spiritual entity capable of interceding for believers, according to certain sayings of the Prophet:

> Recite the Qur'ān, for indeed on the Day of Resurrection it will intercede for those who recite it.[299]

The reading of individual chapters of the Qur'ān similarly represents a form of intercession, and the most common is the recitation of the Opening *sūra* (*al-Fātiḥa*). Besides being recited continuously as part of the obligatory and optional ritual prayers, this chapter also serves as the "closing" formula for all kinds of invocations. Moreover, this *sūra* is recited individually or in groups as spiritual support for distressed or deceased believers, particularly in the context of the visit to cemeteries and graves.

The verse of intercession par excellence is the verse of the Pedestal (*āyat al-kursī*), which, as we have seen, benefits from a singular position compared to all other verses, which results from the Prophet's teaching to his Companions.[300] Starting from the observation that the verse is named after the Pedestal, one may speculate that its importance may be sought in this very mention, associated with intercession. Another saying mentioned earlier, shows the Prophet prostrating himself under the Throne (*'arsh*) and obtaining intercession:

> People will come to me and I will prostrate myself under the Throne [of God] (*fa-asjudu taḥta al-'arsh*). Then it will be said to me, 'O Muḥammad! Lift up your head, intercede, for your intercession will be accepted (*irfa' ra'saka wa-shfa' tushaffa'*), and ask, for it will be given to you.'[301]

The Throne is associated in the *ḥadīth* with God's Mercy:

---

299 Muslim, *Ṣaḥīḥ Muslim*, 2:541.
300 Muslim, *Ṣaḥīḥ Muslim*, 2:546.
301 Bukhārī, *al-Bukhārī*, 4:353–354.

> When God completed the creation, He wrote in the Book that is with Him on the Throne (*fawq al-ʿarsh*): 'My Mercy prevails over My Wrath (*inna raḥmatī ghalabat ghaḍabī*).'[302]

From these notions and others that will be added later, it is possible to outline a cosmological structure of intermediation and intercession that involves the divine Mercy of the Throne (*al-ʿarsh*) and below it, the intercessory power of the Pedestal (*al-kursī*). As we shall see, the latter is placed in Islamic sources in relation to the prophet Muḥammad as the spiritual station that allows him to exercise the highest level of intermediation and intercession for creatures. This is probably why the recitation of the verse of the Pedestal is perceived by Muslims, from the earliest generations, as the highest mode of intercessory request to God.

4 The intercession of fasting

Judging from some *ḥadīth*, fasting (*ṣawm*, *ṣiyām*), particularly ritual fasting during the month of Ramaḍān, also seems to be able to intercede for believers, in the same way as the Qurʾān:

> The fasting and the Qurʾān will intercede for the servant [the believer] on the Day of Judgement (*al-ṣiyām wa-l-qurʾān yashfaʿān li-l-ʿabd*). The fast will say: 'O my Lord, by day I have kept him from food and passions, accept my intercession for him (*fa-shaffiʿnī*)'. The Qurʾān will say: 'I have kept him from sleep by night, accept my intercession for him (*fa-shaffiʿnī*)'. Then their intercession will be accepted (*fa-yushaffaʿān*).[303]

5 The intercession of angels

We have seen some passages in the Qurʾān mentioning that certain creatures can obtain permission to intercede on God's part. Some verses, in particular, suggest that this is primarily the angels:

> Those who bear the Throne (*al-ʿarsh*), and those around it [the angels] glorify their Lord with praise and believe in Him and seek forgiveness for those who believe (*yastaghfirūn li-l-ladhīna āmanū*).[304]

302 Ibid., 4:277–278.
303 Ibn Ḥanbal, *Musnad*, 11:199.
304 Q 40:7.

The same verse then continues with a formula of prayer, forgiveness and protection from the torments of hell that the angels recite for believers according to the divine will.[305]

The intercessory action of the angels is thus manifested through the request for forgiveness (*istighfār*), which is precisely one of the modes of intercession in Islam. The mention of the Throne (*ʿarsh*) in this last verse could support the position that this is precisely the level at which divine mercy is to be located in the Qurʾanic cosmological system.

Other verses show the angels in the exercise of asking for forgiveness:

> The heavens are almost split asunder from above when the angels glorify their Lord by praising him and seek forgiveness for all those on earth (*yastaghfirūn li-man fi-l-arḍ*). Truly God is the Forgiving and Compassionate.[306]

However, another verse reiterates that even angels, defined as "honoured servants" (*ʿibād mukarramūn*), "can only intercede for the one whom He [God] pleases (*wa-lā yashfaʿūn illā li-man irtaḍā*)."[307]

6 The search for the intercession of deities other than God and the "satanic verses"

While it is therefore permissible to seek the intercession of angelic creatures, from the Islamic point of view, men are guilty of a grave transgression if they instead seek the intercession of deities other than God:

> They worship, to the exclusion of God, what can neither hurt them nor benefit them. They say, 'These are our intercessors with God (*hāʾulāʾi shufaʿāʾunā ʿinda Allāh*).' Say, 'Will you tell God what He does not know in the heavens or on earth?' Glory be to Him. May He be exalted far above what they associate with Him.[308]

Islamic sources narrate that seeking the intercession of various deities, particularly the so-called "daughters of Allāh", al-Lāt, al-ʿUzzā and Manāt, was a common practice in pre-Islamic times. However, Muḥammad's preaching, following the instructions conveyed to him by God through the Revelation of the Qurʾān, immediately lashed out against the worship of these deities. The reaction in defence of pil-

---

305 Q 40:8–9
306 Q 42:5.
307 Q 21:26–28.
308 Q 10:18.

grimages and pre-Islamic cults by the notables of the Mecca tribe of the Quraysh was vehement for reasons at once religious, social and economic. In this context, mention should be made of the well-known episode of the "satanic verses", narrated in some classical historical sources, among which we can mention Ibn Isḥāq (d. 767) and Ṭabarī (d. 923), but considered inauthentic by some Muslim scholars.[309] According to these sources, the Prophet would have suffered from the rejection of his preaching by members of his tribe, and for this reason, he would have ardently wished to be able to compromise with them. Because of this "weakness" of his, during the Revelation of some verses of the *sūra* of the Star (*al-Najm*), Iblīs, the foremost of the devilish beings, managed to briefly insert himself between Gabriel and Muḥammad by interpolating a verse. Gabriel had just recited these verses: "What do you think of al-Lāt and al-ʿUzzā, and the other, the third, Manāt?"[310] when Iblīs interpolated the following verse: "These high *gharānīq:* verily, their intercession is approved (*tilka al-gharānīq al-ʿulā wa-inna shafāʿatahunna la-turtajā*)".[311] The rare plural term *gharānīq* is variously interpreted in exegetical sources, which usually converge in identifying in it an epithet in relation to the beauty and rank of these deities.[312] The sources continue by reporting that the Muslim believers who first heard it did not immediately realise the problem, relying on the Prophet's transmission. The non-Muslim members of the Quraysh tribe, on the other hand, were greatly pleased to hear these words, and when the time came for ritual prostration, all, Muslims and non-Muslims alike, bowed together behind the Prophet's leadership, so much so that the Muslims believed for a moment in the conversion of the non-Muslims. However, following this, Gabriel visited the Prophet and warned him that this particular verse was not from his transmission and that it contradicted other verses that had already been revealed, of which the one quoted above is an example. The Prophet was greatly disturbed by this, to such an extent that, according to some Muslim scholars, God revealed this verse to comfort him:

> Whenever We sent a messenger or a prophet before you, and he had the desire [to recite], Satan tampered with his desire. But God annuls Satan's tamperings, and then God confirms His signs. God is Knowing and Wise.[313]

---

309 On this topic, see Shahab Ahmed, *Before Orthodoxy: The Satanic Verses in Early Islam* (Harvard University Press, Cambridge, Massachusetts 2017).
310 Q 53:19–20.
311 Shahab Ahmed, *Before Orthodoxy: The Satanic Verses in Early Islam* (Harvard University Press, Cambridge, Massachusetts 2017), 49.
312 Ibid., 60–64.
313 Q 22:52.

Chapter 5
The Intercession of the Prophet Muḥammad

As we have pointed out, some scholars who have dealt with the notion of intercession have argued that in the Qur'ān, the intercessory function (*shafāʿa*) is not explicitly connected to Muḥammad. Some have interpreted this as a sign that the Prophet's doctrine of intercession only originated in the centuries following his death. However, Muslim exegetes interpret several Qur'anic verses related to intercession as referring to the Prophet himself. Moreover, in the Prophet's sayings, we find a large number of explicit mentions of Muḥammad's function as an intercessor, particularly on the Day of Judgement.

1 The request for forgiveness (*al-istighfār*)

The Qur'ān seems to grant the Prophet, like the angels, to intercede to ask God for forgiveness on behalf of the believers, according to the practice already mentioned (*al-istighfār*). Although Muḥammad's proper name is not mentioned in these verses, exegetes consider that when the Qur'ān uses the formula " messenger" or "prophet" in the third person, it is actually referring to him:

> We did not send any messenger except that he might be obeyed by God's permission. Had they come to yous when they wronged themselves and sought God's forgiveness and the messenger had sought forgiveness for them (*wa-staghfara lahum al-rasūl*), they would have found God relenting and compassionate.[314]

> The believers are only those who believe in God and His messenger and who, when they are with him on some common matter, do not leave till they have sought his permission. Those who ask permission of you – those are the ones who believe in God and His messenger; so if they ask your permission for some affair of theirs, grants it to those whom you wish, and ask forgiveness for them (*wa-staghfir lahum Allāh*). God is Forgiving and Compassionate.[315]

> When it is said to them, 'Come, and the messenger of God will seek forgiveness for you,' (*yastaghfir lakum rasūl Allāh*) they turn their heads. You see them turning away and being haughty.[316]

> O Prophet, when believing women come to you, offering allegiance to you on the basis that they will not associate anything with God nor steal nor fornicate nor kill their children, nor produce any lie they devise between their hands and their feet, nor disobey you in something

314 Q 4:64.
315 Q 24:62.
316 Q 63:5.

https://doi.org/10.1515/9783111500966-010

> recognized as right, accepts their allegiance and seek God's forgiveness for them (*wa-staghfir lahunna-Llāh*). God is Forgiving and Compassionate.[317]

In the following verses, on the other hand, the Qur'anic discourse refers to a second person without making his identity explicit, but exegetes agree that in such cases, the discourse is always addressed to the Prophet:

> It was through some mercy from God that you were lenient with them. Had you been rough and hard-hearted, they would have scattered from around you. Forgives them and seek forgiveness for them (*fa'fu 'anhum wa-staghfir lahum*), and take counsel with them in the affair. Then when you have decided, put your trust in God. God loves those who put their trust [in Him].[318]

> Takes alms from their possessions, by which yous might purify them and make them clean, and send blessings to them (*wa-ṣalli 'alayhim*). Your prayers of blessing are a comfort for them. God is Hearing and Knowing.[319]

> Know that there is no god but God and seek forgiveness for your sin and for the believers, men and women (*wa-staghfir li-dhanbika wa-li-l-mu'minīn wa-l-mu'mināt*). God knows where you turn about and where you lodge.[320]

However, we find in the Qur'ān the affirmation that even the Prophet's intercession can only be exercised if it coincides with the divine Will, and certainly not towards unbelievers:

> Ask forgiveness for them or do not ask forgiveness for them (*astaghfir lahum aw lā tastaghfir lahum*). If you ask forgiveness for them seventy times (*in tastaghfir lahum sab'īn marra*), God will not forgive them. That is because they disbelieve in God and His messenger. God does not guide the people who are reprobates.[321]

2 The prophets' request for forgiveness

In some verses of the Qur'ān, we can observe prophets before Muḥammad exercising intercession. Among them, we find Abraham (Ibrāhīm), whose case is similar to that of Muḥammad, since his willingness to intercede for an unbeliever, albeit in this case his father, does not meet with divine favour. An early verse manifests Abraham's intention in this regard:

---

317 Q 60:12.
318 Q 3:159.
319 Q 9:103.
320 Q 47:19.
321 Q 9:80.

> He [Abraham] said [to his father], 'Peace be on you. I shall ask my Lord to forgive you. He has always shown kindness to me.'[322]

Another verse, however, seems to disapprove of this behaviour and deny divine support for Abraham's intercession:

Except that Abraham said to his father, 'I shall seek forgiveness for you, though I have nothing to help you against God,'[323]

However, this does not imply denying that this possibility can occur outside this specific case, and indeed in the *sūra* of Joseph (Yūsuf), we see his father, the prophet Jacob (Yaʿqūb), begging for forgiveness and interceding for his sons, guilty of plotting against Joseph himself:

> They said, 'Father, ask forgiveness for us for our sin (*yā abā-nā-staghfir lanā dhunūbanā*). We were sinners. He said, 'I shall ask my Lord to forgive you (*sawfa astaghfir lakum rabbī*). He is Forgiving and Merciful.'[324]

3 The Prophet's major intercession on the Day of Judgement (*al-shafāʿa al-ʿuẓmā*)

As we have seen, the Qurʾān provides the possibility of intercession by the Prophet but does not directly relate this intercession to the term *shafāʿa* or terms derived from its root. Nevertheless, *shafāʿa* is the main term used in Islamic religious literature regarding the Prophet's intercession, particularly his intercession on the Day of Judgement. This type of intercession is often referred to as "major intercession" (*al-shafāʿa al-ʿuẓmā, al-shafāʿa al-kubrā*) since it concerns the forgiveness of "major sins" (*al-kabāʾir*), if one excludes the major sin of associating other deities with God (*shirk*), which cannot be forgiven without repentance and conversion. The legitimacy of this practice is based on numerous sayings of the Prophet, for each of which various versions are found in the main collections, and of which I will mention only the most representative:

> The Messenger of God said: 'Verily, God will bring people out of the Fire through intercession (*inna Allāh yukhriju qawm min al-nār bi-l-shafāʿa*).'[325]

---

322 Q 19:47.
323 Q 60:4.
324 Q 12:97–98.
325 Muslim, *Ṣaḥīḥ Muslim*, 1:551.

> I will be the first intercessor in Paradise (*anā awwal shafī' fī-l-janna*). No prophet has been accepted [by such a large number of people] as I have been. Verily there will be a prophet who has been accepted by only one man of his people.[326]

> The happiest people because of my intercession (*as'ad al-nās bi-shafā'atī*) on the Day of Resurrection will be those who have pronounced 'there is no deity but God' with sincerity of heart.[327]

> The Messenger of God said: 'For every prophet there is a special invocation [that will be answered] with which he addresses [God], and I want to keep this invocation to intercede for my community in the Hereafter (*wa urīdu an akhtabi'a da'watī shafā'a li-ummatī fī-l-ākhira*).'[328]

> On the Day of Resurrection people will fall to their knees and each community will follow its prophet and say, 'O such [prophet], intercede! (*yā fulān ishfa'*),' until it will end with intercession to the Prophet [Muḥammad] (*al-shafā'a ilā al-nabī*) and that will be the day when God will raise him to the Station of praise (*yab'athuhu Allāh al-maqām al-maḥmūd*).[329]

> The Prophet said, 'My intercession is especially meant for the great sinners in my community (*shafā'tī li-ahl al-kabā'ir min ummatī*).'[330]

This last saying is perhaps the most widespread in Islamic context concerning the Prophet's intercession, as it touches on the sensitive issue of forgiveness of grave sins. This is why it has become part of the Sunni and Shi'a creeds, as we will see below.

Therefore, should one consider the Prophet's intercession as reserved only for the great sinners among Muslims or for the entire community of believers (*umma*)? Regarding this question, one can find various positions in the sayings of the Prophet. Some sayings seem to support the view that it is indeed only necessary for great sinners:

> I was given the choice between intercession (*al-shafā'a*) or having half of my community (*umma*) enter Paradise and I chose intercession because it is more general and more sufficient. Do you think it is for the pious? No, it is for impure sinners.[331]

Judging by other sayings, however, it is extended to all believers:

> Do you know what choice my Lord has placed before me on this night? We answered: "God and His Messenger know best. He said: "He has given me the choice between entering half of

326 Ibid., 1:565.
327 Bukhārī, *al-Bukhārī*, 8:326.
328 Ibid., 8:183–184.
329 Ibid., 6:223.
330 Abū Dāwūd, *Sunan*,7:119.
331 Ibn Mājah, *Sunan*, 753.

my community into Paradise and intercession, and I have chosen intercession". We said: "O Messenger of God, pray that we may be considered as part of your people". He said, 'It is for every Muslim.'[332]

4 Early historical evidence of belief in the Prophet's intercession

The existence of mentions of the Prophet's intercession from a religious point of view within the poetry of the early Islamic era has been pointed out, as we have seen, by some scholars. The difficulty in establishing their actual antiquity limits their use as a historical source. More certain, however, is the attribution of the inscriptions on the Prophet's *shafāʿa* inside the Dome of the Rock (*qubbat al-ṣakhra*) in Jerusalem. This unique monument was completed in Umayyad times between 691 and 692 and is considered one of the oldest surviving examples of Islamic architecture. Inside the dome, some of the ancient mosaic inscriptions, composed of Qur'anic verses, end with non-Qur'anic formulas related to the intercession of Muḥammad.[333] One of these inscriptions is found on the outside of the octagonal archway, in the north-east band:

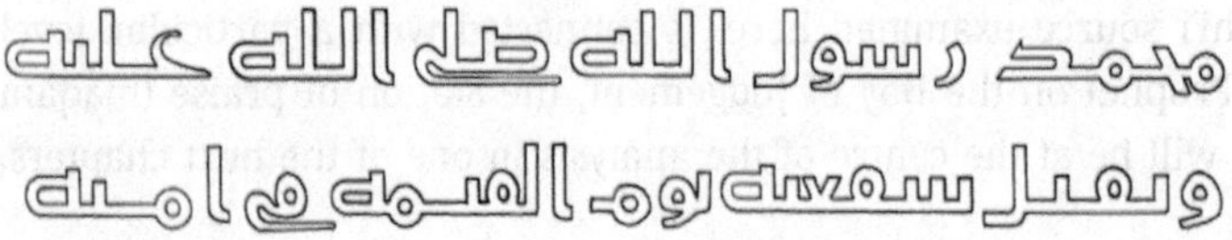

Fig. 1: copy of the original handwriting found inside the Dome of the Rock, Marcus Milwright, The Dome of the Rock and its Umayyad Mosaic Inscriptions (Edinburgh: Edinburgh University Press, 2016), XVII.

> Muḥammad rasūl Allāh ṣallā Allāh ʿalayhi
> wa taqabbal shafāʿatahu yawm al-qiyāma fī ummatihi
> Muḥammad is the Messenger of God, may God bless him.
> and accept his intercession on the Day of Resurrection for his community.

---

332 Ibid., 755.
333 Marcus Milwright, *The Dome of the Rock and its Umayyad Mosaic Inscriptions* (Edinburgh: Edinburgh University Press, 2016), 70–71.

Another inscription is found on a copper plaque that was originally affixed near the east entrance to the dome:

> We ask Thee, our God, by Thy Mercy, by Thy beautiful Names, by Thy noble Face, by Thy immense Power, by Thy perfect Word by which heaven and earth stand together and by which, and by Thy Mercy, we are preserved from the devil and are saved from Thy chastisement on the Day of Resurrection, by Thy abundant Grace, by Thy great Nobility, by Thy Clemency, Thy Power, Thy Forgiveness and Thy Goodness, may Thou bless Muḥammad, Thy servant and Thy prophet, and may Thou accept his intercession (*shafāʿahu*) for his community. May God bless him and grant him peace and the Mercy of God.[334]

These occurrences clearly show the antiquity of the reference to the notion of prophetic *shafāʿa* in the Islamic tradition.

A similar formula is also present, up to the present day, within the Twelver Shiʿa ritual prayer as a supererogatory invocation that completes the attestation of faith (*tashahhud*) before the final greeting:

> [...] and accept his intercession for his community, approach his mediation and raise his spiritual level.[335]

This indicates that the notion examined above, relating to the divine action of raising the spiritual level of creatures, associated with the divine name Rāfiʿ al-darajāt, at least in the Shiʿi source examined here, is connected with a particular level promised to the Prophet on the Day of Judgement, the Station of praise (maqām maḥmūd), which will be at the centre of the analysis in one of the next chapters.

5 The Prophet's intercession before his birth

As we shall see in a later chapter, as the centuries passed, a strong devotion to the prophet Muḥammad spread among Islamic populations, and in some circles esoteric doctrines connected to his cosmic and esoteric dimension developed. According to some of these doctrines, which, as we shall see, show similarities with the doctrines of the ancient world connected to the *logos*, the spiritual nature of Muḥammad is pre-existent to all other creatures. From this premise, interesting narratives have spread, such as the following, which relates the eternity of Muḥam-

334 Ibid., 75.

335 "*wa-taqabbal shafāʿatahu fī ummatihi wa-qrab wasīlatihi wa-rfaʿ darajatihi*", Muḥammad Bāqir al-Majlisī, *Biḥār al-anwār al-jāmiʿa li-durar akhbār al-aʾimma al-aṭhār* (Bayrūt: Dār al-iḥyāʾ al-turāth al-ʿarabī, 1983), 82:288.

mad's nature and prophetic mission to his function as a universal intercessor. This episode is taken from a late but important and widespread biography of Muḥammad, commonly called *al-Sīra al-ḥalabiyya*, composed by ʿAlī ibn Burhān al-Dīn al-Ḥalabī (d. 1635).[336] According to this narration, an ancient Yemenite king named Tabaʿ ibn Ḥassān al-Ḥumayrī, who lived 1,000 years before the Prophet's time, foretold the arrival of Muḥammad and thus drafted a missive addressed to him that contained the following words:

> O Muḥammad, verily I believe in thee, in thy Lord and of all things, and in all that has come from thy Lord, and in all the sacred provisions relating to religious practice and faith (*sharāʾiʿ al-islām wa-l-īmān*), and therefore I affirm this: if I can meet you, I shall rejoice in that; but if I cannot meet you, grant me your intercession on the Day of Judgement (*fa-shfaʿ lī yawm al-qiyāma*), and do not forget me! I am part of the lineage of the first men, I took the covenant of alliance with you before your coming, before God sent you as a messenger, I am part of your religion and the religion of Abraham! (*anā ʿalā millatika wa-millat Ibrāhīm*).

At this point, Tabaʿ would deliver the missive to a wise man of his time, ordering that it be handed down until the time of the Prophet Muḥammad. During the Emigration (*ḥijra*) from Mecca to the future Medina, the Prophet met a certain Abū Laylī, the last person to have inherited the task of transmitting this letter and asked him to hand it over. When he read it, the Prophet said, "Welcome to Tabaʿ, the righteous brother!"[337]

This kind of narrative clearly shows the spread and adaptations of Muḥammad's doctrine of intercession in the context of medieval and pre-modern Islamic societies.

6 The Prophet's intercession during life and after death

While some *ḥadīth* present the characteristics of his intercessory function on the Day of Judgement, other sayings show the Prophet exercising intercession already during his lifetime:

---

336 Catherine Mayeur-Jaouen, "'There Is Matter for Thought': The Episode of the Night Journey and the Heavenly Ascension in the *Sīra ḥalabiyya*, at the Beginning of the Seventeenth Century," in *The Presence of the Prophet in Early Modern and Contemporary Islam: Volume 1, The Prophet Between Doctrine, Literature and Arts: Historical Legacies and Their Unfolding*, ed. Denis Gril, Stefan Reichmuth and Dilek Sarmis (Leiden: Brill, 2022), 115–150.
337 ʿAlī ibn Burhān al-Dīn al-Ḥalabī, *Insān al-ʿuyūn fī sīrat al-amīn al-maʾmūn* (Bayrūt: Dār al-kutub al-ʿilmiyya, 2013), 2:279–280.

> A blind man came to the Prophet and asked him: 'Beg God to heal me'. He replied, 'If you want I will beg for you, but if you prefer, be patient, for that is better for you.' He said: 'Then beg him.' Then he commanded him to perform the ablution thoroughly, and to plead with this supplication: 'O God, I ask and address thee through thy Prophet Muḥammad, the Prophet of mercy. Verily, I have turned to my Lord, through Thee, concerning this need of mine, so that it may be resolved, therefore, O God, accept his intercession for me.'[338]

In Islamic religious literature, this episode is often used to legitimise the recourse to the Prophet's intercession even after his death since this prayer (*du'ā'*) is considered to have been taught by the Prophet himself to believers, without him specifying that its validity would cease following his departure. These same sources, among which we may mention, for example, the famous traditionalist al-Ṭabarānī (d. 971), have this saying followed by another, which contains a later episode, taking place after the Prophet's death, during the caliphate of 'Uthmān ibn 'Affān (r. 644–656). A man came to the caliph seeking to resolve a matter, but 'Uthmān paid no attention and did not attend to his need. Then this man went to the governor of Baṣra at the time, called 'Uthman Ibn Ḥunayf, and complained to him. 'Uthman Ibn Ḥunayf was a Companion of the Prophet, and he was precisely the transmitter of the saying just mentioned about the blind man receiving the Prophet's intercession. The governor ordered the man to perform the ritual ablution and voluntary prayer in which, after pronouncing the initial greeting, he was to utter the same invocation that he had heard from the Prophet when the blind man had come to him. 'Uthman Ibn Ḥunayf then advised the man to return after accomplishing this and afterwards they would go together to the caliph. The man carried out what the governor had ordered him. However, instead of returning to him, he chose to go alone to the caliph. When he reached the door of the caliph's room, the guardian led him by the hand to him. 'Uthmān ibn 'Affān sat him down next to him and asked him what need he wanted to be met since he had forgotten about it until just now. The man informed the caliph of his need, which was immediately granted. The caliph then told him to return to him whenever he had a new need.[339] This episode is often cited in the Sunnite literature of intercession, and the interpretation offered is as follows: thanks to the Prophet's intercession following the invocation,t he caliph 'Uthmān remembers and meets the man's need. According to most Sunni scholars, this is clear proof of the permissibility of this practice and the fact that it actually "works" even after the Prophet's death.

---

338 "*Allāhumma innī as'aluka wa-atawajjahu ilayka bi-nabiyyika Muḥammad nabī al-raḥma innī tawajjahtu bika ilā rabbī fī ḥājatī hādhihi li-tuqḍā lī Allāhumma fa-shaffi'hu fiyya*", Tirmidhī, *Sunan*, 1179.

339 Ṭabarānī, *al-Mu'jam al-ṣaghīr*, 1:173–174.

Another narrative often mentioned in the sources is the following, where an eminent Companion such as ʿAbd Allāh ibn ʿUmar ibn al-Khaṭṭāb (d. 693) is observed seeking help and succour from the Prophet, even after his death:

> Ibn ʿUmar had a leg affected by paralysis, and a man said to him, 'Mention the person you love most (*udhkur aḥabb al-nās ilayka*),' and he replied, 'O Muḥammad! (*yā muḥammad*).'[340]

This narrative ends, in some of the available versions, with the healing of the famous transmitter of traditions, and this attests to its effectiveness according to apologetic literature.[341]

The Sunni religious scholars, as well as the Twelver Shiʿa ones, starting from the sayings just mentioned, thus accept the possibility of the Prophet's intercession during his lifetime. The persistence of the validity of intercession after his death, on the other hand, is an open and controversial question, connected to the more general issue of the status of the deceased, particularly prophets, martyrs and pious men. The importance of this issue is highlighted by the existence of an ancient treatise devoted to this question, entitled "The Life of the Prophets after their Death", composed by the famous Persian theologian and traditionalist Abū Bakr Aḥmad ibn Ḥusayn al-Bayhaqī (d. 1066).[342] This text contains various traditions, which, as we shall see, provide evidence of this belief from the Sunnite point of view, starting with the most famous one, handed down through various chains of transmission:

> The prophets are alive in their graves and praying.[343]

The same idea is conveyed through other variants:

> Verily the prophets are not left in their graves more than forty nights, but [then] they pray before God until the trumpet [of the Day of Judgment] shall be blown.[344]

> A prophet does not stay in his grave for more than forty nights, and then he is resurrected.[345]

---

340 Bukhārī, *al-Adab al-mufrad*, 250.
341 Ibn ʿAsākir, *Tārīkh madīnat Dimashq* (Bayrūt: Dār al-Fikr, 1997), 3:177.
342 Abū Bakr Aḥmad ibn Ḥusayn Bayhaqī, *Ḥayāt al-anbiyāʾ ṣalawāt Allāh ʿalayhim baʿd wafātihim* (al-Madīna al-munawwara: Maktaba al-ʿulūm wa al-ḥikma, 1993).
343 "*al-Anbiyāʾ aḥyāʾ fī qubūrihim yuṣallūn*", *ibid*, 70–74.
344 '*inna al-anbiyāʾ lā yatrukūn fī qubūrihim baʿd arbaʿīn layla wa-lakinnahum yuṣallūn bayn yaday Allāh ḥattā yunfikh fī al-ṣūr*', ibid., 75.
345 "*mā makatha nabī fī qabrihi akthar min arbaʿīn layla hattā yurfaʿ*", ibid., 76–77.

These narratives, in addition to referring to the life of the prophets after death, are also the foundation for mourning practices in Islamic societies, where the custom of remembering the deceased and praying for him forty nights after his departure is widespread. This celebration is called the "fortieth [day]" (*arbaʿīn*) and is analogous to the Catholic masses of trigesima (thirty days) as well as the ceremonies performed in Eastern Orthodox Christianity forty days after a decease. The most famous anniversary of this kind in Islamic context is the one commemorating the death of al-Ḥusayn (d. 680), the Prophet's grandson. It is precisely called *arbaʿīn*, and takes place forty days after the *ʿĀshūrāʾ*, which celebrates, among other things, the actual day of his death. This celebration involves a pilgrimage to his grave in Kerbela, performed in particular by Twelver Shiʿites.[346]

The text of Bayhaqī reports some variants of a narrative relating to Muḥammad's meeting with various prophets preceding him during his Ascension, particularly with Moses. The narratives insist that the various prophets were intent on performing the ritual prayer.[347]

One tradition in particular refers to the post-mortem condition of prophets:

> Verily God has forbidden the earth to consume the bodies of the prophets, upon them be peace.[348]

Regarding the prophet Muḥammad in particular, some *ḥadīth* seem to confirm the possibility of his life after death:

> No one addresses a greeting of peace to me without God returning my spirit so that I in turn may respond with a greeting of peace.[349]
>
> God has angels roaming the earth to bring me greetings from my community.[350]
>
> I am able to hear who sends blessings upon me at my grave and I am informed of who sends blessings upon me from afar.[351]

Bayhaqī later reports a tradition in which the Prophet relates that at the End of Times, in the terrible passage in which every living creature will die before

346 Mahmoud Ayoub, "Arbaʿīn," in *EIr.*
347 Abū Bakr Aḥmad ibn Ḥusayn Bayhaqī, *Ḥayāt al-anbiyāʾ ṣalawāt Allāh ʿalayhim baʿd wafātihim* (al-Madīna al-munawwara: Maktaba al-ʿulūm wa al-ḥikma, 1993), 77–85.
348 *ʿinna Allāh qad ḥarrama ʿalā al-arḍ an taʾkul ajsād al-anbiyāʾ ʿalayhi-l-salām,*' ibid., 88.
349 *ʿmā min aḥad yusallimu ʿalayya illā radda-Llāh ʿilayya rūḥī ḥattā arudda ʿalayhi al-salām,*' ibid., 97.
350 *ʿinnā li-Llāh malāʾika sayyāḥīn fī al-arḍ yuballighūnī ʿan ummatī al-salām,*' ibid., 101.
351 *ʿman ṣallā ʿalayya ʿinda qabrī samiʿtuhu wa Man ṣallā ʿalayya naʾiyā bullightuhu,*' ibid., 104.

being resurrected, some prophets, including himself, will lose consciousness. He will later be the first to regain it, and he will stand before Moses:

> A Muslim and a Jew were insulting each other, the Muslim said, 'By Him who chose Muḥammad in the universe, I take this oath.' The Jew replied: 'He who chose Moses in the universe'. Then the Muslim raised his hand and slapped him. The Jew then went to the Prophet and informed him of the affair between him and the Muslim. The Prophet said: 'Do not prefer me to Moses! Verily, men will be stunned [on the Day of Judgment], and I will be the first to regain consciousness, and then Moses will be attached to the side of the Throne. I shall not know whether he is among those who have been stunned and regain consciousness before me, or among those for whom God has made an exception.'[352]

Another saying, reported by Jalāl al-Dīn al-Suyūṭī (d. 1505), similarly refers to the Prophet's intercession even after his death:

> My life is good for you, for you speak to me and I answer you, and my death is also good for you, for your deeds are presented to me and I praise God for what I see as good, while I ask God's forgiveness on your behalf (*istaghfartu-Llāh lakum*) for what I see as bad.[353]

As far as martyrs are concerned, the evidence, according to the scholars, comes from the Qur'ān itself and relates to the fact that believers who die in battle should not actually be considered as such:

> Do not say of those who are killed in the way of God, 'dead'. No. They are living, but you do not perceive [that].[354]

> Do not reckon those who were killed in God's way as dead: No! [They are] alive with their Lord. They have provision [from Him].[355]

As for the possibility of life in the grave for men more generally, some Muslim scholars rule it out based on a Qur'ānic verse:

> Yous cannot make the dead hear (*innaka lā tusmi'u al-mawtā*), nor can you make the deaf hear the call (*al-du'ā*).[356]

352 "*Lā tukhayyirūnī 'ala Mūsā fa-inna al-nās yaṣ'aqūna yawm al-qiyāma fa-akūnu awwal man yufīq fa-idhā Mūsā bāṭish bi-jānib al-'arsh fa-lā adrī ukāna mimman ṣa'iq fa-afāqa qablī aw kāna mimman istathnā Allāh,' ibid,* 107.

353 Suyūṭī, *al-Jāmi' al-ṣaghīr,* 1:582.

354 Q 2:154.

355 Q 3:169.

356 Q 27:80.

However, leading exegetes of the Qur'ān claim that this verse is expressed through a rhetorical formula, a metaphor that refers specifically only to the call (*al-du'ā'*), the call to Islam, and is addressed to the polytheists of the Prophet's time.[357]

Other sayings seem to support the idea that there remains some connection between the living and the dead, such as the following:

> Verily, when the believer [servant, *'abd*] is laid in his grave and his companions depart from him, he hears the sound of their sandals.[358]
>
> 'Ā'isha reported that the Messenger of God came out in the latter part of the night to go to the [cemetery of] al-Baqī' and said: 'Peace be upon you, O abode of the believers. That which was promised to you for tomorrow [Paradise], you receive it with a little delay; and God willing we shall join you. O God, grant forgiveness to the inhabitants of Baqī' al-Gharqad!'[359]

While the latter sayings refer to deceased Muslims, in another saying, we observe Muḥammad addressing his worst non-Muslim enemies, killed in battle:

> The Messenger of God allowed the bodies of the unbelievers who had fought at Badr to remain unburied for three days. Then he approached them, sat down by their side, called them, and said: 'O Abū Jahl ibn Hishām, or 'Umayya ibn Khalf, or 'Utba ibn Rabī'a, have you not found true what your Lord has promised you [a terrible punishment]? For I have found true what my Lord has promised'. 'Umar, hearing the Prophet's statement, asked him, 'How can they hear and how can they ever respond since they have become rotting corpses?' He replied, 'By Him with whom my soul is kept, you are no more able to hear what I say to them, although they cannot answer.' Then he gave the order and they were dragged and thrown into a pit at Badr.[360]

Based on such indications from primary sources, the majority position among Sunni and Twelver Shi'a Muslim scholars is that the prophet Muḥammad should be considered alive in his tomb, present in the dimension of the intermediary world (*al-barzakh*), and that believers can turn to him, as well as to other prophets and pious men, to obtain his intercession.

357 Abū 'Abd Allāh al-Qurṭubī, *al-Jāmi' li-aḥkām al-Qur'ān wa-l-mubayyin li-mā taḍammanahu min al-sunna wa-āyyi-l-furqān* (Bayrūt: Mu'assasat al-risāla, 2006), 16:205.
358 Muslim, *Ṣaḥīḥ Muslim*, 7:254.
359 Muslim, *Ṣaḥīḥ Muslim*, 3:153. Baqī' al-Gharqad is the cemetery near the mosque in Medina where the Prophet's most important Companions are buried, cf. Werner Ende, *"Baqī' al-Gharqad,"* in *EI*^{3}.
360 Muslim, *Ṣaḥīḥ Muslim*, 7:257–258.

7 The believers' demand for forgiveness

References can be found in Islamic primary sources that intercession can be granted not only to prophets, but also to other men, particularly with regard to Muslim believers' request for forgiveness:

> It is not for the Prophet and those who believe to seek pardon for the polytheists (*mā kāna li-l-nabī wa-l-ladhīna āmanū yastaghfirū li-l-mushrikīn*), even if they were to be near kinsmen, after it has become clear to them that they are companions of the Fire."[361]

Although the expression is phrased in a negative sense, it is evident that believers can join the Prophet in asking for forgiveness (*istighfār*). In the following verse, then, the Qur'ān directly suggests to the believers an intercessory formula of asking for forgiveness:

> Those who have come after them say, 'Our Lord, forgive us and our brothers who have preceded us in the faith, and do not put in our hearts any rancour towards those who have believed. Our Lord, You are Kind and Compassionate.'[362]

The possibility of intercession by believers also emerges from some of the Prophet's sayings, such as the following:

> Verily, in my community there are those who intercede (*man yashfaʿu*) for large groups of people (*li-l-fiʾām*), and among them those who intercede for a tribe (*li-l-qabīla*), and among them those who intercede for a group (*li-l-ʿusba*), and among them those who intercede for a man (*li-l-rajul*), until they enter Paradise.[363]

Among believers, a special category is that of martyrs:

> The Prophet said, 'The intercession of a martyr will be accepted for seventy members of his family.'[364]

361 Q 9:113.
362 Q 59:10.
363 Tirmidhī, *Sunan*, 883.
364 Abū Dāwūd, *Sunan*, 4:176.

8 Ritual prayer for the dead

The ritual prayer for the dead (*ṣalāt al-janāza*), one of the most widely practised rites of passage within Islamic societies, can be considered as one of the modes of intercession, as it appears from some of the Prophet's sayings:

> If a group of one hundred Muslims pray over a deceased person, and they all intercede for him (*kulluhum yashfaʿūn lahu*), their intercession will be accepted (*illā shuffiʿū fīhi*).[365]

The prayer of children towards their parents is also a form of intercession:

> When a man dies, all his works end except three: an almsgiving that continues to bear fruit, a beneficent knowledge that he has left behind him, and a righteous son to pray for him.[366]

More generally, any kind of invocation to God for forgiveness, request for healing and overcoming difficulties with regard to another living person, or request for forgiveness of sins and elevation of spiritual rank concerning a deceased person, is a form of intercession. However, its acceptance by God depends, as we shall see, on the spiritual rank of the person performing it.

In a later chapter, we will examine how Sunni and Shiʿa Muslim scholars systematised the possibility of intercession by different categories of men, starting with these Qurʾanic verses, the sayings of the Prophet, and the practices of the first generations of believers.

9 The prayer of intercession for rain (*ṣalāt al-istisqāʾ*)

Another mode of intercession attested in primary sources is the prayer for the descent of rain (*ṣalāt al-istisqāʾ*), a supererogatory practice that became very common in Islamic societies throughout history. The *ḥadīth* narrates an episode from the Prophet's life when the city of Medina was going through a period of extreme drought. Because of this, a person entered the mosque while the Prophet was busy preaching the Friday prayer, urging him to beg God for rain. At that point, he raised his arms to the sky and repeated the formula three times: "O my Lord, let the rain fall (*Allāhumma-sqinā*)," turning his tunic (*jubba*) inside out as a sign of humility before God.[367]

365 Muslim, *Ṣaḥīḥ Muslim*, 3:126.
366 Ibid., 4:347.
367 Bukhārī, *Ṣaḥīḥ al-Bukhārī*, 2:73–75.

Another tradition related to the request for rain shows the Prophet rejecting a request for intercession:

> A nomadic Arab came to the Messenger of God and said: 'People are suffering, children are hungry, crops have withered and animals have died, ask God to grant us rain (*fa-stasqi-Llāh lanā*), because we seek you as an intercessor with God (*nastashfiʿu bika ʿalā Allāh*) and we seek God as an intercessor with you (*nastashfiʿu bi-Llāh ʿalayka*).' The Messenger of God replied: 'Woe to you! Do you realise what you are saying?' Then he said, 'May God be exalted!' (*subḥāna-Llāh*) and continued to repeat it until the effect of it was visible on the faces of his Companions. Then he added: 'Woe unto you: God is not to be sought as intercessor with anything that He has created. God is immense in respect of that. Woe unto you! Know that the Throne of God is above the heavens – and he pointed with his fingers like a dome above him – which groan because of Him like a saddle because of the rider.'[368]

This tradition is very interesting because it shows the custom on the part of the believers in considering the Prophet as an intermediary vis-à-vis God in the request for rain, but also because it shows the Prophet's vehement reaction in the face of the nomadic Arab who demands not only the Prophet's intercession with God but even God's intercession with the Prophet, putting them on the same level. This clearly cannot be accepted by Muḥammad, who strongly rebukes the nomad and repeatedly exalts God, seeking forgiveness for this kind of careless utterance on the part of believers.

Even after the Prophet's death, supplication for rain through his intercession continued to be practised:

> The people of Medina complained to ʿĀʾisha about the severe drought they were suffering. She said: 'Go to the tomb of the Prophet and open a window to the sky so that there is no ceiling between him and the sky'. They did so, after which the rain was such that the vegetation grew and the dromedaries grew fat. That year was called the year of plenty.[369]

This narrative is also worthy of interest, as it stages the Prophet's intercession through a very concrete spatial symbolism, through the implementation of a connection between heaven and earth that allows the descent of the divine blessing (*baraka*) through the rain.

In another narration, we observe ʿUmar ibn al-Khaṭṭāb wearing the Prophet's robe and performing the prayer for rain,[370] adding to this practice of intercession

---

368 Abū Dāwūd, *Sunan*, 7:103.

369 Dārimī, *Sunan*, 1:56.

370 Jalāl al-Dīn al-Suyūṭī, *Taʾrīkh al-khulafāʾ* (Bayrūt: Muʾassasat ʿIzz al-Dīn, 1992), 140.

through the Prophet the intercession of one of the most eminent living members of his family, namely his uncle al-ʿAbbās ibn ʿAbd al-Muṭṭalib (d. 653):

> 'O God! We used to ask for the intercession of our Prophet towards You (*innā kunnā natawassalu ilayka bi-nabiyyinā*) and You made it rain (*fa-tasqīnā*), and we now ask for the intercession of the uncle of our Prophet towards You (*wa-innā natawassalu ilayka bi-ʿamm nabiyyinā*), make it rain! (*fa-sqinā*)'. And it rained (*fa-yusqawn*).[371]

We may add that the image of rain is a perfect metaphor for intermediation since it descends vertically from above downwards, symbolising, as we have seen, the descent of divine blessing. We must also remember that the verb used in the Qur'ān to indicate the descent of sustenance (*rizq*) from God to humanity is *nazala,* the same verb used to indicate the descent of divine Revelation, and among the different kinds of sustenance we also mentioned water, in the form of rain, hail and snow.

10 The request for help (*al-istiʿāna*) and relief (*al-istighātha*)

Two other terms recur frequently in the terminology of intercession with a very similar meaning, yet showing some differences in usage. The first is *istiʿāna,* meaning "to seek, to ask for help", from the root *ʿ-w-n,* "to help, to assist,"[372] which appears in various forms in the Qur'ān and the Prophet's sayings, most notably in the Opening *sūra* (*al-Fātiḥa*), in the passage "At thee we seek help (*iyyāka nastaʿīn*)."[373] The Prophet, in some sayings, calls God "the One from whom one seeks help (*al-mustaʿān*),"[374] while he states in another saying, "And when you seek help, seek help from God (*wa-idhā-staʿanta fa-staʿīn bi-Llāh*)".[375] Although it is sometimes mentioned in the literature of intercession, this term cannot be included in the technical terminology related to this notion since the believer, through the *istiʿāna* addresses God directly, without intermediaries.

The second term is *istighātha,* from the root *gh-w-th* with the primary meaning of "to call for help and succour",[376] and refers to the request for assistance

371 Bukhārī, *Ṣaḥīḥ al-Bukhārī,* 2:81.

372 Edward William Lane, "*ʿ-w-n,*" in *An Arabic-English Lexicon* (London: Williams and Norgate, 1863–93).

373 Q 1:5.

374 Muslim, *Ṣaḥīḥ Muslim,* 6:246.

375 Tirmidhī, *Sunan,* 902.

376 Edward William Lane, "*gh-w-th,*" *An Arabic-English Lexicon* (London: Williams and Norgate, 1863–93).

from an intermediary, one of the modes of intercession. We find one of the forms of its root in a Qur'anic verse:

> He entered the city at a time when its people were off their guard; and he found two men fighting there, one from his own faction and the other from his enemies. The one who was from his faction sought his help (*fa-staghāthahu*) against the one who was from his enemies; so Moses struck him and finished him off. He said, 'This is of Satan's doing. He is an enemy who clearly leads astray.'[377]

The *ḥadīth* also refers to a request for help in an episode in which Hagar (Hājar), Abraham's concubine, finding herself alone in the desert with her son Ishmael (Ismāʿīl), hears a voice and then asks according to one version "I heard you, can you help me? (*qad asmaʿta in kāna ʿindaka ghiwāth*)"[378] or, according to another version, "Help, if you are well inclined! (*aghith in kāna ʿindaka khayr*)".[379] The presence turns out to be that of Gabriel, who comes to the aid of the mother and child by bringing forth a spring of water with his heel.

We also find the same root in another *ḥadīth:*

> On the Day of Resurrection, the sun will come so close that the sweat will reach halfway up the ears, so when all the people will be in such a condition, they will ask Adam for help, then Moses, then Muḥammad (*istaghāthū bi-Ādam thumma bi-Mūsā thumma bi-Muḥammad*).[380]

The term *istighātha* has thus come into use in the Islamic context, with particular reference to the request for help formulated towards the Prophet, starting with narratives such as the one cited above, where ʿAbd Allāh ibn ʿUmar ibn al-Khaṭṭāb is observed, in the era following the Prophet's death, to seek help and succour through the invocation "O Muḥammad!"

We shall see later how, in the esoteric Islamic doctrines, a figure emerges who, in turn, personifies the role of the one who comes to help when invoked, the "Supreme Helper" (*al-ghawth al-aʿẓam*), so named precisely from the root *gh-w-th.*

In this chapter, we examined the various prerogatives of intercession from primary Islamic sources, and then investigated the specific modalities of the prophet Muḥammad's intercession. In the next chapter, we will address the Prophet's function defined as *tajawwuh*, showing how his role as intercessor acquires royal connotations in religious literature, particularly in relation to his special role on the Day of Judgement.

---

377 Q 28:15.

378 Bukhārī, *Ṣaḥīḥ al-Bukhārī*, 4:377.

379 Ibid., 4:381.

380 Ibid., 2:347–348.

Chapter 6
The *tajawwuh* and the Prophet's royal attributes of intercession on the Day of Judgement

In this chapter, we will discuss the notion of *tajawwuh*, a term derived from the Arabic term *jāh*, with the meaning of "rank, function, dignity," especially in the presence of the sovereign. In ancient Arabic lexicographical dictionaries, we can find the following definition of the term:

> The *jāh* is the position and status vis-à-vis the sovereign (*al-manzila wa-l-qadr ʿinda al-sulṭān*).[381]

Although Arabic linguists often propose Arabic etymologies for this term, it is actually a term of ancient Indo-Persian origin, which is also found in Indian languages. Its meaning in Old Persian and Avestic Persian refers specifically to the place where this rank is expressed and is thus analogous to the Arabic term *maqām*, which, as we shall see, means both "place" and "rank". In avesthetic sources, this term is often equated with a throne or other type of royal seat.[382] In the transition between Pahlavi and Persian, the term *jāh*, while retaining the meaning of "place," began to express the meaning of "rank, degree, function, dignity, greatness, magnificence, honour, reputation, fortune, prosperity." With the latter meaning, it also entered the Arabic lexicon as a synonym for the related term *jalāl*, which, on the contrary, entered the Persian, although the term *jalāl* is more used to denote divine dignity and exaltation, while *jāh* is rather used in relation to creatures.[383]

In the context of the terminology of intercession, the term *jāh* refers to the rank and degree (*al-daraja*) of proximity to God (*al-qurba ilā Allāh*), which enables the Prophet to exercise a special function on the Day of Judgement and more generally allows him to perform the role of universal mediator, which we shall analyse in the next chapter.

---

381 Ibn Manẓūr, *Lisān al-ʿarab* (Bayrūt: Dār al-maʿārif, 1984–1986), 1:733.

382 Mary Boyce, "*Gāh, i. Place,*" in *EIr.*

383 Francis Joseph Steingass, *A comprehensive Persian-English dictionary, including the Arabic words and phrases to be met with in Persian literature, being Johnson and Richardson's Persian, Arabic, and English dictionary revised, enlarged, and entirely reconstructed* (Routledge & Kegan Paul Limited, London 1892), 354.

https://doi.org/10.1515/9783111500966-011

1 The *wasīla* of the Prophet

As noted earlier, a Qur'anic verse exhorts believers to seek intermediation with God (*wasīla*).[384] Alongside the more general dimension of this notion, which we dealt with earlier, there is a more specific dimension connected to the function of the prophet Muḥammad, which will be the focus of the analysis addressed in this chapter.

Since this verse lends itself to interpretation, Qur'anic commentaries, as we have seen, propose proximity to God (*al-qurba ilā Allāh*) as the primary meaning of the term *wasīla*, and thus place this verse in relation to another verse:

> And some part of the night, keep vigil by performing supererogatory prayers. Perhaps your Lord will raise you to Station of praise (*ʿasā an yabʿathaka rabbuka maqāman maḥmūdan*).[385]

Since even this verse is not explicit for whom the promise of the Station of praise is addressed, interpreters, starting with the traditionalist Muḥammad ibn Ismāʿīl al-Bukhārī (d. 870) resort to the Prophet's saying above, as well as other sayings:

> On the Day of Resurrection people will fall to their knees and each community will follow its prophet and say, 'O such [prophet], intercede! (*yā fulān ishfaʿ*),' until it ends with intercession to the Prophet [Muḥammad] (*al-shafāʿa ilā al-nabī*) and that will be the day when God will raise him to the Station of praise (*yabʿathuhu Allāh al-maqām al-maḥmūd*).[386]
>
> The Messenger of God was asked about the word of God: 'Perhaps your Lord will raise you to a Station of praise,' and he said: 'It is intercession (*hiya al-shafāʿa*).'[387]

Other sayings of the Prophet insist on this interpretation, citing what is known as "the prayer of intermediation" (*duʿāʾ al-wasīla*):[388]

> Whoever after hearing the call to prayer recites: 'O God! Lord of this perfect call and of the prayer that will be fulfilled, grant Muḥammad the intermediation (*al-wasīla*) and precellency (*al-faḍīla*), and raise him to a Station of praise (*wa-baʿathahu maqāman maḥmūdan*) that You have promised him,' then my intercession (*shafāʿatī*) will be granted to him on the Day of Resurrection.[389]
>
> When you hear the call to prayer, repeat what is recited, then invoke the blessing upon me (*ṣallū ʿalayya*), because whoever invokes the blessing upon me (*man ṣallā ʿalayya ṣalā*) God

384 Q 5:35.
385 Q 17:79.
386 Bukhārī, *Ṣaḥīḥ al-Bukhārī*, 6:223.
387 Tirmidhī, *Sunan*, 1064.
388 Andrew Rippin, "*Taṣliya*," in *EI²*.
389 Bukhārī, *Ṣaḥīḥ al-Bukhārī*, 1:587.

> will send ten blessings upon him (*ṣallā-Llāh ʿalayhi bihā ʿasharan*). Then ask God to grant me the intermediation (*al-wasīla*), which is a station (*manzila*) in Paradise that belongs only to one of God's servants, and I hope it can be me. If anyone asks that I be given the intermediation (*al-wasīla*), he will be assured of intercession (*ḥallat lahu shafāʿa*).[390]
>
> The Prophet said, 'Ask God to grant me intermediation (*al-wasīla*).' They said: "O Messenger of God, what is intermediation?" He replied: "The highest level of Paradise. No one will reach it except a man, and I hope it will be me.'[391]
>
> Intermediation (*al-wasīla*) is a degree with God (*daraja ʿinda Allāh*) above which there is no other degree, pray to God to grant me intermediation.[392]

The latter narratives propose a precise interpretation of the term *wasīla*, identifying it with a rank in Paradise, the closest to God and the highest in a metaphorical spatial sense, which only one person can access. The *wasīla* is thus the Qurʾanic term for this place, which is also a rank and a station. Instead, the denomination connected to the prophet Muḥammad's function is the Station of praise (*al-maqām al-maḥmūd*), in which we observe the presence of a term (*maḥmūd*) formed from the same root as the name Muḥammad, *ḥ-m-d*, indicating the action of praising or being praised. The further clarification offered by Muḥammad himself is that it is precisely access to this particular level of Paradise that grants him the special possibility of intercession, as appears from the saying mentioned above, in which the Station of praise is interpreted precisely as intercession (*shafāʿa*).

From the earliest Qur'anic commentaries, moreover, a further verse is cited in connection with the *wasīla* verse:

> Your Lord will give to you [something], and you will be satisfied.[393]

Exegetes, among other interpretations, generally assert that this promise from God refers precisely to the special intercession of the prophet Muḥammad on the Day of Judgement. Among these commentaries, we can mention a few, such as the one attributed to the Prophet's famous Companion ʿAbd Allāh ibn ʿAbbās (d. 687), who states that what God will grant the Prophet is "intercession in the Hereafter (*fī al-ākhira min al-shafāʿa*)."[394] Another classical Sunnite commentary, by Abū ʿAbd Allāh al-Qurṭubī (d. 1273), includes the following comments on this verse:

---

390 Muslim, *Ṣaḥīḥ Muslim*, 2:137.
391 Tirmidhī, *Sunan*, 1199.
392 Suyūṭī, *al-Jāmiʿ al-ṣaghīr*, 2:53.
393 '*wa-la-sawfa yuʿṭīka rabbuka fa-tarḍā*', Q 93:5.
394 ʿAbd Allāh Ibn ʿAbbās, *Tanwīr al-miqbās min tafsīr Ibn ʿAbbās* (Bayrūt: Dār al-kutub al-ʿilmiyya, 1992), 651; this commentary is traditionally attributed to the Companion Ibn ʿAbbās (d. 687), but it is probably a late collection of his interpretations.

It is intercession (*shafāʿa*) for the whole of the believers (*muʾminīn*). [...] The Prophet said, 'God will make me intercede for my community (*yushfaʿunī-Llāh fī ummatī*) until He will ask me, 'Are you satisfied, O Muḥammad?' And I will answer, 'O Lord, I am satisfied.'" [...] The Prophet recited God's word in the *sūra* of Abraham (*Ibrāhīm*), 'Those who follow me shall be of my own, and as for those who disobey me, verily Thou art Forgiving, Merciful!,'[395] and the word of Jesus, 'If Thou punish them, verily they are Thy servants,'[396] and then he raised his hands and said, 'O my Lord, my community, my community!' and wept. God then said to Gabriel: 'Go to Muḥammad and say to him: 'God says to thee: 'Verily We shall satisfy thee concerning thy community, and we shall not displease thee!'' [...] When this verse came down, the Prophet said: 'By God! I will not be satisfied until even one of my community is in Hell.'[397]

2 The rank (*al-jāh*)

When Arabic became the official language of Islamic courts, the term *wasīla* became part of the court lexicon, with a specific meaning. This is evident from the primary meaning of this term, proposed in one of the most important lexicographical dictionaries of Arabic, "The Precise and the Great Comprehensive" (*al-Muḥkam wa-l-muḥīṭ al-aʿẓam*) by the Andalusian philologist Ibn Sīda al-Mursī (d. 1066), a meaning later reported as primary also by dictionaries such as "The Tongue of the Arabs" (*Lisān al-ʿarab*):

> *al-Wasīla* is the position (*al-manzila*) in the king's presence, the rank (*al-daraja*), the proximity (*al-qurba*).[398]

This usage reminds us of the importance and prestige accorded to the function of intercession vis-à-vis the sovereign in the context of court life in the pre-modern Christian world,[399] and the same can be said of the pre-modern Islamic world. The main terms used in the terminology of Islamic courts to indicate this privileged position are *wasīla, manzila, daraja, qurba* and *jāh*. The term *jāh*, in particular, will enjoy widespread use in Islamic political terminology throughout the centuries, for instance, by prominent authors such as Ghazālī and Ibn Khaldūn (d.

395 Q 14:36.
396 Q 5:118.
397 Abū ʿAbd Allāh al-Qurṭubī, *al-Jāmiʿ li-aḥkām al-Qurʾān wa-l-mubayyin li-mā taḍammanahu min al-sunna wa-āyyi-l-furqān* (Bayrūt: Muʾassasat al-risāla, 2006), 22:341–342.
398 Ibn Sīda al-Mursī, *'w-s-l'*, *al-Muḥkam wa-l-muḥīṭ al-aʿẓam* (Bayrūt: Dār al-kutub al-ʿilmiyya, 2000).
399 Sean Gilsdorf, *The Favor of Friends. Intercession and Aristocratic Politics in Carolingian and Ottonian Europe* (Leiden: Brill, 2014).

1406).[400] This term is used as a synonym for *wasīla* and also for *maqām*, a very ancient term that has the primary meaning of "place of the feet" and can indicate both a standing and sitting position, as well as a level and rank, both in a proper and metaphorical sense.[401] All these terms ultimately refer to the intercessory position closest to that of the ruler.

3 The metaphor of kingship

In some formulations in the primary sources, the technical terminology of intercession related to the prophet Muḥammad displays an obvious metaphorical dimension. As we have seen above, the rhetorical structure of the Qur'ān makes extensive use of a theological metaphor according to which God, in relation to the cosmology of the divine world, is described as "the King" (*al-Malik*), who rules over various kingdoms. The attribute of God as "King" is particularly connected to the events of the Day of Judgement. Within this cosmology, God as King possesses a Throne (*ʿarsh*) and a Pedestal (*kursī*). However, one should not consider these notions merely metaphorical since they correspond to precise theological and cosmological realities, as reflected in classical exegetical interpretations.[402] Indeed, it should be considered that one of the thorniest theological questions is precisely the meaning of the formula referring to God "set up on the Throne" (*istawā ʿalā al-ʿarsh*), frequently repeated in the Qur'ān.[403] This formula, which, for fear of incurring the theological "sin of anthropomorphism" is not interpreted literally by the theologians – who lean towards the so-called "without [wondering] how" (*bi-lā kayf*) – is part of the metaphor of kingship, which describes God as a "King". Complementing this metaphor are some of the characteristics that the Qur'ān and the *ḥadīth* attribute to the prophet Muḥammad in connection with his function on the Day of Judgement.

---

400 Abdesselam Cheddadi, "Le système du pouvoir en Islam d'après Ibn Khaldûn," in *Annales. Economies, sociétés, civilisations* 3–4 (1980), 534–550.

401 Edward William Lane, "*q-w-m*," *An Arabic-English Lexicon* (London: Williams and Norgate, 1863–93).

402 Jamal Elias, "Throne of God," in *EQ*.

403 There are precisely seven occurrences of this formula in the Qur'an (7:54; 10:3; 13:2; 20:5; 25:59; 32:4; 57:4), on two occasions in verses containing references to intercession (10:3; 32:4).

4 The Prophet between servitude and kingship

In some sayings, the issue of Muḥammad's choice between being a prophet-king (*malik nabī*) or a servant–messenger (*ʿabd rasūl*) appears:[404]

> Gabriel was seated with the Prophet, and he looked up to heaven as an angel descended. Gabriel said: 'Verily, this angel has never descended since the day he was created, and [he will not descend again] before the Hour [of Judgement].' Said [the angel who had descended], 'O Muḥammad, your Lord has sent me to you asking whether you wish to be a prophet–king (*malik nabī*) or a servant–messenger (*ʿabd rasūl*).' Gabriel said, 'Be humble before your Lord, O Muḥammad.' He [the Prophet] said, 'I prefer to be a servant–messenger (*ʿabd rasūl*).'[405]

In other traditions, we observe the Prophet's renunciation of the royal characteristics of temporal power, starting with his habit of eating sitting on the ground in a simple manner, without following the customs of the courts connected to political power, which prescribed eating while leaning or reclining, using luxurious vessels.[406] During the Friday sermon, moreover, he did not sit on the pulpit (*minbar*), as a king sitting on a throne would do, but remained standing, and when, on one occasion, he held a staff (*qaḍīb*), almost as if it were a sceptre, he was rebuked by an angel.[407] The idea that transpires from the sources, however, is that this was not an actual choice on the part of the Prophet, but rather his conforming to the divine Will, communicated to him by the angels.

Starting with sayings similar to this, a critique of kingship developed in the formative phase of Islam, which finds space in the so-called ascetic literature (*zuhd*), and left a deep impression in the classical Sunni tradition. The political idea of sovereignty in Islamic societies has always shown this tension between the religious ideal of power shown by the behaviour of the Prophet and the first four caliphs and the practice of "royal" power in the various courts of later

---

404 Samuela Pagani, "Roi ou serviteur? La tentation du Prophète, ou le choix d'un modèle," in *Archives de sciences sociales des religions*, 178 (2017), 43–68.

405 Ibn Ḥanbal, *Musnad*, 12:76–77; cf. also the other very similar versions of this narration transmitted by ʿAbd al-Razzāq al-Sanʿānī (d. 826) in the *Muṣannaf*, Samuela Pagani, "Roi ou serviteur? La tentation du Prophète, ou le choix d'un modèle," in *Archives de sciences sociales des religions*, 178 (2017), 52–53, 57.

406 Patrizi, Luca. "The Metaphor of the Divine Banquet and the Origin of the Notion of Adab," in *Knowledge and Education in Classical Islam. Religious Learning between Continuity and Change*, edited by Sebastian Günther (Leiden: Brill, 2020) 1:526; "Roi ou serviteur? La tentation du Prophète, ou le choix d'un modèle," in *Archives de sciences sociales des religions*, 178 (2017), 51–52.

407 Ibid., 52–54.

Islamic history.[408] This religious and sober idea of power continued to be encouraged by the *'ulamā'* class through the centuries, with the notable exception of Ibn Taymiyya (d. 1328), who instead attempted a compromise between the prophetic and royal dimensions in his "The Caliphate and the Monarchy" (*al-khilāfa wa-l-mulk*). According to Ibn Taymiyya, the figures of Joseph, David and Solomon show how it is possible to unite the prophetic function with the royal one, in the same way as it is possible to unite in the Islamic era, the caliphal function with the royal one. On the part of the Syrian scholar, these arguments probably derive from an effort to legitimise and defend the Sunnite institutions contemporary to him in the face of the Alid drifts of his era.[409]

As we shall see from the primary sources, the characteristics associated with temporal power that seem to have been denied by God to the Prophet during his lifetime are instead restored to him in the Hereafter and particularly in the context of his eschatological function on the Day of Judgement.

5 The Station of praise (*al-maqām al-maḥmūd*)

As we have seen, the idea emerges from the Qur'ān and the *ḥadīth* that God will grant the Prophet a special rank (*al-wasīla*) on the Day of Judgement, and he will be elevated to a Station of praise (*al-maqām al-maḥmūd*), from where he will be able to exercise the highest degree of intercession granted to a creature. This special rank and station will take the form of a royal seat (*sarīr, kursī*) in close proximity to God, or, according to some bolder interpretations, the Prophet will sit directly beside God on his Throne (*'arsh*). The transmission of these kinds of traditions and interpretations by some Muslim scholars has caused great controversy in Islamic religious circles, especially since the time of Ṭabarī (d. 923), who included them in his Qur'anic commentary. Following is the interpretation he reported, attributed to the exegete Mujāhid ibn Jabr (d. 722):

> Regarding the verse 'Perhaps your Lord will elevate you to a Station of praise,' Mujāhid said, 'He will make him sit on the Throne (*yujlisuhu 'alā al-arsh*).'[410]

Some traditions mention instead a seat next to God, destined for the Prophet:

---

408 Ibid., 48–55.

409 Ibid., 55–56.

410 Muḥammad Ibn Jarīr al-Ṭabarī, *Tafsir Ṭabarī: Jāmi' al-bayān 'an ta'wīl āyy al-Qur'ān*, 25 vols (Jīza: Hajr li-l-ṭibā'a wa-l-nashr, 2008.) 25:145.

> Whoever invokes blessing upon Muḥammad (*man ṣallā ʿalā Muḥammad*) saying: 'O God, grant him the seat next to you on the Day of Resurrection (*Allāhumma unzil-hu al-maqʿad al-muqarrab ʿindaka yawm al-qiyāma*),' then my intercession with him is assured (*wajabat lahu shafāʿatī*).[411]
>
> A seat (or pedestal, *kursī*) will be placed for the Prophet at the right hand of God.[412]

Although no reference is made to a seat, another tradition seems to confirm this interpretation:

> Abū Hurayra reported that the Messenger of God said, 'I am the first for whom the earth will be opened, and then I will be adorned with garments drawn from the robes of Paradise and I will stand at the right hand of the Throne (*aqūmu ʿan yamīn al-ʿarsh*). In that place there will be no creature but me.'[413]

Since some of these traditions, although not contained in the main canonical collections, cannot be rejected from the point of view of the authenticity of their transmission, Muslim scholars have been sharply divided over the centuries on their acceptance. In his commentary, Ṭabarī expands on the issue, concluding that although the formulation of these traditions is somewhat conntroversial from a theological point of view, there is no basis for rejecting them. This would later become one of the main themes around which the controversy over the alleged "sin of anthropomorphism" of the adherents of the ḥanbalite school would revolve, against which numerous Sunni scholars not belonging to this school would lash out. One of these hotly debated issues concerns the action of God sitting on the Throne and its interpretation. Another controversy arises from the fact that the last of the reported traditions seems to show similarities with the Christian doctrine mentioned earlier, according to which Jesus ascended into heaven and sits at the right hand of the Father. This is why its detractors include it in the traditions "infiltrated" by converts from Judaism and Christianity, the so-called "Israelite traditions" (*isrāʾiliyyāt*).[414] Without being able to go into detail on such a complex issue, which has already been analysed in other studies,[415] we can state that some of these interpretations, at least from a metaphorical point of view, seem to

---

411 Ibn Ḥanbal, *Musnad*, 28:201.

412 Nīsābūrī, *al-Mustadrak ʿalā al-ṣaḥīḥayn*, 4:612–613.

413 Tirmidhī, *Sunan al-Tirmidhī*, 1199.

414 Roberto Tottoli, "Origin and Use of the Term *Isrāʾiliyyāt* in *Muslim Literature*," *Arabica* 46 (1999), 193–209.

415 Claude Gilliot, *Exégèse, langue et théologie en islam: L'exégèse coranique de Tabari* (Paris: Librarie Philosophique J. Vrin, 1990) 250–254.

agree with the characteristics of the symbolism of kingship attributed to the Prophet on the Day of Judgement and analysed in this chapter. The interpretation of the Station of praise as a royal seat next to the divine Throne, in any case, appears on several occasions in the works of the Sunni scholars. A relevant example is the long passage in a treatise on the invocation of blessing on the Prophet attributed to the famous Persian linguist and scholar Majīd al-Dīn al-Fīrūzābādī (d. 1414), to which we will return later, in which he reports and validates several traditions related to this interpretation.[416]

As Christiane Gruber has pointed out, in art produced at the Turkish and Persian Islamic courts from the thirteenth century onwards, in some rare miniatures within illustrated manuscripts, the Prophet is depicted with his legs crossed on a throne:

> In the earliest images that have come down to us, the Prophet is depicted as a monarch on a throne, with his facial features fully visible and surrounded by a variety of motifs such as angels, rays of light and heavenly scent. These many iconographic details contribute to what might be called a visual discourse on sacred kingship through which Muḥammad is depicted as both prophet and king.[417]

These depictions, however, must probably be associated with legitimising the political power that encouraged their production, rather than the royal symbolism associated with the Prophet's eschatological function.

On the other hand, a detail mentioned in some traditions appears to be related to the Prophet's royal symbolism. This refers to a particular garment reserved for him on the Day of Judgement, which shows similarities with the iconography seen earlier, relating to the ascension into Heaven of Jesus and Mary, depicted as a king or queen, respectively, in royal attire.

We have just mentioned the first of these traditions, in which the Prophet states that on the Day of Judgement, before being placed "at the right hand of the Throne" he will be "adorned with garments taken from the robes of Paradise."[418]

The second tradition also refers to the Prophet's dress:

416 Majīd al-Dīn Muḥammad ibn Ya'qūb al-Fīrūzābādī, *al-Ṣilāt wa al-bushr fī al-ṣalāt ʿalā khayr al-bashar* (Dimashq: Dār al-Qur'ān, 1966) 72–73.

417 Christiane Gruber, "Images," in *Muhammad in History, Thought, and Culture: An Encyclopedia of the Prophet of God*, edited by Coeli Fitzpatrick, Adam Walker (Santa Barbara: ABC-CLIO, 2014) 286–294.

418 See *above*, p.

> The people will be gathered on the Day of Resurrection, I and my community will be on a hill and my Lord will clothe me in a green robe (*fa-yaksūnī Rabbī ḥullat khaḍrā'*), then He will give me permission (*yu'adhdhan lī*) [to intercede]. Then I will say what God wills me to say, and this is the Station of praise.[419]

In these traditions, we observe God's investiture of the Prophet with celestial garments, which is similar to the royal rituals of investiture, the latter a term whose etymology refers precisely to covering with garments and ornaments.

To conclude this discussion, it is necessary to point out that in the Shi'i sources, we find mention of certain divine seats reserved for the leading figures of the People of the Household (*ahl al-bayt*), the family of Muḥammad extended to 'Alī, on the Day of Resurrection:

> When the Day of Resurrection comes, 'Alī will sit on al-Firdaws, which is a mountain higher than the whole of Paradise. On its summit is the Throne of Light and before him flow the waters of the Tasnīm. No one can pass over the Bridge (*ṣirāṭ*) except after accepting his authority (*walāya*) and that of his descendants. 'Alī will then stand over the Bridge, allowing those who love him to enter Paradise and those who detest him to be consigned to Hell.[420]

> Thus God addressed the Prophet on the night of his heavenly journey: 'As for thy daughter, I shall make her stand near my throne where she will be told, 'Behold, God hath given thee power over His creatures. Whosoever hath wronged thee and thy children, thou mayest judge them as thou wishest; for God will accept thy verdict concerning them.'[421]

> When the Day of Resurrection shall come, the throne of God will be adorned with every beautiful ornament. There will be brought two platforms of light, the length of each being one hundred miles, and placed one on the right and the other on the left of the throne. Ḥasan and Ḥusayn will be seated each on one of them, thus they will adorn the throne of God as would two earrings adorn the face of a woman.[422]

The same symbolism of the divine seat finds further and peculiar development in the spiritual and eschatological dimension relating to the Prophet's pulpit (*minbar*).

---

419 Abū Bakr Ibn Abī Dāwūd, *al-Ba'th wa-l-nushūr: al-ḥayā ba'd al-mawt* (al-Qāhira: Maktabat al-turāth al-islāmī, 1986) 43–44.

420 Mahmoud Ayoub, *Redemptive Suffering in Islam. A Study of the Devotional Aspects of 'Āshūrā' in Twelver Shī'ism* (The Hague-Paris-New York: Mouton Publishers, 1978) 202.

421 Ibid., 215.

422 Ibid., 201.

6 The *minbar* as the Prophet's royal seat

In the light of the considerations developed so far, it is possible to explore some symbolic values latent in one of the most important religious and political emblems of Islam, as well as one of the oldest and most relevant models of Islamic architecture: the *minbar.*

Ever since the time of the first mosque founded in Medina, the Prophet used to deliver his discourse (*khuṭba*), during the communal Friday prayer (*ṣalāt al-jumuʿa*), on an elevated object to facilitate listening. It had always been the custom for Arabs to lie down on the ground, so taking a seat on an elevated object denoted the presence of a particular authority.

Initially, the Prophet used a palm tree trunk for this purpose, but at some point around the year 629, it was decided to opt for something more evolved, a wooden artefact consisting of "two steps and a seat (*maqʿad*), similar to a throne,"[423] which took the name *minbar,* from a root meaning "elevated or raised object," and can simultaneously indicate the idea of "raising the voice".[424] Both meanings appear semantically appropriate and complementary. The Prophet's *minbar* was made of Medinese tamarisk wood by a craftsman, a Byzantine or Coptic slave. When the Prophet first climbed onto it, abandoning the palm tree trunk, according to some traditions, the latter emitted groans similar to those of a dromedary or a child, and Muḥammad was forced to console him by touching him and exhorting him with kind words.[425]

According to ancient Arabic historiographical and literary sources, the term *minbar,* which for some linguists is of ancient Ethiopian origin, is analogous to other terms denoting a simple seat (*majlis*), or a throne or royal seat (*sarīr, takht, kursī*), and only took on a meaning analogous to pulpit with its use.[426] Indeed, it is possible to translate *minbar* as pulpit (from Latin *pulpitum*, parapet), term borrowed from the Christian lexicon, indicating an object that shares an identical end use with it, namely the delivery of a religious sermon.

After Muḥammad's death, his *minbar* became part of his relics, which, as we shall see later, were considered a vehicle of divine blessing (*baraka*) and intercession. Moreover, at a stage when the caliph himself still delivered the Friday sermon, it became a symbol of temporal authority during the period of the four

---

423 Andrew Petersen, "Minbar," in *Dictionary of Islamic architecture*, edited by Andrew Petersen (London and New York: Routledge, 1996), 191–192.

424 Edward William Lane, "*n-b-r*," *An Arabic-English Lexicon* (London: Williams and Norgate, 1863–93).

425 Bukhārī, *Ṣaḥīḥ al-Bukhārī*, 3:179–180; Burton-Page, John et al. "Minbar," in *EI*^{2}.

426 Ibid.

"rightly guided" caliphs, who out of respect for the Prophet, stopped at the second step during their sermons. The first Umayyad caliph Muʿāwiya I (r. 661–680) was intent on bringing the *minbar* to his new capital, Damascus, to use it as a royal throne, but this was prevented by the protests of the dignitaries of Medina, while according to other sources, it was blocked by miraculous natural events such as earthquakes and eclipses.[427] He then had a throne built and was the first to use it among the rulers of the Islamic empires. The connection between *minbar* and the royal throne is also evident since, in the early phase of Islamic empires, it was the place next to which court dignitaries took the covenant of alliance (*bayʿa*) with the new caliph.[428]

Historiographical sources state that Muʿāwiya decided to modify the Prophet's original *minbar* in Medina, ordering the number of its steps to be increased to six. At the same time, he decreed that all mosques in the Umayyad Empire be equipped with a *minbar*, thus giving rise to the general use of this religious device in Islamic places of worship.[429] The Prophet's *minbar* was preserved in the Medina mosque until the thirteenth century, when it was destroyed by fire.[430] In the early stages of its history, the Prophet's *minbar* was so precious in the eyes of Muslims that it was covered with a cloth, similar to the *kiswa* of the Kaʿba in Mecca and the Prophet's tomb in Medina.[431]

From this time on, the *minbar* gradually acquired a standardised form within Islamic architecture, regularly taking its place to the right of the *miḥrāb*, the niche indicating the direction of Mecca, in which the *imām* prays. The classical structure of the *minbar*, starting at least from the Fatimid era (909–1171), provides for an entrance at its beginning, with or without a door, while two handrails protect the steps closed on the sides, ending in a platform, often surmounted by a dome. When a door is in place, it remains locked and is exclusively opened on Fridays to admit the *imām*. Small columns are often present both at the entrance and under the dome. The number of steps has gradually increased over the ages, sometimes reaching as high as seventeen.[432] Some very old *minbar*s have survived to the

427 Heba Mostafa, "The Early Mosque Revisited: Introduction of the *Minbar* and *Maqṣūra*," in *Muqarnas: An Annual on the Visual Cultures of the Islamic World* 33 (2016), 7.
428 Ibid., 9.
429 Andrew Petersen, "Minbar," in *Dictionary of Islamic architecture*, edited by Andrew Petersen (London and New York: Routledge, 1996), 191–192; Burton-Page, John et al. "Minbar," in EI^2.
430 Jean Sauvaget, *La Mosquée Omeyyade de Médine: Étude sur les origines architecturales de la mosquée et de la basilique* (Paris: Vanoest, 1947), 85–89.
431 Burton-Page, John et al. "Minbar," in EI^2.
432 Andrew Petersen, "Minbar," in *Dictionary of Islamic architecture*, edited by Andrew Petersen (London and New York: Routledge, 1996), 191–192.

present day, serving as an architectural archetype for those built later. The oldest and most precious *minbar* is the one still present in the al-Qayrawān mosque in Tunisia, protected in glass. According to available sources, it was built in the Aghlabid period during the reign of the ruler Abū Ibrāhīm Aḥmad (r. 856–63) with Indian teak wood, which came from Baghdad. Some specialists claim that its characteristic decoration, typical of late Umayyad art, would instead indicate that it was either made in the Near East, particularly in Iraq, and later brought to al-Qayrawān or produced by craftsmen from Iraq.[433] Another ancient *minbar* that is particularly valuable from an artistic point of view is that of the al-Kutubiyya mosque in Marrakesh, Morocco, built in Andalusia in the twelfth century with inlaid wood.[434]

If we return to the Prophet's *minbar*, sources indicate that he used to ascend the final platform during the Friday sermon. Some traditions mention a very special episode, closely related to his function as an intercessor for rain, with some variations from the above versions:

> Al-Walīd ibn ʿUtba, who was governor of Medina, sent me to Ibn ʿAbbās to question him about the prayer for rain of the Messenger of God (*ṣalāt rasūl Allāh fī-l-istisqāʾ*). He said: 'The Messenger of God came in modest and humble attire, supplicating, until he reached the place of prayer. Then he went up to the pulpit (*minbar*), but did not deliver the sermon (*khuṭba*) as usual. He made many invocations and supplications and said 'God is greater' (*takbīr*). Then he performed an oration consisting of two movements as is done during the Feast (*thumma ṣallā rakʿatayn kamā yuṣallī fīʿīd*).'[435]

Some details of this episode deserve a brief analysis. First of all, the image of the ladder as a symbol of ascension is widespread in the universal imagery, and we have already observed its characteristics in the ancient Islamic tradition. It is also worthy of interest that when the Prophet has to perform his intercessory prayer for rain, he ascends to the highest level of the *minbar*. This action indicates that for the Prophet, the *minbar* symbolises ascension, coming closer to God, and the highest platform of the *minbar* represents on earth what his Station of praise (*al-maqām al-maḥmūd*) represents in the Hereafter. Some *ḥadīth* attributed to the Prophet add further details of this symbolism:

---

433 Nadège Picotin and Claire Déléry. "Fragments d'histoire du *minbar* de Kairouan," in *The Aghlabids and their Neighbours. Art and Material Culture in Ninth-Century North Africa*, edited by Glaire D. Anderson, Corisande Fenwick, and Mariam Rosser-Owen (Leiden: Brill, 2018), 208–209.
434 Jonathan M. Bloom, et al., eds. *The Minbar from the Kutubiyya Mosque* (New York: The Metropolitan Museum of Art; Madrid: Ediciones El Viso, S.A.; Rabat: Ministère des Affaires Culturelles, Royaume du Maroc, 1998).
435 Abū Dāwūd, *Sunan Abī Dāwūd*, 2:367–368.

> That which is between my house and my pulpit is a garden of Paradise, and my pulpit is on my basin.[436]

> Between my house and my pulpit is a garden of Paradise, and my pulpit is on one of the canals of Paradise.[437]

> Verily the pillars of this pulpit of mine are established in Paradise.[438]

As we shall see later, the area of the mosque in Medina between the house – later to become the tomb – of the Prophet and the *minbar*, belongs materially, according to the Islamic conception derived from the *ḥadīth*, to the Hereafter.

Considering the importance of the given word and oaths in ancient Arab society, the sacredness of the *minbar* further emerges from a saying of the Prophet according to which anyone who swears falsely before it will be condemned to Hell.[439]

In order to perform the intercessory prayer for rain, the Prophet ascends his *minbar*, performing a metaphorical and spiritual ascent to the Station of praise (*al-maqām al-maḥmūd*), from where he can exercise his intercession at the highest level. The sources enrich this episode with a detail: this intercession worked so well that the following week it rained a lot, so much so that the Prophet was forced, during the following Friday prayer, to implore God in the same way, but this time to stop the rain.[440]

From a time not easily definable, out of respect for the Prophet, it has been the custom for the person delivering the Friday sermon not to climb up to the final platform of the *minbar* but only halfway up the steps and to remain standing during the sermon. This is precisely because the platform represents the Prophet's Station, which only he can access. It is probably for this reason that it became customary to build on the final platform of the *minbar* a canopy with columns surmounted by a dome (*qubba*). This detail of Islamic architecture usually denotes the presence of a shrine built over a tomb or relic and ultimately indicates, like the dome over his tomb in Medina, the presence of the Prophet himself. This type of architectural iconography, in honour of the Prophet's Station, has its counterpart in Christian art, where one often observes the presence of a royal canopy (*cibori-*

---

436 *"mā bayna baytī wa-minbarī rawḍā min riyāḍ al-janna wa-minbarī ʿalā ḥawḍī"*, Bukhārī, *Ṣaḥīḥ al-Bukhārī*, 2:184.

437 *"mā bayna baytī wa-minbarī rawḍā min riyāḍ al-janna wa-minbarī ʿalā turʿa min turaʿ al-janna"*, ʿAlī ibn Abū Bakr al-Haythamī, *Majmuʿ al-zawāʾid*, 8:438.

438 *"inna qawāʾim minbarī hādhā rawātib fī al-janna,"* Nasāʾī, *Sunan*, 266–267.

439 Abū Dāwūd, *Sunan Abī Dāwūd*, 5:150.

440 Bukhārī, *Ṣaḥīḥ al-Bukhārī*, 2:91–92.

um), sometimes surmounted by a crown, as a symbol of the presence of the sacred and the relationship between heavenly and earthly kingship.[441]

From an in-depth analysis of the religious and historical characteristics of the *minbar*, a precise symbolic dimension emerges, referring to the Prophet's function of intermediation and intercession:

> The supreme function of the *minbar*, therefore, is to be a bond and an intermediary between earth and Heaven. The minbar provides an elevation for the word or promise of Paradise, of pardon and of love of God. The elevation is furnished by steps which are symbolic in their number. This function, accomplished by a piece of ritual furniture, is performed by a man who is central in Muslim liturgy, the khāṭib and/or the imam.[442]

A further dimension that emerges from this analysis, from the primary meaning of the *minbar* as a royal seat and its architectural features, is that it appears as an earthly image of Muḥammad's royal seat in the Hereafter, the *waṣīla* or Station of praise, from which he will exercise his intercession on the Day of Judgement.

The dimension of elevation connected to the *minbar*, considering the possibility of the elevation of spiritual degrees as represented by the divine name *Rāfiʿ al-darajāt* discussed above, also appears in the sources as a prototype of the path of spiritual ascent. A greater example is the vision described by al-Ḥakīm al-Tirmidhī (d. 869), a celebrated theorist of the notion of holiness (*walāya*) and precursor of doctrinal Sufism.[443] In his autobiography, he recounts a phase in his life when he was in constant spiritual retreat and, at one point, had a dream-like vision of the Prophet:

> I was in this spiritual state (*ḥāl*), when I saw, as in a dream, the Messenger of God enter the congregational mosque (*al-masjid al-jāmiʿ*) of our city. I entered following his steps (*ʿalā athar-ihi*), being obliged to follow them. He continued walking until he entered the central area (*al-maqṣūra*), and I was on his steps, very close to him, as if I were clinging to his back, putting my steps in the exact place where he put his, until he entered the central area. Then he went

441 Manuel Castiñeiras, "The Baldachin-Ciborium. The shifting meanings of a restricted liturgical furnishing in Romanesque art," in *The Regional and Transregional in Romanesque Europe*, edited by J. McNeill and R. Plant (London: Routledge, 2021), 47–67.

442 Naima Chikhaoui, "The Minbar: Symbol of Verticality and Elevation," in *Sacred Web: A Journal of Tradition and Modernity* 14 (2004), 101.

443 Sufism is the most common name for the spiritual path in Islam, which usually involves an initiation with a master (*shaykh*), and can take an individual form, or be organised in the confraternity system (*ṭuruq*). Sufism has produced an abundant and relevant doctrinal and normative literature, and at least in the context of pre-modern Islamic societies, numerous religious authorities were at the same time affiliated with a Sufi brotherhood. For an introduction to Sufism, see Carl William Ernst, *Sufism. An Introduction to the Mystical Tradition of Islam* (Boulder: Shambhala, 2016).

up to the pulpit (*minbar*), and I went up following his steps. When he went up a step, I went up in his steps, until he sat on the highest step (*istawā ʿalā aʿlāhā daraja*), and I sat on the step below the one he was sitting on, by his two feet (*ʿinda qadamayhi*), and my right side was in the direction of his face, while my face was facing the doors to the marketplace, and my left side was facing the people. Then I awoke from my dream, and I was in that spiritual state (*ḥāl*).[444]

This vision is extremely interesting, since, in addition to reiterating the conception of the spiritual path in Islam as an imitation of the prophetic path, as well as the conception of the spiritual ascent of the friends of God or saints (*awliyāʾ*) as an imitation of the Prophet's Ascension (*miʿrāj*), both of which are attested by specialists in Sufism, it points precisely to the *minbar* as one of the symbols of this ascension. Indeed, this vision identifies each step of the staircase as a single station to be traversed and finally shows the Prophet sitting on the final platform as if on a throne, using the terminology seen earlier (*istawā ʿalā*), with his two feet on the lower step. The station of the Prophet's feet, on the other hand, represents the station where al-Tirmidhī sits, the highest station reachable by other men. As we shall see later, in the terminology of Sufism this station is called the "station of proximity" (*maqām al-qurba*). Since this is the great mosque of the city in which Tirmidhī lived, namely Termez in present-day Uzbekistan, and not the mosque of Medina, one may consider that in this vision, every mosque and every *minbar* potentially represents an image of the Prophet's mosque, and the central area (*maqṣūra*) represents the sacred area of the mosque of Medina (*rawḍa*).

In conclusion, and direct connection with the next topic, I will add a curious detail related to the Prophet's *minbar*. According to the al-Andalus-born geographer and traveller Ibn Jubayr (d. 1217), at the top of the right side of his *minbar*, where he rested his hand, there was a hollow silver cylinder, oblong in shape, which was able to rotate, capable of holding an interlocking object. When the Prophet was delivering his speech, sometimes his grandsons al-Ḥasan (d. 670) and al-Ḥusayn (d. 680), sons of ʿAlī ibn Ṭālib (d. 661) and his daughter Fāṭima (d. 632), would play with this cylinder. It is unclear what it might have contained, and specialists propose two objects: the spear (*ʿanaza*) of the Prophet, a model for the sword that would later come into use for the *imām* during the Friday discourse, or the banner (*liwāʾ*) of the Prophet, since, at least in some late cases, banners are observed hanging from the sides of *minbars*.[445]

---

444 al-Ḥakīm al-Tirmidhī, "*Naṣṣ risāla budūwwu sha'n Abī ʿAbd Allāh Muḥammad al-Ḥakīm al-Tirmidhī*," in *Kitāb khatm al-awliyāʾ*, ed. ʿUthmān Ismāʿīl Yaḥyā (Bayrūt: al-Maṭbuʿat al-kāthūliyya, 1965), 16.

445 Jean Sauvaget, *La Mosquée Omeyyade de Médine. Étude sur les origines architecturales de la mosquée et de la basilique* (Paris: Vanoest, 1947), 85–89.

We shall now introduce other attributes that Islamic tradition grants to the Prophet concerning his eschatological function, among which we find, to begin with, a banner.

Fig. 2: The The *minbar* of the Medina mosque in the Umayyad period, from Jean Sauvaget, La Mosquée Omeyyade de Médine. Étude sur les origines architecturales de la mosquée et de la basilique (Paris: Vanoest, 1947), 88.

7 The Banner of praise (*liwā' al-ḥamd*)

These attributes include the Banner of praise, a celestial image of the Prophet's earthly banner, mentioned in some *ḥadīth:*

> I will be the lord (*sayyid*) of the sons of Adam on the Day of Judgement, and I am not boasting. I will hold the Standard of Praise (*liwā' al-ḥamd*) and I am not boasting. On that day all the prophets, from Adam onwards, will be under my banner. And I am the first for whom the earth will be opened, and I am not boasting.[446]

In the eschatological context, the Banner of praise (*liwā' al-ḥamd*) must certainly be placed in relation to the Station of praise (*maqām maḥmūd*) since it shares the same root (*ḥ-m-d*) with the latter expression, as well as with the name Muḥammad. The banner is a symbol of royal authority and is therefore a sign of the Prophet's authority over all creatures, as their lord, *sayyid*, a term denoting supreme authority in the pre-Islamic and Islamic Arabic context.

8 The heavenly Basin (*al-ḥawḍ*)

A further attribute of the Prophet on the Day of Judgement is his function connected to the heavenly Basin (*al-ḥawḍ*). Although the term *ḥawḍ* does not appear in the Qur'ān, it does appear in a large number of *ḥadīth*, in some of which it is related to the Qur'anic notion of *kawthar:*

> The Messenger of God dozed for a moment and smiled. They asked him, "Messenger of God, why did you smile?" He replied, "A *sūra* has just been revealed to me," and then recited, "In the name of God, Clement and Merciful. Verily, We have granted you *kawthar*...", to the end. When the recitation was over, he asked, "Do you know what *kawthar* is?" They replied, "God and His Messenger know more." He said: "It is a river that my Lord, the Exalted, has promised to bestow in Paradise: associated with it is a great good and a basin (*ḥawḍ*), to which my people will approach on the Day of Resurrection. There will be vessels as numerous as the stars in the sky.'[447]

Based on sayings similar to this, it has become customary to call this basin *al-ḥawḍ al-kawthar.* Other sayings mention two heavenly rivers instead:

---

446 Tirmidhī, *Sunan al-Tirmidhī*, 1199.

447 Abū Dāwūd, *Sunan Abī Dāwūd*, 7:125.

> In it [the *ḥawḍ*] will flow two streams that have their sources in Paradise, one of gold and the other of silver.[448]

The connection between this station in Paradise and intercession emerges from other traditions:

> Al-Naḍr ibn Anas ibn Mālik narrated from his father, who said: 'I asked the Prophet to intercede for me (*sa'altu al-nabī an yashfa'a lī*) on the Day of Judgement. He replied: 'I will do it.' I said, 'O Messenger of God! Where shall I seek you?' He replied, 'Seek Me! The first time on the Bridge (*ṣirāṭ*).' I asked: 'If I do not meet you on the Bridge?' He said, 'Then look for me at the Balance (*mīzān*).' I asked, 'What if I do not meet you at the Balance?' He said, 'Then seek me at the *ḥawḍ*, for indeed I shall not fail in these three places.'[449]

The Prophet will wait for the believers at the heavenly Basin, but only some will be allowed to approach it and drink from its waters:

> I will precede you to the basin (*innī faraṭukum 'alā al-ḥawḍ*), and whoever passes by there will drink from it, and whoever drinks from it will never thirst again. People will come to me whom I will recognise, and they will recognise me, but a barrier will be placed between me and them.[450]

Several *ḥadīth* report the characteristics of the celestial basin, also indicating its vastness through the names of various locations far apart and the hyperbolic number of vessels for drinking its water:

> My basin (*ḥawḍī*) has the width of a month's walk. Its water is whiter than milk, its smell is more pleasant than musk, and its cups are as numerous as the stars of heaven, and he who drinks from it will never thirst again.[451]
>
> Between the two sides of my basin (*ḥawḍī*) there will be a distance as between San'ā' and Medina.[452]

The term *ḥawḍ* derives from the terminology of the nomadic Arabs and already appears in the *Mu'allaqāt*, famous pre-Islamic poems, where it indicates the source of water at which dromedaries quench their thirst.[453] According to ancient Arabic

448 Muslim, *Ṣaḥīḥ Muslim*, 6:108–109.
449 *Tirmidhī, Sunan al-Tirmidhī*, 881.
450 Bukhārī, *Ṣaḥīḥ al-Bukhārī*, 8:332.
451 Ibid., 8:333.
452 Muslim, *Ṣaḥīḥ Muslim*, 6:136.
453 The term appears in the poem attributed to Ṭarafa ibn al-'Abd, plural (*ḥiyāḍ*), verse 75, p. 144, and in the poem attributed to Zuhayr ibn Abī Sulmā, singular (*ḥawḍ*), verse 5, p. 172; singular

linguists, the etymological meaning of one of Islam's main theological metaphors, the notion of *sharīʿa*, indicates precisely the source to which men or dromedaries are led, and thus the term *sharīʿa* is cited as a synonym for *ḥawḍ*.[454] Within this metaphor, therefore, Muḥammad is the one who leads the believers to the heavenly Basin. This is evident from several sayings, such as the following, similar to others mentioned earlier:

> By Him in whose hands is my soul, I will remove people from my basin as one removes stray dromedaries from the basin.[455]

The heavenly Basin certainly possesses an eschatological dimension related to future events, but at the same time, if one considers certain *ḥadīth*, it would seem to be already part of the cosmology of the invisible world, which the Prophet is able to perceive:

> I will go before you and be your witness [on the Day of Judgement], and, I swear by God, I am looking at my basin (*ḥawḍī*) right now.[456]

Another important dimension of this metaphor relates to the idea that the *ḥawḍ* is part of a celestial structure in the invisible world, which has its terrestrial counterpart, as mentioned above:

> The Prophet said: 'That which is between my house and my pulpit is a Garden of Paradise, and my pulpit is on my basin.'[457]

Islamic tradition, based on the words of the Prophet, therefore holds that this area of the mosque in Medina called the "Garden" (*rawḍa*), venerated for this reason to this day, is materially part of Paradise. This belief gave rise to the idea that it is possible to reproduce this celestial structure on Earth. This is evident from the configuration of places of worship and Islamic court architecture, which almost invariably include gardens with a basin in the centre, called *ḥawḍ*. Particularly in Persian art, the central basin took on a very distinctive specific form, precisely by the name of *ḥawḍ al-kawthar*. This specific form then also became a very recurrent

(*ḥawḍ*), verse 53, p. 194, in *The Muʿallaqāt for Millenials. Pre-Islamic Arabic Golden Odes*, Arabic text and translation, (King Abdulaziz Center for World Culture [Ithra], Al Dhahran, 2020).

454 Ibn Manẓūr, *Lisān al-ʿarab*, Dār al-maʿārif, Bayrūt 1984–1986, 2237.

455 *"wa-lladhī nafsī bi-yadihi laʾadhūdanna ʿan ḥawḍī rijālan kamā tudhād al-gharība min al-ibil ʿan al-ḥawḍ"*, Bukhārī, *Ṣaḥīḥ al-Bukhārī*, 3:332.

456 Ibid., 4:520.

457 *'mā bayna baytī wa-minbarī rawḍa min riyāḍ al-janna wa-minbarī ʿalā ḥawḍī'*, ibid., 2:184.

motif in figurative art. The basin motif within the garden became an architectural motif, particularly in relation to court architecture.[458]

This might allow us to consider the *ḥawḍ*, from a metaphorical point of view, as a further royal attribute granted to the Prophet on the Day of Judgement. In any case, the image of the *ḥawḍ al-kawthar* is closely connected to the Prophet's intercessory function, as is evident from an interpretation by Jaʿfar al-Ṣādiq (d. 765), a Muslim scholar and descendant of the Prophet, who is held in very high esteem by both Sunnis and Shiʿites, who venerate him in particular as the sixth Imām. When asked about the meaning of the term *kawthar*, he is said to have replied:

> It is intercession for Thy [the Prophet's] community (*al-shafāʿa li-ummatika*).[459]

Another significant detail about the *ḥawḍ*, found in the sources, is the existence of other heavenly basins bestowed on other prophets besides Muḥammad:

> Verily for every prophet there is a basin (*ḥawḍ*), and they compete to see the one at which they will arrive [more believers]. I hope that mine will be the one with the most arrivals.[460]

> For every prophet there is a basin (*ḥawḍ*), except for Ṣāliḥ, for his basin is the udders of his camel.[461]

This last variant, despite not being considered authentic by all transmitters, is very interesting, as it relates the water of the heavenly Basin to the descent of milk into the udder, which, as we have seen, is one of the ancient meanings contained in the root *n-z-l*, with the meaning of descent of a spiritual order.

In Shiʿa traditions about the Day of Judgement, the image of the heavenly Basin is often present. Associated, however, with the People of the Household (*ahl al-bayt*). In particular, the *ḥawḍ al-kawthar* is under the control of ʿAlī:

> The Prince of the Faithful [ʿAlī] will stand at [*ḥawḍ*] *al-kawthar* with a staff of thorns (*awsaj*) *in his* hand, with which he will destroy our enemies. Then the enemy will declare, "But I profess the two *shahāda* [I am a Muslim!]"; ʿAlī will reply, "Go to your 'such' *imām* and ask him to intercede for you." The man will reply, 'My *imām* whom you named has disowned me (*tab-*

458 An example of this can be found in Wayne Edison Begley, "The Myth of the Taj Mahal and a New Theory of Its Symbolic Meaning," in *The Art Bulletin* 61, 1 (1979), 14.

459 ʿAbd al-Raḥmān al-Sulamī, *Ḥaqāʾiq al-tafsīr. Tafsīr al-Qurʾān al-ʿazīz*, (Bayrūt: Dār al-kutub al-ʿilmiyya, , 2001), 2:422.

460 Tirmidhī, *Sunan al-Tirmidhī*, 884.

461 Abū ʿAbd Allāh al-Qurṭubī, *Kitāb al-tadhkira bi-aḥwāl al-mawtā wa-umūr al-ākhira* (al-Riyāḍ: Maktabat dār al-minhāj, 2004), 1:213; Ṣāliḥ is one of the so-called "Arab prophets" mentioned in the Qurʾān, where the story of the she-camel sent to him by God is told in various passages (Q 7:73–79; 1:61–68; 26:141–59; 27:45–53).

> *arra'a*).' But ʿAlī will reply, 'Go back and ask the one whom you accepted as your master (*walī*) and whom you preferred over all other creatures; if he is indeed the best of men, ask him to intercede for you, for the best of men is the one who can intercede.' Man will say: "I am dying of thirst!". But ʿAlī will reply, 'May God increase your thirst and never quench it.'[462]

According to the view from Shiʿa sources, moreover, the *ḥawḍ* is not only a source of water but is a living being that possesses human feelings and will rejoice when a person who loves the People of the House approaches it and will not only quench his thirst, but will also make him taste food so delicious that he will never want to leave this place again.[463]

9 In the presence of the King: the Prophet as mediator and universal intercessor

As a partial conclusion to analysing a series of primary sources in Islam concerning the Prophet's eschatological function linked to intercession, we can propose a few initial considerations. The first is as follows: although the function of prophet-king (*malik nabī*), granted to some prophets previous to him, does not seem to have been granted by God to the Prophet Muḥammad during his earthly life, a royal function is clearly granted to him in the Hereafter, judging from the analysis of the eschatological sources. On the Day of Judgement, when God will install Himself on His Throne as a King to judge all creatures endowed with free will, the prophet Muḥammad will enjoy a primary role as a universal mediator and intercessor, bestowed with the royal attributes represented by the Station of praise, the Standard of Praise and the heavenly Basin.

This symbolic system is expressed comprehensively in a treatise attributed to Ghazālī, entitled "That which is precluded to those who are not of his people (*al-Maḍnūn bihi ʿalā ghayr ahlihi*)." This text is one of his philosophical works that Muslim scholars and contemporary specialists disagree on attributing to him, although a more recent study has produced solid arguments in favour of its authenticity.[464] One chapter of this treatise is entitled "Section on Intercession" (*faṣl fī-l-*

462 Mahmoud Ayoub, *Redemptive Suffering in Islam. A Study of the Devotional Aspects of ʿĀshūrāʾ in Twelver Shīʿism* (The Hague-Paris-New York: Mouton Publishers, 1978), 209.
463 Ibid., 206.
464 Muhammad Afifi Al-Akiti, "The Good, the Bad, and the Ugly of Falsafa: Al-Ghazālī's *Maḍnūn*, *Tahāfut*, and *Maqāṣid*, with Particular Attention to their Falsafī Treatments of God's Knowledge of Temporal Events." In *Avicenna and his Legacy: A Golden Age of Science and Philosophy*, edited by Yitzhak Tzvi Langermann (Turnhout: Brepols, 2010), 51–100.

shafāʿa), and in it, Ghazālī explores the spiritual and royal dimension of the Prophet's intermediary function:

> The intercession of the prophets (*al-anbiyāʾ*) and the saints (*al-awliyāʾ*), is an expression of the light that emanates from the divine Presence on the prophetic essence (*ʿibāra ʿan nūr yashruq min al-ḥaḍra al-ilāhiyya ʿalā jawhar al-nubuwwa*), which spreads from it to all essences that relate to the prophetic essence by the power of love (*li-shiddat al-maḥabba*), by much perseverance in prophetic traditions (*al-sunan*), and by the abundance of the practice of remembrance (*al-dhikr*) through the invocation of blessing upon the Prophet (*al-ṣalā ʿalayhi*).

He then proposes a complex metaphor between the material Light, which descends on specific points and not everywhere, and the divine Light, which descends directly on only some men. On the other hand, other men need the Prophet's intermediation to access the divine Light. To better clarify this passage, Ghazālī resorts precisely to the metaphor of kingship:

> For example, a vizier, being a trustworthy man, is a favourite of the attentions of a king, who therefore pardons some of the sins of a person who is a friend of the vizier. The person concerned escapes punishment, not because the vizier's personality is identical to that of the king, but because the person, by ties of friendship, is linked to the vizier, who is linked to the king. If there had not been intercession between the king and the offender, the king would not have pardoned the criminal. There are several traditions that show that those who love the Prophet, invoking divine blessings upon him or visiting his grave or answering the call to prayer or praying for him after the call to prayer, deserve the Prophet's recommendations. This intercession means the reflection of light in an indirect way.[465]

Another author, who comes from a very different intellectual background from Ghazālī, such as that of the Iberian peninsula under Islamic rule, ʿAbd al-Jalīl ibn Mūsā al-Qaṣrī al-Anṣārī (m. 1211–12), takes a highly original look at the royal characteristics of intercession in his theological work "The Branches of Faith" (*Shuʿab al-īmān*).[466] He introduces the categories of intercessors with the following words:

> Intercession (*shafāʿa*), on earth and in the Hereafter, is divided into three groups: the angels (*al-malāʾika*), the prophets (*al-anbiyāʾ*) and the believers among the people of the spiritual rank (*al-muʾminūn ahl al-jāh*).[467]

---

465 Abū Ḥāmid al-Ghazālī, *al-Maḍnūn bihi ʿalā ghayr ahlihi*, in *Majmūʿat rasāʾil al-imām al-Ghazālī*, ed. Ibrāhīm Āmīn Muḥammad (al-Qāhira: al-Maktaba al-tawfīqiyya, 2002), 371–372.
466 José Bellver, "*Ascetics and Sufis,*" in *The Routledge handbook of Muslim Iberia*, ed. By Maribel Fierro (Routledge, Abingdon, Oxon – New York 2020), 328.
467 ʿAbd al-Jalīl al-Qaṣrī, *Shuʿab al-īmān* (Bayrūt: Dār al-kutub al-ʿilmiyya, 1995), 605.

Given the analogy between the spiritual rank and the earthly rank, he describes the relationship between God and Muḥammad in this way:
The proximity (*qurba*) of the Prophet in relation to God, in Paradise, is like the position of the vizier in relation to the King (*manzilat al-wazīr min al-malik*): in the level of intermediation (*fī darajat al-wasīla*) he mediates (*yatawassala*) and intercedes (*yashfaʿu*) by fulfilling needs, raising the ranks (*rafaʿa al-darajāt*) and granting permission for the noble visit [to the ruler, as a metaphor for God] and the vision of the noble face [of the ruler, as a metaphor for God], and the opening of the doors of the sacred area, and more.[468]

Later, in the sixteenth century, the famous Egyptian scholar ʿAbd al-Wahhāb al-Shaʿrānī (d. 1565), who often uses the royal metaphor in his work, described the Prophet's intercession in similar words in his work entitled "The Muhammadan Covenants" (*al-ʿUhūd al-muḥammadiyya*):

> Know, dear brother, that the shortest path to reach the Presence of God (*ḥaḍrat Allāh*) is that of invoking blessings upon the Prophet (*al-ṣalā ʿalā al-nabī*), so he who has not served the Prophet exclusively and asks to enter the Presence of God, asks the impossible, because due to his ignorance of the rules required of God the Most High (*adab maʿa Allāh taʿālā*), the chamberlains of the divine Presence (*ḥujjāb al-ḥaḍra*) will not grant him entry. Such a person can be compared to a peasant (*al-fallāḥ*) who asks to enter the sultan's presence without an intermediary! (*al-ijtimāʿ bi-l-sulṭān bi-ghayr wāsiṭa*).[469]

To better specify this metaphor, at the end of this chapter, it may be useful to reproduce a very evocative passage from Tor Andrae's seminal work discussed above, which shows the great attention he paid to the royal dimension of Muḥammad's intercessory function:

> The popular conception of God among Muslims is inseparably connected to the image of the king and his court; God is the King of kings on a grand scale. Seated on his throne, the Mighty One has his *dīwān*. To the right and left are the dignitaries and great men of the kingdom. But absolutely not in random order; the place that corresponds to their dignity, their *manzila* with the king, is precisely determined by the king, and closer to the king himself, more determined. *Manzila* and *qurba* are the recurring designations for the position of prophets and pious men in relation to God; *qurba* here does not mean, as for the mystics, the proximity to the intimate unity, the *unio mystica*, but the honourable proximity of the ruler. The closest of all, to the right of the king, is the vizier himself. This is the place Muḥammad occupies when, clothed in the robe of honour, he stands at the right hand of the throne, 'where no one else stands, and where all men envy him'. For the position of honour is at the same time an expression of the personal favour the ruler has

---

468 Ibid., 208.
469 ʿAbd al-Wahhāb al-Shaʿrānī, *Lawāqiḥ al-anwār al-qudsīyya fī bayān al-ʿuhūd al-muḥammadiyya* (Bayrūt: Dār al-kutub al-ʿilmiyya, 2005), 224.

for that person: he has influence, *wasīla,* with the ruler according to the measure of his *manzila* and *qurba.* Happy is the inferior who can count on the *wasīla* of one of the majors, happier if he can count on the *wasīla* of the vizier himself. 'Pray that I be given the *wasīla,*' Muḥammad intimates to the worshippers. When the ruler wants to honour a favourite, he demands respect for him and humble submission from his subjects (cf. Esther 3), and honours him in a special way, before all others, with the special kindness of the Oriental when he wants to show magnanimity (cf. Esther 6). In this way, God honoured the Prophet. All his lofty qualities, all his spiritual dignity, are honours that God has bestowed with generous kindness on his Chosen One.[470]

Fig. 3: *ʿasā an yabʿathaka maqaman maḥmūdan*
"Perhaps your Lord will raise you to a Station of praise," Q 17:79
Calligraphy, Turkey, nineteenth century.

---

470 Tor Andrae, *Die person Muhammeds in lehre und glauben seiner gemeinde* (Stockholm: Norstedt & Toner, 1917), 260 (tr. by the author).

Chapter 7
Intercession according to the main currents of Islam

After examining the Islamic primary sources related to intercession, it is possible to move on to an analysis of the theological opinions of the various subdivisions within Islam in relation to this notion. We will then begin with the opinion expressed by the religious authorities of Sunnism and move on to that of Twelver Shiʿism, while also briefly mentioning the controversies on intercession found in Sunnite sources concerning the opinion of minority groups such as the Kharijites and Muʿtazilites.

1 Intercession according to Sunnism

The belief in intercession is invariably present in the Sunnite creeds, starting with the oldest, the aforementioned "The Greatest Understanding" (*al-Fiqh al-akbar*), attributed to Abū Ḥanīfa al-Nuʿmān (d. 767), the highest authority of the ḥanafite legal school, where we find this formulation:

> The intercession (*shafāʿa*) of the prophets is real, just as real and certain is the intercession (*shafāʿa*) of our Prophet towards those sinful believers and towards those among them who have committed grave faults deserving of punishment.[471]

We also find a similar formulation in the *Waṣiyya* of Abū Ḥanīfa:

> The intercession of our prophet Muḥammad is a reality for all who are believers among the people of Paradise, even if one is guilty of grave sins.[472]

Furthermore, in the *Fiqh al-akbar*, we find the belief in the basin:

> The basin of the Prophet is truth (*wa-ḥawḍ al-nabī ḥaqq*).[473]

471 Abū Ḥanīfa al-Nuʿmān, *Imām Abū Ḥanīfa's Al-Fiqh al-Akbar Explained by Abū 'l-Muntahā al-Maghnīsāwī with Selections from ʿAlī al-Qārī's Commentary, including Abū Ḥanīfa's Kitāb al-Waṣiyya* (London-Santa Barbara: White Thread Press, 2014), 187.
472 Ibid., 188.
473 Abū Ḥanīfa al-Nuʿmān, *Waṣiyyat al-īmām Abī Ḥanīfa al-Nuʿmān* (Bayrūt: Dār Ibn Ḥazm, 1997), 60.

https://doi.org/10.1515/9783111500966-012

In his collection of theological opinions entitled "The opinions of Muslims and the divergences of those who pray" (*Maqālāt al-islāmiyyin wa-khtilāf al-muṣallīn*), Abū al-Ḥasan al-Ashʿarī (m. 936), the highest authority of the Ashʿarite theological school, states, against the opinion of the Muʿtazilites, that for the Sunnis (*ahl al-sunna wa-l-istiqāma*) the intercession (*shafaʿa*) of the Prophet is reserved for the great sinners of his community. This is why God will extract from Hell those monotheistic Muslims (*ahl al-qibla muwaḥḥidīn*) who have committed great sins, after they have spent some time in the fire.[474] He also reports the Sunnites' belief that the Prophet will have a basin with which he will only quench the thirst of believers and not unbelievers.[475]

Abū Manṣūr al-Māturīdī (d. 944), the foremost authority of the Māturīdite school of theology, in his "Book of Divine Unity" (*Kitāb al-tawḥīd*), argues that all Muslims will enter Paradise through the Prophet's intercession, and only unbelievers will be rejected. Sinless believers will not have to face the Judgement (*ḥisāb*), while those with lesser sins will enter Paradise after being judged. The Khorasanian theologian also argues, against the opinion of the Muʿtazilites, that the Prophet will intercede for the great sinners of his community, who will thereby emerge from Hell after having stayed there for some time.[476]

The main Sunnite creeds include the notion of intercession (*shafāʿa*), not limiting it to prophets but also granting it to other categories of people. In the creed attributed to Aḥmad al-Ṭaḥāwī (d. 933), *al-ʿAqīda al-Ṭaḥāwiyya*, which is considered the canonical creed of Ashʿarism, we find this formulation:

> The intercession that God has deferred for them [to those who have performed mortal sins] is truth, as is narrated in the traditions (*wa-l-shafāʿa allatī-ddakharahā lahum ḥaqq kamā ruwiya fī al-akhbār*).[477]

> People who have committed mortal sins in the community of Muḥammad will not remain in the fire forever, as long as they are monotheists. Among them are also the unrepentant who, despite this, have gone to meet God as recognised believers. They are in His judgement and His decree. If He wills, He forgives them and absolves them by His grace, as He said in His Book: 'Surely, God does not forgive idolatry, but He forgives everything else to whom He pleases.'[478] Or, if He wills, He punishes them in the Fire with His justice, and then removes

474 Abū al-Ḥasan al-Ashʿarī, *Maqālāt al-Islāmiyyīn wa-ikhtilāf al-muṣallīn*, edited by Helmut Ritter (Wiesbaden: Franz Steiner, 1963), 474.

475 Ibid., 473.

476 Ulrich Rudolph, *Al-Māturīdī and the Development of Sunnī Theology in Samarqand* (Leiden: Brill, 2015) 114, 213.

477 Aḥmad *al-Ṭaḥāwī, The Creed of Imam al-Ṭaḥāwī. Translated, Introduced, And Annotated by Hamza Yusuf* (Berkeley: Zaytuna Institute, 2008), 59.

478 Q 4:48.

> them with His mercy and through the intercession of intercessors among the people who are obedient to Him (*wa shafāʿat al-shāfiʿīn min ahl ṭāʿatihi*), and then sends them to His Paradise.[479]

As can be seen, the category of intercessors is is rather broad, not limited to prophets but also devout believers. In this creed, too, we find mention of the Prophet's heavenly Basin:

> The basin, with which God has honoured him, through which there is relief for his community, is truth (*al-ḥawḍ alladhī akramahu-Llāhu taʿāla bihi ghiyāth^{an} li-ummatihi ḥaqq*).[480]

The Iraqi jurist and traditionalist Abū Bakr al-Ajurrī (d. 970), in his "Book of Divine Law" (*Kitāb al-sharīʿa*), devotes an entire chapter to intercession (*shafāʿa*).[481] He begins with a section entitled "The Obligation of Faith in Intercession" (*wujūb al-īmān bi-shafāʿa*), quoting the Qur'anic verses related to it, stating that those who deny the possibility of intercession based on certain Qur'anic verses make a serious misinterpretation, since these verses do not refer to believers, but to disbelievers.[482] The following section, which contains many previously mentioned sayings, is devoted to the issue of the Prophet's intercession on the Day of Judgement.[483] At this point, Ajurrī enumerates and analyses the categories of persons authorised to intercede besides the Prophet in a section entitled "The Intercession of the Wise Men and Martyrs on the Day of Judgement".[484] The Iraqi scholar reports several versions of a saying of the Prophet in relation to the first of these categories:

> There are nine peculiarities (*khiṣāl*) with God for the martyr: he is forgiven (*yughfir lahu*) from the first gush of blood; he is shown his seat (*maqʿad*) in Paradise; he is adorned with the garment of faith (*ḥillat al-īmān*); he is protected from punishment in the grave (*ʿadhāb al-qabr*); he is reassured in the time of greatest terror (*al-fazaʿ al-akbar*); on his head is placed the crown of dignity (*tāj al-waqār*); his precious stones (*yāqūta*) are better than the world and

479 Aḥmad *al-Ṭaḥāwī, The Creed of Imam al-Ṭaḥāwī. Translated, Introduced, And Annotated by Hamza Yusuf* (Berkeley: Zaytuna Institute, 2008), 69.

480 Ibid., 59.

481 Abū Bakr al-Ajurrī, *Kitāb al-sharīʿa*, (al-Riyāḍ: Dār al-waṭan, 1997) 1198–1252. Ibn Abī Yaʿlā (d. 1131) counts al-Ajurrī among the ḥanbalite scholars, cf. Ibn Abī Yaʿlā, *Ṭabaqāt al-ḥanābila, Ṭabaqāt al-ḥanābila* (al-Qāhira: Maṭbaʿat al-sunnat al-muḥammadiyya, 2016) 1:220; Ibn Khallikān (d. 1282) instead counts him among the shāfiʿites, cf. Ibn Khallikān, *Wafayāt al-aʿyān wa-anbāʾ abnāʾ al-zamān* (Bayrūt: Dār ṣādir, 1978) 2:345.

482 Ibid., 1205.

483 Ibid., 1212–1242.

484 Ibid., 1243–1252.

> what it contains; he is married to seventy-two heavenly brides (*ḥūr al-ʿayn*); he can intercede for seventy of his close relatives.[485]

Ajurrī draws the possibility for martyrs to intercede from this saying, which also mentions the precise number of persons towards whom this intercession can be exerted. It is also worth noting the evident reference to a kind of royal investiture in Paradise for the martyr.

Another saying of the Prophet allows Ajurrī to confirm the possibility of the intercession of prophets in general and to add the category of the scholars:

> Three [categories of people] will intercede on the Day of Resurrection (*yashfaʿu yawm al-qiyāma thalātha*): the prophets (*al-anbiyāʾ*), then the scholars (*al-ʿulamāʾ*), then the martyrs (*al-shuhadāʾ*).[486]

A further category proposed by Ajurrī is that of those who know the Qurʾān by heart (*ḥuffāẓ*, sing. *ḥāfiẓ*):

> Whoever recites the Qurʾān and learns it by heart in its entirety, God will make him enter Paradise and intercede (*shaffāʿahu*) for ten members of his family who would have deserved Hell.[487]

Finally, Ajurrī adds another category: the People of the House of the Messenger (*ahl bayt al-rasūl*):

> A man of my community, through intercession, will bring into Paradise as many people as there are members of the tribes of Rabīʿa and Muḍar.[488]

In the second version reported by al-Ajurrī, the person is specified:

> ʿUthmān Ibn ʿAffān (d. 656) will intercede on the Day of Judgement [for as many people as there are members of the tribes] of Rabīʿa and Muḍar.[489]

As we have seen, usually by People of the Household (*ahl al-bayt*) is meant the wives, children and descendants of Muḥammad. However ʿUthmān, besides having married two daughters of the Prophet consecutively, is also part of the same family

485 Ibid.,1243.
486 Ibid., 1246.
487 Ibid., 1246–1247.
488 Ibid., 1247; in ancient Arabic culture, these are regarded as two tribes distinguished by the large number of individuals within them.
489 Ibid., 1249.

as Muḥammad on his mother's side, who was a granddaughter of the Prophet's grandfather.

The Iraqi scholar adds some versions of a narration (*khabar*) that is not part of the canonical collections and which is attributed to Kaʿb al-Aḥbār (d. 652):

> Kaʿb took the hand of al-ʿAbbās [ibn ʿAbd al-Muṭṭalib] and said, 'Save me by intercession.' Asked [al-ʿAbbās], 'But isn't intercession only valid for prophets?' or 'And I can intercede?' Replied [Kaʿb], 'Of course, there is no People of the Household of the Prophet who do not have the power of intercession.'[490]

The section on intercession ends with a peremptory saying, attributed to the famous Companion Anas Ibn Mālik (d. 712), placed by Ajurrī as a warning: "He who refuses *shafāʿa* will not be entitled to it."[491]

Finally, in the next section, entitled "Faith in the heavenly Basin (*ḥawḍ*) that was granted to the Prophet," Ajurrī quotes numerous sayings, already mentioned here, to corroborate this doctrine.[492]

Another work shortly after Ajurrī's, the 'Commentary of Sunni Creeds from the Qur'ān, from the sunna and the majority consensus of the Companions of the Prophet" (*Sharḥ uṣūl iʿtiqād ahl al-sunna wa-l-jamāʿa min al-kitāb wa-l-sunna wa-ijmāʿ al-ṣaḥāba*), compiled by the Persian theologian and traditionalist Abū al-Qāsim al-Lālakāʾī (m. 1027),[493] contains a large number of sayings of the Prophet concerning intercession (*shafāʿa*),[494] the Station of praise (*maqām maḥmūd*)[495] and the heavenly Basin (*ḥawḍ*).[496]

Lālakāʾī's disciple, Abū Bakr al-Bayhaqī (d. 1066), also includes the Prophet's *shafāʿa* on the Day of Judgement among the main points in his creed, also quoting a large number of *ḥadīth* to validate it.[497] In the next point, he also refers to the belief in the Prophet's heavenly Basin.[498]

---

490 Ibid., 1250–1252.
491 Ibid., 1252.
492 Ibid., 1253–1269.
493 Livnat Holtzman, "al-Lālakāʾī, Abū al-Qāsim," in *EI*[3].
494 Abū al-Qāsim al-Lālakāʾī, *Sharḥ uṣūl iʿtiqād ahl al-sunna wa-l-jamāʿa min al-kitāb wa-l-sunna wa-ijmāʿ al-ṣaḥāba* (Iskandariyya: Maktabat dār al-baṣīra, 2001), 925–945.
495 Ibid., 946–949.
496 Ibid., 950–957.
497 Abū Bakr Aḥmad ibn Ḥusayn al-Bayhaqī, *The Creed of Imam Bayhaqī, An Abridged Translation of al-Iʿtiqād wa-l-hidāya ilā sabīl al-rashād*, tr. by Nasir Abdussalam (London: Turath Publishing, 2017), 162–170.
498 Ibid., 177.

After him, one of the main Sunnite authorities, if not the main one, Ghazālī, in his major work entitled "The Revival of the Sciences of Religion" (*Iḥyā' ʿulūm al-dīn*), in the chapter devoted to Sunnite belief, summarises the categories of people who are granted intercession:

> And we believe in the intercession (*shafāʿa*) of the prophets (*al-anbiyā'*),[499] the scholars (*al-ʿulamā'*), the martyrs (*al-shuhadā'*), as well as the rest of the believers (*sā'ir al-mu'minīn*), in accordance with the rank (*jāh*) and position (*manzila*) of each one with God. And the remnant of the believers lacking an intercessor (*wa-man baqiya min al-mu'minīn wa-lam yakun lahu shafīʿ*) will be extracted [from Hell] according to God's favour, a believer will not remain in the fire for ever, but whoever has in his heart the weight of an atom of faith (*mithqāl dharra min al-īmān*) will be extracted from it.[500]

Among the points of belief, Ghazālī also mentions the belief in the Prophet's heavenly Basin through a description that, as will be clearly observed, builds on the *ḥadīth* mentioned earlier:

> And we believe in the basin to which one is led (*al-ḥawḍ al-mawrūd*), the basin of Muḥammad, from which believers will drink before entering Paradise, after being permitted to cross the Bridge (*al-ṣirāṭ*). He who drinks a single sip of it will never thirst again. Its width is the distance of a month's journey, and its waters are whiter than milk and sweeter than honey. Around it are jugs (*abārīq*) as numerous as the stars of heaven, and in it flow two springs from the *kawthar*.[501]

In the chapter devoted to death and the Hereafter, Ghazālī then reports a large number of traditions on intercession and on the Prophet's heavenly Basin.[502]

Some prominent Muslim scholars devoted specific treatises to the notion of *shafāʿa*, with the main aim of defending the Sunni position against the views of other schools, such as the Kharijites or Muʿtazilites. Among them, we may mention "The Major Intercession on the Day of Judgement" (*al-Shafāʿa al-uẓmā fī yawm al-*

---

499 In some manuscripts, after the category of prophets also appears the category of saints (*al-awliyā'*). It is unclear whether this is an interpolation or a censorship (cf. the term *al-awliyā'* in footnote in Abū Ḥāmid al-Ghazālī, *Iḥyā' ʿulūm al-dīn* (Jadda: Dār al-minhaj, 2011) 1:340). In the theological and mystical system developed by Ghazālī, the role of the saints is certainly central, and thus the eventual inclusion of this category after that of the prophets would be perfectly consistent with his doctrine.

500 Abū Ḥāmid al-Ghazālī, *Iḥyā' ʿulūm al-dīn* (Jadda: Dār al-minhaj, 2011), 340.

501 Ibid., 1:339–340.

502 *Ibi*, 9:573–585; Abū Ḥāmid al-Ghazālī, *The Remembrance of Death and the Afterlife – Kitāb Dhikr al-mawt wa-mā baʿdahu – Book XL of the Revival of the Religious Sciences – Iḥyā' ʿulūm al-dīn, tr. with an Introduction and notes by T.J. Winter* (Cambridge: Islamic Texts Society, 2015), 210–219.

qiyāma), by Fakhr al-Dīn al-Rāzī (d. 1209). This text focuses particularly on analysing Qur'anic verses related to *shafā'a* due to its author's specialisation in Qur'anic exegesis. Rāzī's strictly theological and philosophical approach influences the commentary on these verses. He argues that, according to Sunni doctrine, the *shafā'a* is not intended for unbelievers but for believers who have deserved Hell but will remain there for a certain duration before being extracted from it thanks to the Prophet's special intercession. Subsequently, again based on Qur'anic interpretations and some of the Prophet's sayings mentioned earlier, Rāzī upholds the classical Sunnite position on *shafā'a*, criticising in detail the position of the Mu'tazilites, who instead deny this possibility for believers destined for Hell, as we shall see in the next chapter.[503]

Another important text is "The Confirmation of Intercession" (*Ithbāt al-shafā'a*) by Shams al-Dīn al-Dhahabī (d. 1348), which is specifically dedicated to the Prophet's *shafā'a*. This treatise, by contrast, reveals its author's specialisation as a traditionalist and is essentially built on a large number of *ḥadīth* that deal with this topic. In the introduction, the Damascene scholar states his intention to refute the non-Sunni position of the Mu'tazilites, Murji'ites, and Kharijites.[504] After quoting the Qur'anic verse mentioned above, according to which on the Day of Judgement, "It will not profit them [the disbelievers] the intercession of the intercessors" (*fa-mā tanfa'uhum shafā'at al-shāfi'īn*),[505] al-Dhahabī states:

> Know that to the unbelievers, however, the intercession of intercessors will be of great benefit! The modes of intercession of our Prophet are seven.
>
> The first is his general major intercession for the creatures (*shafā'atuhu al-kubrā al-'āmma fī al-khalā'iq*), at the time when creation will yearn for it, and he will intercede for the people of the halt (*fa-yashfa'u fī ahl al-mawqif*)[506] to decree their fate, and this is the Station of praise (*maqām maḥmūd*) that will make the first and the last happy.
>
> The second is his intercession (*shafā'atuhu*) when he prostrates himself and praises his Lord, saying: 'My community!', and God answers him: 'Let those of your community who will have no account to render enter through the right gate of Paradise,' and the saying is authentic (*ṣaḥīḥ*).
>
> The third is his intercession (*shafā'atuhu*) to bring the rest of the people of Paradise into Paradise, as transmitted by Muslim.

503 Fakhr al-Dīn al-Rāzī, *al-Shafā'a al-uẓmā fī yawm al-qiyāma* (al-Qāhira: al-Maktaba al-azhariyya li-l-turāth, 1988), 38–57.
504 Shams al-Dīn al-Dhahabī, *Ithbāt al-shafā'a* (al-Riyāḍ: Maktaba aḍwa' al-salaf, 2000), 19–20.
505 Q 74:48.
506 Those who stand between the Resurrection and the Judgement.

> The fourth is his intercession (*shafāʿatuhu*) for those who enter Hell because of capital sins (*ahl al-kabāʾir*). He [the Prophet] said, 'A limit will be set for me, and I will bring them out of the fire and let them enter Paradise.' [The saying continues] until the Prophet says: 'O my Lord, no one is left in the fire except the one who is blocked by the Qurʾān, that is, the one who is eternally condemned.'[507]
>
> The fifth is his intercession (*shafāʿatuhu*) for a portion of the people of Hell (*ahl al-nār*), until their punishment is alleviated, as per the saying conveyed by Abū Saʿīd [al-Khudrī] that the Prophet was mentioning his uncle Abū Ṭālib and said: 'Perhaps my intercession (*shafāʿatī*) will help him so that he will be placed in a shallow place in Hell (*ḍaḥḍāḥ min al-nār*), with fire reaching his ankles and boiling his brain.' In [another] saying al-ʿAbbās said, 'Messenger of God, verily Abū Ṭālib has defended you and helped you; will this bring him advantage?' He replied, 'Yes, I found him in the abysses of fire (*ghamarāt al-nār*) and pulled him out to the shallow part (*ḍaḥḍāḥ*).'
>
> The sixth is intercession (*shafāʿatuhu*) for people destined to enter Hell because of their sins, and [the Prophet] will intercede for them, and they will not enter the fire but Paradise.
>
> The seventh is: [The Prophet] will intercede to elevate the spiritual level of some and increase their bliss (*yashfaʿu fī rafaʿa darajāt aqwām wa-ziyāda naʿīmahum*), as per the saying of Umm Salama that the Prophet made an invocation for Abū Salama when he died, saying: 'O my Lord, forgive Abū Salama and raise his spiritual rank among those who are well guided.'[508]

This brief, non-exhaustive overview of the views of primary Sunni authorities in relation to intercession clearly shows how this notion, in its most inclusive version, is an integral part of classical Sunni doctrine.

2 Intercession according to Kharijites and Muʿtazilites

As we stated earlier, Sunni theology was structured and canonised to react to the challenges brought by some minority movements to the majority positions of Muslim scholars. Likewise, it is possible to say that the inclusion of intercession in Sunni creeds and theological literature can be precisely described as a reaction to these movements' opposition to this belief.[509] The most prominent among these movements are the Kharijites and the Muʿtazilites. According to Sunni sources, the Kharijites reject the belief in intercession in particular, even in relation to the Prophet's intercession on the Day of Judgement for those in Hell due to grave

---

507 "...he who is blocked by the Qurʾān" refers to the one who associates other deities with God, meaning that the proof against him will be the numerous verses in the Qur'an that warn against the worst of sins in Islam, which, unlike the other major sins, has no chance of being forgiven by God without the sinner's repentance.

508 Shams al-Dīn al-Dhahabī, *Ithbāt al-shafāʿa* (al-Riyāḍ: Maktaba aḍwaʾ al-salaf, 2000), 20–22.

509 This is, for example, the view expressed by Arent Jan Wensinck in *The Muslim Creed. Its Genesis and Historical Development* (New York: Barnes & Noble, 1932), 180.

sin (*ahl al-kabāʾir*). This is because, according to their beliefs, anyone who commits a grave sin is considered a disbeliever (*kāfir*) and is destined to enter the fire of Hell without being able to leave.

The Muʿtazilites also reject the belief that the Prophet can intercede for those in Hell due to their belief that anyone who dies without repenting of a grave sin they have committed is undoubtedly destined for Hell and will not be forgiven. This is consistent with their doctrine of divine Justice (*al-ʿadl*) and the doctrine of promise and punishment (*al-waʿd wa-l-waʿīd*), according to which both the promise of reward for good deeds and punishment for sins are a certainty, and therefore no intercession could intervene to change the divine Will.[510]

Some traces of this controversy around intercession seem to emerge as early as the ninth century, particularly in the sayings attributed to Aḥmad Ibn Ḥanbal (d. 855). As is well known, the celebrated scholar stood in direct opposition to the theses of the Muʿtazilites, so much so that he suffered imprisonment during the inquisition (*miḥna*) instituted by the Abbasid caliph al-Maʾmūn (r. 813–833). In the "Commentary on the Fundamentals of Beliefs," Lalākāʾī mentions Ibn Ḥanbal's position on this controversy, particularly in relation to the Kharijite arguments:

> I said to Abū ʿAbd Allāh – that is, Aḥmad ibn Ḥanbal: 'What was narrated by the Prophet concerning intercession (*shafāʿa*)?' He replied, 'These authentic sayings we believe and accept, just as we believe and accept all that was narrated by the Prophet with good chains of transmission.' I asked him: 'Will some people come out of hell?' He replied: 'Yes. If we do not accept what the Messenger came with and reject him, then we are rejecting God's command. God said: 'And whatever the Messenger gives you, then take it. And what he forbids you, then refrain from it."[511] I asked, 'What about intercession (*shafāʿa*)?' He replied, 'How many traditions are narrated by the Prophet concerning intercession (*shafāʿa*) and the basin (*ḥawḍ*)! These people reject them and speak [vainly], and this is the opinion of a group of Kharijites, that God in truth will not bring anyone out of Hellfire after they have entered it. All praise is due to God who has preserved us from that with which he tested them.'[512]

As we have seen, Abū al-Ḥasan al-Ashʿarī (d. 936), in his collection of theological opinions, along with the position of the Sunnis quoted above, also reports the position of the Muʿtazilites, according to whom the intercession (*shafāʿa*) of the

510 Maria Massi Dakake, *The Charismatic Community: Shiʿite Identity in Early Islam* (Albany: State University of New York Press, 2007), 137.

511 Q 59:7.

512 Abū al-Qāsim al-Lālakāʾī, *Sharḥ uṣūl iʿtiqād ahl al-sunna wa-l-jamāʿa min al-kitāb wa-l-sunna wa-ijmāʿ al-ṣaḥāba* (Iskandariyya: Maktabat dār al-baṣīra, 2001), 945.

Prophet can only elevate the spiritual levels of believers, while nothing can save grave sinners from eternal fire.[513]

Also during the tenth century, we observe the re-emergence of this controversy at the beginning of the chapter on intercession in Ajurrī's *Kitāb al-sharīʿa:*

> Know, may God bless you, that the disapproval of intercession (*al-munkar li-shafāʿa*) is based on the attestation that the one who enters Hell no longer leaves it, and this is the position with which the Muʿtazilites have disavowed it. The arguments that we shall mention, on the other hand, draw their foundation from the Book of God, from the customs of the Messenger of God, from the customs of the Companions and those who followed them in excellence, as well as from Muslim scholars. The Muʿtazilites differ in this totally, not considering the customs of the Messenger of God, and of the Companions.[514]

In the eleventh century, we discovered an indirect reference to the muʿtazilite view on intercession in the text entitled "Commentary on the Five Foundations" (*Sharḥ al-uṣūl al-khamsa*), attributed, albeit erroneously, to al-Qāḍī ʿAbd al-Jabbār (d. 1024–1025), one of the major figures of the Muʿtazilite school.[515] This text is, instead, to be ascribed to the Zaydite Aḥmad ibn Abū Hāshim Ḥusaynī (d. 1034), but it actually contains the otherwise lost text of the muʿtazilite theologian, of whom it is a commentary.[516] The author premises that all scholars accept the Prophet's intercession for his community, although they differ on the specific categories of believers for whom it is intended. The opinion that emerges from the text is that it is reserved only for believers not guilty of serious sins. This is because forgiving a grave sinner who has not repented of his sin would be like a father forgiving the unrepentant murderer of his own son, who may be considering killing another of the same father's children. At the same time, interceding for a grave sinner would harm the very honour of the Prophet.[517]

In the same historical period, the renowned al-Andalus scholar ʿAlī Ibn Ḥazm (d. 1064), in his theological and heresiographical treatise entitled "Judgment concerning religions, inclinations, and sects" (*al-Faṣl fī-l-milal wa-l-ahwāʾ wa-l-niḥal*),

---

513 Abū al-Ḥasan al-Ashʿarī, *Maqālāt al-Islāmiyyīn wa-ikhtilāf al-muṣallīn*, edited by Helmut Ritter (Wiesbaden: Franz Steiner, 1963), 474.

514 Abū Bakr al-Ajurrī, *Kitāb al-sharīʿa* (al-Riyāḍ: Dār al-waṭan, 1997), 1198.

515 Gabriel Said Reynolds, "The Rise and Fall of Qadi ʿAbd al-Jabbar," in *International Journal of Middle East Studies* 37, 1 (2005), 3–18.

516 Aḥmad ibn al-Ḥusayn ibn Abī Hāshim Mānkdīm, (misattribution to ʿAbd al-Jabbār ibn Aḥmad), *Sharḥ uṣūl al-khamsa*, edited by ʿAbd al-Karīm ʿUthmān (al-Qāhira: Maktabat wahba, 1965), 687–793; on the attribution of this text, see the clarifications of Wilferd Madelung, "ʿAbd al-Jabbār B. Aḥmad," In *EIr.*

517 Martin J. McDermott, *The Theology of al-Shaikh al-Mufid (d. 413–1022)* (Beirut: Dar al-Mashreq, 1978), 255.

he introduces the notion of intercession (*shafāʿa*), stating that it is rejected by the Kharijites and the Muʿtazilites, as well as by all those who, like the latter, follow the doctrine that a person can no longer leave Hell after entering it. Ibn Ḥazm then reports the Qur'anic verses that are used by those who deny intercession, analysing them one by one and finally upholding the Sunnite doctrine that they can only be referred to as unbelievers (*kuffār*), whereas in truth, God will authorise some people to exercise intercession.[518]

In the twelfth century, the Muʿtazilite position emerged sharply from the Qur'anic commentary "The Revelator" (*al-Kashshāf*) by Maḥmūd al-Zamakhsharī (d. 1144).[519] The difference between the Mutaʿzilite and the Sunnite view is particularly evident if one compares the interpretations of the passages relating to intercession in Zamakhsharī's commentary and that of al-Bayḍāwī (d. 1309), written two centuries later. This is because, as is well known, the latter is largely inspired by the former while attempting to "rectify" the Mutaʿzilite interpretations in a Sunnite key or to eliminate them directly.[520] However, Zamakhsharī does not reject intercession altogether but instead states that it can only have the effect of increasing divine Grace for believers, as is evident from a verse in the Qur'ān,[521] while as far as grave sinners are concerned, no kind of intercession will be accepted by God in their regard. Bayḍāwī, on the other hand, in his commentary on the same verses, argues that even grave sinners fall into the category of believers, and for this reason, intercession also concerns them, will be accepted by God and will bring them out of Hell, while it will not serve to increase divine Grace for believers. He states that the Station of praise (*maqām maḥmūd*) promised to the Prophet corresponds to the Station of intercession (*maqām al-shafāʿa*), adding further that the Prophet's intercession is part of his duty towards his community.[522]

Bayḍāwī returns to the polemic with the Muʿtazilites in his theological text "The Ascent of Lights in the Analysis of Opinions" (*Ṭawāliʿ al-anwār min maṭāliʿ*

518 Ibn Ḥazm al-Ẓāhiri al-Andalusī, *al-Faṣl fī al-milal wa-l-ahwāʾ wa-l-niḥal* (al-Qāhira: Maktabat al-salām al-ʿāliyya, 1929), 4:53–54.

519 Andrew J. Lane, *A Traditional Muʿtazilite Qur'ān Commentary: the Kashshāf of Jār Allāh al-Zamakhsharī* (Leiden: Brill, 2006); Kifayat Ullah, *Al-Kashshāf. Al-Zamakhsharī's Muʿtazilite Exegesis of the Qur'ān* (Berlin/Boston: De Gruyter, 2017).

520 ʿAbd Allāh Ibn ʿUmar al-Bayḍāwī, *The Lights of Revelation and the Secrets of Interpretation. Hizb I of the Commentary on the Qur'ān by al-Bayḍāwī, Arabic Edition & English Translation with Introduction and notes by Gibril Fouad Haddad* (Manchester: Beacon Books, 2016).

521 "That God may recompense them with the fairest of what they have done and increase their recompense from His bounty. God provides for those whom He wishes, without reckoning." Q 24:38.

522 Lupti Ibrahim, "The Place of Intercession in the Theology of al-Zamakhsharī and al-Bayḍāwī," in *Bulletin of Christian Institutes of Islamic Studies* 4 (1981), 27–35.

al-anẓār). In this treatise, he develops similar arguments on the Sunnite view of intercession, further elaborated by Maḥmūd al-Iṣfahānī's (d. 1348) commentary on the same text.[523]

Some of the theological conceptions of the Kharijites were inherited from the Ibadites, which is why, to this day, the official doctrine of Ibadism rejects the use of intercession. In one of the main Ibadite theological texts, "The Book of the Collection of Questions and Clarification of Opinions" (*Kitāb al-mujāz fī taḥṣīl al-su'āl wa-takhlīs al-maqāl*), compiled by Abū Zakariyyā' al-Warjilānī (d. before 1174), we indeed find a refutation of the Prophet's intercession for grave sinners.[524]

3 Intercession according to Twelver Shiʿism

As we observed from some examples in the previous chapter, in the formative phase of Islamic theology, the presence and influence of Muʿtazilism is evident in the theological literature. For this reason, scholarly literature has often assumed a direct influence of Muʿtazilism not only on the emergence of Sunnite theology but also on the development of the theology of other currents, of Twelver Shiʿism, and likewise medieval Jewish theological thought.[525]

In particular, the question of the relationship and possible mutual influences between Twelver Shiʿism and Muʿtazilism has been widely debated, both by ancient Muslim authors and modern scholars. What can be gleaned from this literature is that a certain commonality of theological theses is undeniable, even when considering only a few specific personalities in specific historical periods. At the same time, it is possible to identify a similar number of theological arguments that openly differentiate the two schools.[526]

One of the main topics of open disagreement between the two currents, as reflected in ancient polemical literature, is precisely the belief in the Prophet's intercession for the great sinners of his community on the Day of Judgement. Indeed, in the context of Twelver Shiʿism, intercession is a fundamental article of faith that, to

523 ʿAbd Allāh Ibn ʿUmar Bayḍāwī; Maḥmūd ibn ʿAbd al-Raḥmān Iṣfahānī, *Nature, Man and God in Medieval Islam Abd Allah Baydawi's Text, Tawaliʿ al-Anwar Min Mataliʿ al-Anzar, Along with Mahmud Isfahani's commentary Mataliʿ al-Anzar, Sharh Tawaliʿ al-Anwar, ed. and tr. by Edwin Elliott Calverley and James W. Pollock*, Volume One (Leiden: Brill, 2002), 1073–1078.

524 Valerie J. Hoffman, *The Essentials of Ibāḍī Islam* (Syracuse-New York: Syracuse University Press, 2012), 22.

525 Hussein Ali Abdulsater, *Shiʿi Doctrine, Muʿtazili Theology: Al-Sharīf al-Murtaḍā and Imami Discourse* (Edinburgh: Edinburgh University Press, 2017), 3.

526 Ibid., 1–7.

this day, has not been questioned even by the most rationalist currents. A strong convergence between Sunnism and Twelver Shiʿism can be observed on intercession, and this will be, as we shall see, one of the main reasons for the strong controversy unleashed by the various branches of the Islamic Reformation against both camps. However, it is necessary to point out an obvious difference, which consists in identifying the categories of intercessors.

One of the earliest and most important of the Twelver creeds is "The Book of Creeds" (*Risālat al-iʿtiqādāt*), compiled by Ibn Bābawayh al-Qummī, known as Shaykh Ṣadūq (d. 991), who in his time was one of the major opponents of the Āl-e Nowbakht, a family of Imamite scholars with a marked Muʿtazilite tendency. In the chapter devoted to intercession (*shafāʿa*), Shaykh Ṣadūq states that it is reserved for Muslims who have committed major or minor sins without repentance before death, while those who have repented do not require intercession, for as ʿAlī ibn Abī Ṭālib stated, "There is no intercessor more effective than repentance (*al-tawba*)."[527] To the categories of intercessors belong first and foremost the prophets (*anbiyāʾ*) and their heirs (*awṣiyāʾ*), the Imāms, but also simple devout believers, who may intercede for a large number of other believers.[528] Belief in the heavenly Basin (*ḥawḍ*) also finds its place in this creed, and traditions almost identical to those found in Sunni sources are cited, with the difference that the one who will give drink to the believers while preventing his enemies from accessing the basin, will be ʿAlī ibn Abī Ṭālib.[529]

The most prominent disciple of Shaykh Ṣadūq, Shaykh Mufīd (d. 1022), in his commentary on his master's creed, only adds a brief reference to intercession in the chapter on the meaning of the Qurʾanic term *al-Aʿrāf* (Qurʾān 7:46). He states that this designation refers to a specific place in the eschatological cosmology where those among the believers will stay while waiting to enter Paradise through the intercession (*shafāʿa*) *of* the Prophet and his descendants, ʿAlī ibn Abī Ṭālib and the Imāms.[530]

In another theological text by Shaykh Mufīd, entitled "The Main Theses of the Selected Doctrines" (*Awāʾil al-maqālāt fī al-madhāhib al-mukhtārāt*), he adds some details:

---

527 Asaf Ali Asghar Fyzee, A *Shiʿite Creed, A translation of Risālatuʾl-Iʿtiqādāt of Muḥammad b. ʿAlī Ibn Bābawayhi al-Qummī known as Shaykh Ṣadūq* (Oxford: Oxford University Press, 1942), 63.

528 Ibid., 67–68.

529 Ibid., 66–67.

530 Muḥammad ibn Muḥammad al-Nuʿmān al-Shaykh al-Mufīd, *The Emendation of A Shiʿite Creed, a translation of Taṣḥīḥu ʾl-Iʿtiqād of Abū ʿAbdillāh Muḥammad ibn Muḥammad ibn Nuʿmān, Known ash-Shaykh al-Mufīd (336/948 or 338/950–413/1022)*, tr. by ʿIrfān ʿAbdu ʾl-Ḥamīd (Tehran: World Organisation for Islamic Services (WOFIS), 2006), 2:69.

> The Imamites agree that the Messenger of God will intercede (*yashfaʿu*), on the Day of Judgement, for a group of his community who will have committed grave sins (*li-jamāʿat min murtakibī al-kabāʾir min ummatihi*), and that the Prince of the Believers [ʿAlī] will intercede (*yashfaʿu*) for sinners among his partisans (*aṣḥāb al-dhunūb min shīʿatihi*), and that the Imāms of Muḥammad's family will intercede (*yashfaʿūn*) in the same way, and God will save through their intercession (*bi-shafāʿatihim*) many sinners; they also agree on the intercession of the Messenger (*shafāʿat al-rasūl*) the Murjiʾites (*al-murjiʾa*) except Ibn Shabīb and a group among the People of the *ḥadīth*.[531] The Muʿtazilites (*al-muʿtazila*) are united in opposing this, and they claim that the intercession of the Messenger of God (*shafāʿat rasūl Allāh*) is reserved for the obedient and that there will be no intercession for those who deserve punishment among all creatures.[532]

This conception of intercession runs through the theological history of Twelver Shiʿism, transmitted by various later Shiʿi scholars, until it came together in the work of the leading authority of Safavid-era Shiʿism, Muḥammad Bāqir al-Majlisī (d. 1699). In his monumental collection of *ḥadīth* and interpretations of the Qurʾān titled "Seas of Lights: The Collection of the Pearls of the Pure Imāms Traditions" (*Biḥār al-anwār al-jāmiʿa li-durar akhbār al-aʾimma al-aṭhār*), Majlisī devotes a chapter to intercession (*shafāʿa*). The large number of traditions related to intercession gathered here shows the importance of this notion in the context of Twelver Shiʿism. These traditions are often almost identical to those reported in the previously mentioned Sunni collections, the only difference is that they report the Imām and the People of the House of the Prophet as transmitters and beneficiaries, not the Companions of the Prophet. Here are some examples of these traditions:

> The Messenger of God said: 'There are three categories of people who will intercede with God (*yashfaʿūn ilā Allāh*), and their intercession will be accepted: the prophets (*al-anbiyāʾ*), then the scholars (*al-ʿulamāʾ*), then the martyrs (*al-shuhadāʾ*).'"

531 Shaykh Ṣadūq here uses the denomination "Murjiʾites" to refer to certain Sunni ḥanafite theologians, so called, in the first historical phase of theological elaboration, because they "deferred" (from the root *r-j-ʾ*) judgement on the apostasy of a believer guilty of grave sin, referring the final judgement to God. The second reference is probably to the muʿtazilite theologian Muḥammad Ibn Shabīb (d. ninth c.); the third reference is to the current of the *ahl al-ḥadīth*, the Sunnite scholars in religious sciences who, from the eighth-ninth c. onwards, considered that authority from a legal point of view, after the Qurʾān, was to be found in the sayings of the Prophet (*ḥadīth*), rejecting the recourse to opinion (*al-raʾy*), which was gaining ground especially within the future ḥanafite legal school and the ashʿarite and māturidite theological schools.

532 Muḥammad ibn Muḥammad al-Nuʿmān al-Shaykh al-Mufīd, *Awāʾil al-maqālāt fi al-madhāhib al-mukhtārāt* (Bayrūt: Dār al-kitāb al-islāmī, 1983), 50.

> The Messenger of God stated, 'Whoever does not believe in my basin (*ḥawḍī*), God will not let him attain it; whoever does not believe in my intercession (*shafāʿatī*) God will not let him attain it.'[533]

> The Messenger of God said: 'Verily, my intercession (*shafāʿatī*) is for those of my community who have committed grave sins. As for those who have behaved well, against them there shall be nothing.'[534]

> The Messenger of God said: 'There is no better intercession than repentance (*al-tawba*). Intercession will be granted to the prophets, the heirs [the Imāms], the believers and the angels. As for the believers, they will be granted intercession [for a number of people] such as the tribes of Rabīʿa and Muḍar, and the lowest of the believers is the one who will intercede for thirty people. There will be no intercession for the people of doubt and associationism, nor for the people of unbelief and denial, but only for the believers among the people of divine Unity.'[535]

As we can see, some of these traditions, attributed to the Prophet, are quite similar to some Sunni traditions mentioned earlier. Other traditions, on the other hand, although in some cases displaying identical content, either grant a central role to the main personalities of Twelver Shiʿism or are traditions directly attributed to them:

> ʿAlī narrated that Fāṭima asked the Messenger of God, 'O Father, where shall I meet you on the Day of Judgement, the Day of Fears, the Day of Great Fright?' The Prophet replied, 'O Fāṭima, at the Gate of Paradise, I will carry the Banner of praise (*liwāʾ al-ḥamd*) where I will intercede for my people with my Lord.' She said: 'O Father, if I do not meet you there?' He replied, 'At the heavenly Basin (*al-ḥawḍ*), where I will quench the thirst of my community.' She said, 'If I do not meet you there?' He replied, 'At the Bridge (*ṣirāṭ*), where I will stand up and say, 'Lord, secure my community." She said, 'If I do not meet you there?' He replied, 'At the Balance (*mīzān*), where I will say, 'Lord, secure my community." She said, 'If I do not meet you there?' He replied: 'Seek me at the side of Hell, where I will prevent the sparks of its flame from touching my community.' Then Fatima was satisfied, peace be upon her, upon her father, her husband and her children.'[536]

> Jaʿfar al-Ṣādiq said: 'When the Day of Judgement comes, God will gather the First and the Last into one plain, and a great darkness will engulf them, so they will invoke their Lord and say: 'O Lord! Turn away this darkness from us!" He said: 'Then will come a people with a light that will go before them, illuminating the land of the Day of Judgement. The people of the gathering will say: 'They are the prophets of God,' but a call will come to them from the Presence of God: 'They are not prophets. The people gathered will say: 'They are angels. A call will come to them from the Presence of God: 'They are not angels, they are not angels!' The assembled peo-

533 Muḥammad Bāqir al-Majlisī, *Biḥār al-anwār al-jāmiʿa li-durar akhbār al-aʾimma al-aṭhār*, 110 vols. Bayrūt: Dār al-iḥyāʾ al-turāth al-ʿarabī, 1983), 8:34.
534 Ibid., 8:34.
535 Ibid., 8:58.
536 Ibid., 8:35.

ple will say: 'They are martyrs'. The call will answer them from the Presence of God: 'They are not martyrs, they are not martyrs. They will say, 'Who are they?' The call will answer them: 'O people of the gathering, answer! O people of the gathering, ask them: 'Who are you?' The people of the gathering will say, 'Who are you?' They will say, 'We are the Alawites (*al-ʿalāwiyyūn*), we are the progeny of Muḥammad, God's Messenger, we are the sons of ʿAlī, friend of God (*walī Allāh*), we are the chosen ones by God's benevolence, we are the trustworthy peacemakers.' The call will be answered by the Presence of God Almighty and Majestic: 'Intercede (*ishfaʿū*) for your beloved ones, for your friends and for your partisans (*shīʿatikum*). Thus, they will intercede.'[537]

Jaʿfar al-Ṣādiq said: 'Our partisans (*shīʿatunā*) are created by the light of God and will return to Him. By God! You will join us on the Day of Judgment, we will be asked to intercede and we will intercede, and by God, you will be asked to intercede and you will intercede, and there will be no man among you for whom a Hell will not be placed on his left and a Paradise on his right, whereby he will make his loved ones enter Paradise and his enemies enter Hell.'[538]

The Prophet said: 'When I will be at the Station of praise (*al-maqām al-maḥmūd*), I will intercede for those of my community who have committed grave sins, and God will grant me intercession for them. By God! I will not intercede for those who will cause harm to my progeny! (*lā tashaffaʿtu fī-man ādhā dhurriyyatī*).'[539]

Jaʿfar al-Ṣādiq stated, 'He who denies three things is not among our partisans (*laysa min shīʿatinā*): the Ascension of the Prophet (*al-miʿrāj*), the questioning in the grave (*al-masāʾil fī-l-qabr*), and intercession (*al-shafāʿa*).'[540]

Jaʿfar al-Ṣādiq said: 'The Prophet's intercession concerns his community, our intercession concerns our partisans (*shīʿatunā*), and the partisans' intercession concerns their families.'[541]

Jaʿfar al-Ṣādiq said: 'The first to intercede on the Day of Judgement for his community will be the Messenger of God, and the first to intercede for his family members and children will be the Prince of Believers [ʿAlī], and the first to intercede for the Muslims of Byzantium will be Ṣuhayb, and the first to intercede for the believers of Ethiopia will be Bilāl.'[542]

---

537 Ibid., 8:36–37.
538 Ibid., 8:37.
539 Ibid.
540 Ibid.
541 Ibid., 8:42.
542 Ibid., 8:43. Ṣuhayb ibn Sinān (d. c. 657) was an Arab of Greek culture who lived for twenty years as a prisoner in Byzantium, and when he was released he reached Mecca and became one of the first Muslims. In the Islamic tradition he is considered, in the words of the Prophet, the "forerunner of the Byzantines" (*sābiq al-rūm*), just as Bilāl is considered the forerunner of the Abyssinians and Salmān the forerunner of the Persians, cf. Ahmad Shboul, "Greek destinies among Arabs: Rumi Muslims in Arab-Islamic civilization," in *Modern Greek Studies (Australia & New Zealand)* 14 (2010), 288–290.

> The Prophet said: 'There are five intercessors: the Qur'ān; the bond of kinship (*al-raḥim*); loyalty (*al-amāna*); your Prophet (*nabiyyikum*); the People of the House of your Prophet (*ahl bayt nabiyyikum*).'[543]

> The Prophet said: 'I see my daughter Fāṭima coming on the Day of Judgement on a mount of light. On her right will be seventy thousand angels, on her left seventy thousand angels and behind her seventy thousand angels who will guide the female believers (*al-mu'mināt*) of my community to Paradise. Similarly, any woman who prays during the day and night five ritual prayers, fasts in the month of Ramaḍān, makes the pilgrimage to the Sacred House of God, pays ritual alms from her possessions, obeys her husband, and considers ʿAlī as my successor, will enter Paradise through the intercession of my daughter Fāṭima.'[544]

> The Prophet said: 'Do not disdain the poor people among the partisans of ʿAlī and their descendants (*fuqarā' shīʿat ʿAlī wa-ʿitratahi*), for one man among them will intercede [for a great number of people] as the tribes of Rabīʿa and Muḍar.'[545]

The chapter ends with an appendix (*tadhnīb*) that includes Majlisī's commentary, in which he summarises the Twelver Shiʿites' belief in intercession. He begins by stating that all Muslim scholars agree on the validity of the Prophet's intercession (*shafāʿa*). However, while the Muʿtazilites consider the beneficiaries of this intercession to be the believers who are granted greater reward, others claim that it is the sinners. The position of the Shiʿites, Majlisi argues, is that intercession consists in the forgiveness of sinners, even when they have committed greater sins. At the same time, Shiʿites believe that intercession is not limited to the Prophet but is also incumbent upon the Imāms after him and all devout believers to whom God has granted permission to intercede. Majlisī, showing a certain openness, ends his chapter with a quotation from the commentary of the collection of Muslim's authentic *ḥadīth* (*Sharḥ ṣaḥīḥ Muslim*) by the Sunni scholar Yaḥyā al-Nawawī (d. 1277), who in turn, cites the Qāḍī ʿIyāḍ's opinion from the *al-Shifā*'.[546]

543 Muḥammad Bāqir al-Majlisī, *Biḥār al-anwār al-jāmiʿa li-durar akhbār al-a'imma al-aṭhār*, 110 vols. Bayrūt: Dār al-iḥyā' al-turāth al-ʿarabī, 1983), 8:43.

544 Ibid., 8:58–59.

545 Ibid., 8: 59.

546 Ibid., 8:62–63.

Chapter 8
Muḥammad as Mediator: Devotion to the Prophet

According to the opinion of the Sunni and Shiʿite Twelver scholars, as we have seen, the Prophet not only holds the privilege of the major intercession on the Day of Judgement but also exercises a constant function of mediation towards believers since, like the other prophets, he lives in the intermediary world (*al-barzakh*). For this reason, a strong devotion to him has progressively developed within Islamic societies, focusing on his role as a mediator between God and believers. This perception of Muḥammad's function is reflected in the religious literature and emerges at the same time through certain practices, especially widespread in Sunni circles. It is crucial, therefore, to emphasise how devotion to the prophet Muḥammad occupies a fundamental place in the religious life of Muslim peoples. The impact of the Prophet's figure on the thinking, and especially on the religious practices of Muslim societies is too evident to be underestimated. This dimension has been effectively described by Marion Holmes Katz:

> Nevertheless, believing Muslims throughout the centuries have not merely acknowledged Muḥammad's prophethood and followed his teachings; they also have experienced him as an intimately known and intensely beloved presence in their lives. Indeed, in well-authenticated reports, the Prophet is said to have declared that no one is truly a believer unless he loves the Prophet more than his own parent or child. This sense of deep love and personal connection to the Prophet has been generated in many ways, including a rich tradition of devotional poetry describing the Prophet's physical beauty, moral perfection, and abundant miracles. It has also been evoked and sustained by many ritual activities.[547]

Within Islamic societies, a number of practices related to devotion to the Prophet have developed in both cultured and popular circles, especially in Sufi circles. These practices use the terminology of secular love since, in the Sunnite Islamic tradition, Muḥammad is habitually called the "beloved of God (*ḥabīb Allāh*)" and is thus at the same time the object of love and devotion of Muslim populations.

547 Marion Holmes Katz, "The Prophet Muhammad in Ritual," in *The Cambridge Companion to Muhammad*, edited by Jonathan E. Brockopp (New York: Cambridge University Press, 2010), 139.

https://doi.org/10.1515/9783111500966-013

1 Intercession in devotional practices towards the Prophet

This devotion is conveyed through religious formulas and practices, as well as through poetry, especially sung poetry. As we shall see, the Prophet's function as mediator and intercessor is inevitably present in this heritage. The study of devotion to the prophet Muḥammad in Islam and the practices associated with it has not, however, enjoyed particular attention from specialists. It is only in recent years that numerous researches devoted to this topic have appeared.[548]

2 The visit to the Prophet's tomb and the request for intercession

The Prophet Muḥammad died in Medina in 632 and was buried in his home, which was separated from the first mosque only by a wall. Also buried alongside the Prophet were his two Companions, Abū Bakr (d. 634) and ʿUmar (d. 644), who had succeeded him in leading the community of believers. Over time, the practice of visiting (*ziyāra*) Muḥammad's tomb developed, although, from the outset, there was resistance from a number of Muslim scholars. Controversy gravitated around certain traditions attributed to the Prophet that prohibited the construction of raised tombs in masonry and pointed to the veneration of the tombs of prophets and saints by other religions, particularly Judaism and Christianity, as a bad example. At the same time, however, other traditions seemed to specifically promote visiting the Prophet's mosque in Medina. According to one of these traditions, it was one of only three mosques it was meritorious to visit, along with those in Mecca and Jerusalem. Other traditions added that a prayer in the mosque in Medina was worth as much as thousands of prayers in another mosque, except for the prayer in the mosque in Mecca, which was even more meritorious. Moreover, as we have seen, a specific part of the mosque in Medina was considered part of Para-

548 For a summary on this issue, see Ruggero Vimercati Sanseverino, "Theology of Veneration of the Prophet Muḥammad. Knowledge and love in the *Shifā'* of al-Qāḍī ʿIyāḍ (d. 544/1149) between *ḥadīth*, philosophy and spirituality," in *The Presence of the Prophet in Early Modern and Contemporary Islam, Volume 1, The Prophet Between Doctrine, Literature and Arts: Historical Legacies and Their Unfolding*, edited by Denis Gril, Stefan Reichmuth and Dilek Sarmis (Leiden: Brill, 2021), 153–196. In this direction, the three planned volumes of *The Presence of the Prophet in Early Modern and Contemporary Islam* series represent the final outcome of a research project finally devoted to this fundamental topic.

dise, between the Prophet's house and thus between his tomb and his pulpit.[549] Another kind of tradition, as we have seen, stated that those who visited the Prophet's tomb would undoubtedly obtain his intercession, as would those who died in Medina:

> Whoever succeeds in dying in Medina, let him die there, for I will intercede for those who die there (*fa-innī ashfaʿu li-man yamūtu bihā*).[550]

Controversy aside, the visit to Muḥammad's tomb has become a custom among Muslim populations over time, approved by most religious scholars, and the ruling dynasties – until the Saʿūd dynasty came to power in the twentieth century – have always favoured this visit, through the architectural development of the mosque and the construction of the famous Green Dome (*al-qubba al-khaḍrā'*), which has itself become an iconographic symbol associated with the presence of the Prophet.

In the most important text on Islamic prophetology, "The Healing through the Presentation of the Rights of the Chosen One" (*al-Shifā' bi-taʿrīf ḥuqūq al-muṣṭafā*) by al-Qāḍī ʿIyāḍ (d. 1149), an entire chapter is devoted to the visit to the Prophet's tomb. The author begins by stating that this visit is a custom (*sunna*) of Muslims, on whose validity there is a majority consensus among scholars (*ijmāʿ*).[551] After presenting a number of *ḥadīth* related to the visit, especially traditions related to intercession, al-Qāḍī ʿIyāḍ states that the objective for those who visit the mosque of Medina is prayer in the Prophet's mosque, given the merits set forth above, as well as seeking blessings (*tabarruk*) at the sacred area of the mosque (*rawḍa*), the pulpit (*minbar*) and the tomb of the Prophet, the place where he sat, which his hands touched and where he walked, and the places where his Companions lived.[552] He adds that some Companions used to visit the tomb of the Prophet and mentions, for example, ʿAbd Allāh ibn ʿUmar ibn al-Khaṭṭāb (d. 693), who used to touch the seat of the Prophet's pulpit (*maqʿad al-nabī min al-minbar*) and then pass his hands over his face. When the mosque was empty, the Companions would touch the knob of the pulpit (*rummanat al-minbar*) with their right hand, which was near the tomb, and then turn towards the direction of Mecca (*qibla*) and perform invocations.[553]

---

549 Harry Munt, *The Holy City of Medina: Sacred Space in Early Islamic Arabia* (New York: Cambridge University Press, 2014), 127–147.
550 Tirmidhī, *Sunan al-Tirmidhī*, 1269.
551 Qāḍī ʿIyāḍ al-Yaḥṣubī, *al-Shifā' bi-taʿrīf ḥuqūq al-*muṣṭafā, ed. ʿAbduh ʿAlī Kūshak (Dubai: Jā'izat Dubay al-dawliyya li-l-Qur'ān al-karīm, 2013), 582.
552 Ibid., 585.
553 Ibid., 586–587.

This attitude of the Companions towards the relics of Muḥammad clearly shows us how, even after his departure, the search for even a material connection with the Prophet remained in close association, as we shall see, with his function as mediator and intercessor.

3 The search for blessing and intercession through the Prophet's relics

The sacred dimension of the Prophet's body has been the subject of an in-depth study by Denis Gril, who shows how it derives primarily from its function as a receptacle for Islam's sacred text. The Companions of the Prophet, as evidenced by a number of *ḥadīth*, sought contact with his body with the firm conviction that this represented direct access to the sacred. By virtue of the universal mediator function embodied by the Prophet, contact with his sacred body constituted immediate and tangible access to the intercessory function he dispensed.[554] The intrinsic sacredness of Muḥammad's body is described in the primary sources of Islam through the root *b-r-k*, which expresses the idea of blessing (*baraka*) and whose pursuit is indicated by the term *tabarruk*. After the Prophet's death, this material blessing remains accessible to the believer in two ways: the first, as we have seen, is the visit to the Prophet's tomb in Medina and the most direct contact possible with the material parts that came into contact with his sacred body; the second is the search for proximity to his bodily relics, as well as to the objects that came into contact with his sacred body or relics.[555]

Numerous *ḥadīth* refer to devotion to the Prophet's relics. The Companions tried in every way to make contact with the Prophet's sacred body by touching or kissing it.[556] They would also try to retrieve the substances released from his body, such as the water the Prophet used for his ablutions, his sweat, his saliva,

554 Denis Gril, "Le corps du Prophète," in *Revue des mondes musulmans et de la Méditerranée* 113–114 (2006), 39, 49, 54.

555 On the Prophet's relics, cf. Luca Patrizi, "La vénération des reliques du prophète Muḥammad en Islam entre dévotion et fondement du pouvoir," in *The Presence of the Prophet in Early Modern and Contemporary Islam, Volume 3, Prophetic Piety in Islam: History and Anthropology*, edited by Nelly Amri, Rachida Chih and Stefan Reichmuth. (Leiden: Brill, 2023), 223–249; Adam Bursi, *Traces of the Prophets: Relics and Sacred Spaces in Early Islam* (Edinburgh: Edinburgh University Press, 2024).

556 Denis Gril, "Le corps du Prophète," in *Revue des mondes musulmans et de la Méditerranée* 113–114 (2006), 48–49.

and the blood that resulted from his "wet cupping" (*ḥijāma*),[557] in order to ingest or preserve them.

Similarly, the Companions sought to obtain bodily relics of the Prophet, such as hairs, and contact relics of various kinds, the most important of which are clothes, shirts, cloaks and sandals.

Some *ḥadīth* show that upon the Prophet's death, some Companions kept some of these relics and soon began to use them to cure infirmities by drinking or smearing water on their bodies that had been specially put in contact with them. Some Companions, moreover, at the point of death, demanded to be buried with the Prophet's hair on their eyes, mouth and under their tongue.[558]

In this context, the Prophet's garments enjoy a special status and display a role that is at once devotional, talismanic and political. The transmission of a garment, particularly a cloak as a vehicle of religious and spiritual inheritance, is a recurring element in the history of the Abrahamic religions. The Prophet's cloak, in particular, is closely linked to the practice of intercession. Indeed, as we have seen, some *ḥadīth* show the Prophet wearing his cloak (*burda*) backwards, to perform the prayer of invocation of rain. After the Prophet's death, the practice of invoking rain was continued by the Companions, and some narratives report that ʿUmar ibn al-Khaṭṭāb would seek the Prophet's intercession by wearing his cloak while performing this prayer.[559] According to other *ḥadīth*, one of the Prophet's garments, a robe (*jubba*), was kept by one of his wives, ʿĀʾisha, and then inherited by the latter's sister, Asmāʾ, who used the water from washing this garment to cure the sick.[560]

These practices were transmitted through the centuries: we can find a very representative episode of the recourse to the Prophet's intercession and succour through his relics in the historiographical literature of the medieval period. In 1520, due to the delay of the flooding of the Nile, the Ottoman governor of the time, Khāʾir Bey (r. 1517–1522), asked the authorities representing the four legal schools, the scholars, and the most important Sufi masters of his time to spend the night in prayer at the Nilometer, the flood-measuring device located in Cairo. However, as the level continued to fall, the governor himself went to the Ni-

557 Wet cupping is a technique of ancient medicine, recommended and practised by the Prophet, still in use today among some Muslim peoples, which involves small incisions in the skin and the subsequent application of glass cups in a vacuum, with the aim of draining corrupted blood and regenerating the blood system, cf. Cristina Álvarez Millán, "Bloodletting and cupping," in *EI*[3].

558 Brannon Wheeler, *Mecca and Eden: ritual, relics, and territory in Islam* (Chicago and London: The University of Chicago Press, 2006), 72.

559 Jalāl al-Dīn al-Suyūṭī, *Taʾrīkh al-khulafāʾ* (Bayrūt: Muʾassasat ʿIzz al-Dīn, 1992), 140.

560 Muslim, *Ṣaḥīḥ Muslim*, 5:432–433.

lometre accompanied by Qur'anic reciters, who recited the Qur'ān several times before completing the reading of the main *ḥadīth* collection, the *Ṣaḥīḥ* of Bukhārī. Since even this did not seem to yield the desired results, the governor brought with him the Prophet's relics that were kept in the madrasa al-Ghūriyya and ordered them to be immersed in the water of the Nilometre cistern, accompanying the act with prayers of intercession to the Prophet. At that point, according to sources, the level rose to the required sixteen cubits, allowing the dam to be opened and the thanksgiving celebrations to begin.[561]

This episode, among the many that can be traced in the sources, shows that in pre-modern Islamic societies, the belief that the Prophet's intercession was one of the most direct methods of obtaining the hoped-for help and salvation from God was deeply rooted. For this reason, there was a gradual spread of a specific practice through which the believer could turn his spiritual orientation on the Prophet and subsequently obtain his intercession with God: the invocation of blessing on the Prophet.

4 The invocation of blessing on the Prophet (*al-ṣalā ʿalā al-nabī*) as intercession

Among the various traditions associated with intercession mentioned in the previous chapters, one in particular shows the relationship between intercession and the invocation of blessing on the Prophet:

> When you hear the call to prayer, repeat what is recited, then invoke the blessing upon me (*ṣallū ʿalayya*), because whoever invokes the blessing upon me (*man ṣallā ʿalayya ṣalā*) God will send ten blessings upon him (*ṣallā-Llāh ʿalayhi bihā ʿasharan*). Then ask God to grant me the intermediation (*al-wasīla*), which is a station (*manzila*) in Paradise that belongs only to one of God's servants, and I hope it can be me. If anyone asks that I be given the intermediation (*al-wasīla*), he will be assured of intercession (*ḥallat lahu shafāʿa*).[562]

The invocation of blessing on the Prophet, in Arabic *al-ṣalā ʿalā al-nabī* or *taṣliya*, often called "prayer on the Prophet" in modern Western languages, is one of the most famous Islamic practices that form part of the *dhikr*, the "remembrance of God," which consists of the mention of divine names and religious formulas.[563] Al-

561 Jean-Charles Ducène, "Rites religieux et crue du Nil en Égypte Médiévale," in *Acta orientalia belgica* 23 (2010), 70–71.

562 Muslim, *Ṣaḥīḥ Muslim*, 2:137.

563 Cristina De La Puente, "The Prayer Upon the Prophet Muhammad (Tasliya), a Manifestation of Islamic Religiosity," in *Medieval Encounters* 5, 1 (1999), 121–129.; Michele Petrone, "Prayer on the

though it is not obligatory, it is part of the strongly recommended practices, since a divine exhortation to perform it is found in a Qurʿanic verse:

> Verily, God and the angels send blessing upon the Prophet (*yuṣallūna ʿalā al-nabī*); O you who believe, invoke blessing and peace upon him (*ṣallū ʿalayhi wa-sallim taslīman*).[564]

According to Muslim exegetes, this verse was revealed to the Prophet in the second year of the Hegira (*hijra*), on the night of the Ascension (*al-miʿrāj*), at the time when he was at the aforementioned "distance of two arcs or less" (*qāb qawsayn aw adnā*).[565] The central term in this verse is the verb *ṣallā/yuṣallī*, from the root *ṣ-l-w*, which, according to Muslim linguists and religious scholars, has three meanings. The first is general: "to pray, to perform a prayer, to worship, to venerate God," while the second is "to perform a *ṣalā*," the Islamic ritual prayer. As for the third meaning, when the verb *ṣallā* is followed by the preposition "on, upon" (*ʿalā*), classical Arabic dictionaries propose several solutions: if the action of the verb comes from God, it means Mercy (*raḥma*); if it comes from the angels, it means invocation (*duʿāʾ*) and request for forgiveness (*istighfār*); if, on the other hand, the subject is God or the angels, and the object is the Prophet, it means "blessing (*baraka*), sending blessings on him, magnifying him, conferring honour on him;" if the subject is a man, and the object is the Prophet, it means "invoking divine blessing on him, magnifying him, conferring honour on him."[566] The voluminous dictionary *Tāj al-ʿarūs*, compiled by Murtaḍā al-Zabīdī (d. 1790), which selects and incorporates the main meanings proposed by previous dictionaries, reports the view that *ṣalā* is derived from the Hebrew word *ṣalūtā*. The origin of the root meaning, according to the *Tāj al-ʿarūs*, is connected to invocation (*al-duʿāʾ*) and then to mercy (*al-raḥma*) and blessing (*baraka*), the *ṣalā* that comes from the angels is a request for forgiveness (*al-istighfār*) and invocation (*al-duʿāʾ*); if it comes from God and the angels, it is above all magnification (*taʿẓīm*) and veneration (*takrīm*).[567]

Prophet between Devotion and Scholarship," in *Oriente moderno* 102 (2022), 1–35; Mehdi Sajid, "Spiritual Legacy, Sufi Identity, and Mystical Knowledge in Taṣliya formulae," in *Die Welt des Islams* (2022), 1–30.

564 Q 33:56.

565 Constance E. Padwick, *Muslim Devotions: A Study of Prayer-Manuals in Common Use* (London: S.P.C.K, 1961), 154.

566 Edward William Lane, "*ṣ-l-w*," *An Arabic-English Lexicon* (London: Williams and Norgate, 1863–93).

567 Murtaḍā al-Ḥusaynī al-Zabīdī, "*ṣ-l-w*," *Tāj al-ʿarūs min jawāhir al-qāmūs* (al-Kuwayt: Muʾassasat al-kuwayt li-l-taqaddum al-ʿilmī, 2001).

This practice spread gradually over the centuries, and from the twelfth century onwards, treatises dedicated to it began to appear, as well as the first collections of invocations of blessing on the Prophet.[568] One of these earliest texts is the "Book of the Notification of the Benefit of the Invocation of Blessing and Peace on the Prophet" (*Kitāb al-iʿlām bi-faḍl al-ṣalāt ʿalā al-nabī wa-l-salām*) by Muḥammad ibn ʿAbd al-Raḥmān al-Numayrī (d. 1150). It is a collection of sayings of the Prophet and Companions, focusing on the *ṣalā ʿalā al-nabī* and the various versions of this invocation found in the traditions.[569]

Among these, some are related to intercession, such as the following, attributed to Ibn ʿAbbās:

> O my Lord, accept the major intercession of Muḥammad (*shafāʿat Muḥammad al-kubrā*), grant his request [of the *wasīla*] in the Hereafter and the Hereafter, and raise his level as high as possible, just as with Abraham and Moses.[570]

> Whoever invokes the blessing upon me (*man ṣallā ʿalayya*) in this way: 'O my Lord, grant him the seat next to Yours (*al-maqʿad al-muqarrab ʿindaka*) on the Day of Judgement, my intercession becomes obligatory for him (*wajabat lahu shafāʿatī*).'[571]

The aforementioned Fīrūzābādī (d. 1414) also composed a treatise on the *ṣalā ʿalā al-nabī*, entitled "The Bond and the Good News: On the Invocation of Blessing on the Best of Creatures" (*al-Ṣilāt wa-l-bushr fī al-ṣalāt ʿalā khayr al-bashar*), in which he proposes an interpretation on the nature of this invocation:

> *Allāhumma ṣalli ʿalā Muḥammad* means: 'O God, magnify him in this low world (*ʿaẓẓimhu fī-l-dunya*), by the exaltation of his mention (*bi-iʿlā dhikrihi*), the clear manifestation of his calling as well as by making his law permanent; and in the Hereafter by accepting his intercession for his community (*bi-tashfīʿihi fī ummatihi*) and multiplying his reward and recompense, and the manifestation of benefit for the first and the last through the Station of praise, and his preference for the close ones and the people of vision.'[572]

Another treatise entitled "The Astonishing Word About the Invocation of Blessing on the Beloved Intercessor" (*al-Qawl al-badīʿ fī al-ṣalā ʿalā al-ḥabīb al-shafīʿ*), was composed by the Egyptian scholar Muḥammad ibn ʿAbd al-Raḥmān al-Sakhāwī

568 Michele Petrone, "Prayer on the Prophet between Devotion and Scholarship," in *Oriente moderno* 102 (2022), 1–35.

569 Muḥammad ibn ʿAbd al-Raḥmān al-Numayrī, *Kitāb al-iʿlām bi-faḍl al-ṣalāt ʿalā al-nabī wa-l-salām* (Bayrūt: Dār al-kutub al-ʿilmiyya, 2009).

570 Ibid., 59.

571 Ibid., 61.

572 Majīd al-Dīn Muḥammad ibn Ya'qūb al-Fīrūzābādī, *al-Ṣilāt wa al-bushr fī al-ṣalāt ʿalā khayr al-bashar* (Dimashq: Dār al-Qur'ān, 1966), 65.

(d. 1497). In this text, the relationship between this practice and intercession emerges clearly, starting with the title itself. He comments on the Qur'anic verse on the divine order in relation to the invocation on the Prophet in this way:

> The aim [of this verse] is to inform the believers about the rank (*manzila*) of His Prophet, who is with Him in the Supreme Assembly (*'indahu fī al-malā' al-a'lā*), praising him to the close angels (*yuthnī 'alayhi 'inda al-malā'ika al-muqarrabīn*), and therefore the angels send blessings upon him (*al-malā'ika yuṣallūn 'alayhi*). After that, he commanded the inhabitants of the lower world to invoke blessing and peace upon him (*al-ṣalā 'alayhi wa-l-taslīm*), to unite praise towards him from the inhabitants of the two worlds, upper and lower.[573]

In another passage, Sakhāwī indicates the function of the *ṣalā 'alā al-nabī:*

> al-Ḥalīmī[574] stated that the aim in invoking the blessing on the Prophet is to get closer to God the Most High, obeying his commandment, and respecting the Prophet's right over us. Ibn 'Abd al-Salām[575] said: 'Our *ṣalā 'alā al-nabī* is not an intercession on our part towards him (*shafā'at minnā lahu*), since we cannot intercede for a being similar to him. However, God has commanded us to reciprocate those who bestow favours and goodness upon us, and if we are unable to reciprocate in like manner, we must reciprocate with invocations (*al-du'ā'*). This is because God knows that we are incapable of reciprocating the favour of our Prophet. He has instructed us to invoke blessings upon him to reciprocate his goodness and bounty upon us, for there is no excellence greater than the excellence of the Prophet.'[576]

Sakhāwī therefore states that the *ṣalā 'alā al-nabī* is not to be understood as an act of intercession on the part of the one who recites it with regard to the Prophet, since there is no creature whose spiritual rank is above his, and therefore no one can be in a position to intercede with him. Instead, this invocation takes the form of the believer's plea that the intercession of Muḥammad to be accepted by God, and results, as we have seen, in returning towards the person he invokes in the form of as many blessings[577].

This is also the opinion Cristina De La Puente expresses at the end of her study on the *ṣalā 'alā al-nabī:*

> The practice of praying over Muḥammad seems to be linked to the evolution within Islam of veneration for the Prophet's charismatic personality, and especially to the belief that Muslims

573 Muḥammad ibn 'Abd al-Raḥmān al-Sakhāwī, *al-Qawl al-badī' fī al-ṣalā 'alā al-ḥabīb al-shafī'* (al-Madīna al-munawwara: Mu'assasat al-rayyān, 2002), 85.
574 Abū 'Abd Allāh al-Ḥalīmī (d. 1012–13).
575 'Izz al-Dīn ibn 'Abd al-Salām (d. 1262).
576 Muḥammad ibn 'Abd al-Raḥmān al-Sakhāwī, *al-Qawl al-badī' fī al-ṣalā 'alā al-ḥabīb al-shafī'* (al-Madīna al-munawwara: Mu'assasat al-rayyān, 2002), 83.
577 Andrew Rippin, *Taṣliya*, in *EI*[2].

> need the Prophet's mediation between his community and God. The *taṣliya* is not just a eulogy, but a request, and perhaps its actual meaning is simple: to ask God that He Himself pray to Muḥammad, so that Muḥammad will be made aware of the believers' love and be able to mediate for them on the Last Day.[578]

From the above considerations, a very close connection can thus be observed between the *ṣalā ʿalā al-nabī* and the Prophet's intercessory function. Likewise, it is possible to find numerous references to intercession in devotional literature towards the Prophet.

5 Intercession in devotional literature towards the Prophet

A strand of Islamic religious literature, starting with the biographical genre on the Prophet's life (*al-sīra al-nabawiyya*), focuses on the so-called "proofs of prophethood" (*dalāʾil al-nubuwwa*), or on the Prophet's "qualities" and "characteristics" (*shamāʾil, khaṣāʾiṣ*). This literature arose on the impetus of the encounter between the Islamic tradition and other religions, aiming to counter the controversy surrounding the differences between Muḥammad and the central figures in other religions, particularly with the figure of Jesus from a Christian and Islamic perspective. Moreover, this literature was born precisely on the back of Muslims' growing devotion to Muḥammad. Coming from the sphere of religious scholars, this literary production also shows that this devotion is not confined to the so-called "popular" sphere but is absolutely transversal, shared by all categories of people in the context of pre-modern Islamic societies.[579]

In this literature, a *ḥadīth* is inevitably cited which, among the "proofs" and "characteristics" of Muḥammad's prophecy, claims that five were given exclusively to him, and among them we find his intercession:

> I was given five things (*uʿṭītu khamsa*) that were not given to any prophet before me. I was attended with terror [in the hearts of enemies] for a distance of one month's journey. The land has been made for me a place of prayer and purification [with reference to pulveral ablution, *tayammum*], so that when the time for prayer comes, any man in my community may pray; spoils have been made lawful for me; each prophet was sent exclusively to his na-

578 Cristina De La Puente, "The Prayer Upon the Prophet Muhammad (Tasliya), a Manifestation of Islamic Religiosity," in *Medieval Encounters* 5, 1 (1999), 129.
579 Michele Petrone, "'Special Features of the Prophet' (*Khaṣāʾiṣ nabawiyya*) From Jurisprudence to Devotion," in *The Presence of the Prophet in Early Modern and Contemporary Islam, Volume 1, The Prophet Between Doctrine, Literature and Arts: Historical Legacies and Their Unfolding*, edited by Denis Gril, Stefan Reichmuth and Dilek Sarmis (Leiden: Brill, 2021), 197–228.

tion, whereas I have been sent to all mankind; intercession has been granted to me (*uʿṭītu al-shafāʿa*).[580]

In one of the earliest works of this literature, "The Nobility of the Chosen One" (*Sharaf al-muṣṭafā*), composed by Abū Saʿd al-Kharkūshī (d. 1016), we find a chapter devoted to the Banner of praise of the Prophet and its connection to intercession on the Day of Judgement:

> ʿAbd Allāh ibn Salām asked the Messenger of God: "What are the characteristics of the Banner of praise?" He replied, "Its length is like a march of a thousand years, its tip is made of ruby (*yāqūt al-ḥamrāʾ*), its handle is made of silver (*fiḍḍa bayḍāʾ*), its ferrule is made of emerald (*zumurrud al-ḥaḍrāʾ*). It consists of three elements, one in the east, one in the west, and one in the centre, on which three lines are engraved: the first is 'In the name of the Merciful and Clement God', the second is 'Praise be to God, Lord of the Worlds', and the third is 'There is no divinity but God, and Muḥammad is the Messenger of God'. The length of each line is a million years, and the width is a million years.'
>
> When the Messenger of God shall wave the Banner in the Plains of Judgement, the fire shall not affect any of the people of Hell, until it is drawn from them.
>
> The Banner of God's Messenger will wave on the Day of Judgement, and for as long as it waves, the chastisement of the people of Hell will be lightened, because of its blessing, rank and station (*bi-barakatihi wa-jāhih wa-manzilatihi*).
>
> An announcement shall be heard coming from the Throne (*al-ʿarsh*), the Throne of the Merciful, Lord of the Worlds: 'Where is the Arab prophet, from the tribe of the Quraysh, the unlettered (*ummī*), a native of the Tihāma,[581] of the sacred area of Mecca, Muḥammad son of ʿAbd Allāh, seal of the prophets and lord of the messengers?" He will then resurrect the Prophet and he will be given the Banner of praise (*liwāʾ al-ḥamd*), he will grasp it, and Adam and all his descendants among the prophets and messengers and all the devout believers, martyrs and saints will be under the Banner of the Prophet, occupying the part of the Garden that they will. He will be the first of the prophets and messengers to enter Paradise, his community will be the first of all communities to enter Paradise. When the proclamation of Muḥammad will take place, he will be offered the Banner of praise and he will be granted all the Gardens of Paradise, of which he will be able to occupy the part that he will want, and with him will be his wives among the women of Paradise in addition to those whom he will marry among the heavenly brides in the Hereafter, and with him will be his earthly offspring, and all the people of Paradise will be grouped together.'[582]

580 Bukhārī, *Ṣaḥīḥ al-Bukhārī*, 1:484–485.
581 Coastal region of the Arabian Peninsula contiguous to Ḥijāz, the region of Mecca and Medina.
582 Abū Saʿd ʿAbd al-Mālik ibn Abū ʿUthmān Muḥammad al-Kharkūshī, *Manāḥil al-shifāʾ wa-manāhil al-ṣafā bi-taḥqīq kitāb sharaf al-muṣṭafā* (Makkat al-mukarrama: Dār al-bashāʾir al-islāmiyya, 2003), 6:125–126.

The chapter continues with a list of all those who will bear a Banner on the Day of Judgement, in addition to the Prophet, to lead their respective groups, among whom we may mention the martyrs (*al-shuhadā'*) and the pious men (*al-sāliḥīn*).[583] The final chapter of Kharkūshī's text is then dedicated to intercession (*shafā'a*), and in it the Persian scholar reports a long series of traditions related to it.[584]

We have already mentioned several times what is considered to be the most important of the treatises devoted to devotion to Muḥammad, entitled "The Healing through the Presentation of the Rights of the Chosen One" (*al-Shifā' bi-ta'rīf ḥuqūq al-muṣṭafā*) by al-Qāḍī 'Iyāḍ (m. 1149). Interestingly, some of the texts we will discuss, refer to "healing" (*shifā'*) in relation to the Prophet. This healing is at once literal, as we shall see, for example, with regard to the *qaṣīdat al-Burda*, and spiritual, according to the metaphor of treatment and healing that is often found in Islamic religious literature. In this treatise, which systematises material from the literature of "proofs" and "characteristics", there are numerous interesting references to the Prophet's intercession. It is divided into four parts, and in the first part, al-Qāḍī 'Iyāḍ introduces the content of the third chapter, as follows:

> About what is conveyed in the authentic and well-known traditions concerning the immensity of his measure with his Lord and his station (*bi-'aẓīm qadrihi 'inda rabbihi wa-manzilatih*), and what is reserved for him in the two worlds due to his nobility. [The scholars] are agreed that he is the noblest of men, the chief of the sons of Adam (*sayyid walad Ādam*), the best of men as regards station with God (*afḍal al-nās manzila 'inda Allāh*),[585] and whose spiritual level is highest and closest to Him (*wa-a'lāhum daraja wa-aqrabuhum zulfā*).'[586]

In this passage, the author introduces a fundamental notion which is common to find in devotional literature on the Prophet, particularly in the invocations and litanies: the notion of *qadr*, "measure," which we have already analysed with regard to certain Qur'anic occurrences in relation to the "Night of Measure" (*laylat al-qadr*). In this sense, as we have seen, it represents the "divine measure" that descends from enormous reserves (*khazā'in*),[587] and on this night, it descended upon Muḥammad, who therefore participates in the "divine measure." The term "station" (*manzila*), which we see associated with the Prophet in this passage, can also mean the receptacle in which a divine descent (*tanzīl*) takes place. In

583 Ibid., 6:127–135

584 Ibid., 6:185–189.

585 Another manuscript contains the version "the best of creatures with God".

586 al-Qāḍī 'Iyāḍ al-Yaḥṣubī, *al-Shifā' bi-ta'rīf ḥuqūq al-*muṣṭafā, ed. 'Abduh 'Alī Kūshak (Dubai: Jā'izat Dubay al-dawliyya li-l-Qur'ān al-karīm, 2013), 213.

587 Q 15:21.

the words of al-Qāḍī ʿIyāḍ, however, the term "measure" refers to the Prophet and is accompanied by the term "immense" (*ʿaẓīm*), which is usually associated with God in the Qurʾān, but is also associated in a specific passage with Muḥammad. According to exegetes, the following verse refers precisely to the Prophet: "Verily, your character is immense."[588] There is indeed a relationship between "immensity of measure" and "station", since they appear side by side in this text and in other litanies. In this sense, it is conceivable that it could refer to the measure of the Prophet's spiritual rank (*daraja*), as well as his rank of proximity to God, which allows him to exercise his special intercession, as Tor Andrae had already proposed in a passage mentioned above:

> For the position of honour is at the same time an expression of the personal favour the ruler has for that person: he has influence, *wasīla*, with the ruler according to the measure of his *manzila* and *qurba*.[589]

The text of al-Qāḍī ʿIyāḍ further specifies the theme of the following section:

> About what is conveyed regarding the mention of his place (*makāna*) with God, his election (*al-iṣṭifāʾ*), the elevation of his mention and preference (*rifʿat al-dhikr wa-al-tafḍīl*), and his mastery over the sons of Adam, and about what is reserved for him in this lower world of the prerogatives of his spiritual levels (*mazāyā al-rutab*), and of the blessing of his good name (*wa-barakat ismihi al-ṭayyib*).[590]

Here again, the notion of station and rank, connected to election, is central, and we also find a reference to spiritual degrees.

Continuing the analysis of this text, we find the narration of other *ḥadīth* related to intercession:

> When Adam rebelled, he said, 'O God, forgive my error by the right (*bi-ḥaqq*) of Muḥammad! Accept my repentance!' God answered him, 'Whence do you derive your knowledge of Muḥammad?' He replied, 'I saw written everywhere in the Garden: 'There is no deity but God, Muḥammad is the Messenger of God.' Thus I knew that he was the most honoured of creation in Thy sight.' At this point God forgave him. This is said to be the interpretation of God's words: 'Adam received words from his Lord and God accepted his repentance.'[591]

---

588 "*Wa-innaka laʿalā khuluq ʿaẓīm,*" Q 68:4.

589 Tor Andrae, *Die person Muhammeds in lehre und glauben seiner gemeinde* (Stockholm: Norstedt & Toner, 1917), 260 (tr. by the author).

590 al-Qāḍī ʿIyāḍ al-Yaḥṣubī, *al-Shifāʾ bi-taʿrīf ḥuqūq al-*muṣṭafā, ed. ʿAbduh ʿAlī Kūshak (Dubai: Jāʾizat Dubay al-dawliyya li-l-Qurʾān al-karīm, 2013), 213.

591 Q 2:37.

> Adam said: 'When Thou hast created me, I raised my head to Thy Throne, and upon it was written: 'There is no other deity but God, Muḥammad is the Messenger of God,' so I knew that there would be no one of more immense measure before Thee (*aʿẓam qadr ʿindaka*) than he whose name Thou hast set beside Thy.' God then revealed to him: 'By My Power and Majesty, he is the last of the prophets among your descendants. Had it not been for him, I would not have created you. Adam is said to have been given the nickname (*kunya*) of 'Father of Muḥammad' (Abū Muḥammad). Some say he was 'Father of humanity' (Abū-l-bashar).[592]

One section is specifically devoted to intercession and the Station of praise, and in it, in addition to the main traditions, al-Qāḍī ʿIyāḍ also reports some lesser-known narratives, such as the following:

> He will stand at the right hand of the Throne (*innahu qiyāmuhu ʿan yamīn al-ʿarsh*), at a station where there will be no one but him. The first and the last will envy it.[593]
>
> *Minbar*s shall be set up for the prophets, on which they shall sit. My *minbar* will remain empty, I will not sit on it and I will remain before my Lord. God will ask me: 'What do you want me to do with your community?' I will answer: 'O Lord, hasten their judgment.' He will call them together and they will be judged. Some of them will enter the Garden through His mercy and others through my intercession (*bi-shafāʿatī*). I shall continue to intercede until He gives a written order [of forgiveness] to the men for whom the fire was decreed, until the Firekeeper says: 'O Muḥammad! You have left no room for the wrath of your Lord against your community!'[594]

We mentioned earlier traditions according to which each prophet will have his own heavenly Basin on the Day of Judgement. To this, we now add the idea of a *minbar* reserved for each prophet, and it is interesting to note that in the *ḥadīth*, as we have seen, a close relationship emerges between the heavenly Basin and the *minbar*, almost as if they served the same function, or were part of the same cosmological system or structure.

The text of al-Qāḍī ʿIyāḍ goes on to report a tradition that extends the Prophet's role as intercessor on the Day of Judgement not only to humans but to the whole of creation, taking plants and minerals into account as well:

> I will intercede on the Day of Resurrection for most of the stones and trees of the earth.[595]

---

592 al-Qāḍī ʿIyāḍ al-Yaḥṣubī, *al-Shifāʾ bi-taʿrīf ḥuqūq al-*muṣṭafā, ed. ʿAbduh ʿAlī Kūshak (Dubai: Jāʾizat Dubay al-dawliyya li-l-Qurʾān al-karīm, 2013), 223–224.

593 Ibid., 270.

594 Ibid., 277.

595 Ibid., 278.

Another section of the same chapter is devoted to intercession and the Station of praise. After conveying some traditions, al-Qāḍī ʿIyāḍ develops the theme of the relationship between the Prophet's name, his rank, his station, and the act of magnifying him through praise:

> God calls him in His Book Aḥmad and Muḥammad. One of the special characteristics that God has bestowed upon him is that He has caused his names to contain praise for him, so that the immensity of his gratitude is contained in his mention. His name Aḥmad is derived from the elative form (*afʿal*), in order to intensify the attribute of praise. Muḥammad, on the other hand, is a passive participle (*mufaʿʿal*), which intensifies the great amount of praise. He is the most exalted among those who praise and the best among those who are praised and the person who deserves the most praise. He is the most praised of the praised and the one who praises the most. On the Day of Resurrection he will have the Banner of praise as the completion of the perfection of praise to him. In that place he will be known by the attribute of praise. His Lord will raise him to the Station of praise, as He has promised Him. The first and the last generations will praise him for his intercession for them. On that day, the Prophet will begin with the praise that, as he said, 'to no one else has been bestowed'. In the books of the prophets, his community is called 'the praisers' (*al-ḥammādiyyin*), so it is appropriate that he is called Muḥammad and Aḥmad.[596]

Two other names in connection with praise (*al-ḥamd*) mentioned in this chapter are al-Ḥamīd and al-Maḥmūd, two forms of the same root.[597]

A section of this chapter is devoted to explaining the various names attributed to Muḥammad, some of which refer to his intercessory function. One group is connected to the rank, station and divine favour that enable intercession: "the possessor of mediation" (*ṣāḥib al-waṣīla*), "the possessor of divine favour" (*ṣāḥib al-faḍīla*), "the one who performs ascension" (*ṣāḥib al-miʿrāj*), "he who rides the *burāq*" (*rākib al-burāq*), "the possessor of the high spiritual degree" (*ṣāḥib al-daraja al-rafīʿa*), "the possessor of the Station of praise" (*ṣāḥib al-maqām al-maḥmūd*). One group is instead related to intercession itself: "the possessor of intercession" (*ṣāḥib al-shafāʿa*), "the accepted intercessor" (*al-shafīʿ al-mushaffāʿ*). Finally, another group is connected to the royal characteristics of his intercessory function: "the possessor of the heavenly Basin to which one is brought" (*ṣāḥib al-ḥawḍ al-mawrūd*), "the possessor of the crown" (*ṣāḥib al-tāj*), "the possessor of the banner" (*ṣāḥib al-liwāʾ*), "the possessor of the staff" (*ṣāḥib al-qaḍīb, ṣāḥib al-hirāwa*), "the possessor of proof and power" (*ṣāḥib al-ḥujja wa-l-sulṭān*). The author goes on to explain some of these attributes in detail:

596 Ibid., 286.
597 Ibid., 294–295.

> The meaning of staff (*al-qaḍīb*) is the sword (*al-sayf*), as is explained in the Gospel: 'He shall have a staff of iron with which he shall fight as well as his community'. This could be the long, thin stick that the Prophet wielded and that the caliphs now use.[598] As for the other staff (*al-hirāwa*) mentioned, it is indeed a staff (*al-ʿaṣā*). I believe it is the staff mentioned in the saying of the heavenly Basin (*al-ḥawḍ*): 'I will drive people away from it with my staff for the People of Righteousness'. As for the crown (*al-tāj*), the turban (*al-ʿimāma*) is meant. At that time, it was only in use among the Arabs. The turban is the crown of the Arabs.[599]

In the second part of the *al-Shifāʾ*, al-Qāḍī ʿIyāḍ dwells on two other categories of intercessors besides the Prophet. The first is the family (*āl*) of Muḥammad, the love for which may be diriment on the Day of Judgement and even grant a spiritual level close to that of the Prophet himself:

> Recognition (*maʿrifa*) of Muḥammad's family is immunity from Hell (*barāʾa min al-nār*); love (*maḥabba*) for Muḥammad's family is permission to cross the Bridge (*jawāz ʿalā al-ṣirāṭ*); friendship (*walāya*) for Muḥammad's family is protection from punishment (*amān min al-ʿadhāb*).[600]

> Whoever loves me and loves these two – and pointed to Ḥasan and Ḥusayn, their father [ʿAlī] and their mother [Fāṭima] – will be with me in my spiritual degree (*darajatī*) on the Day of Judgement.[601]

The second category of intercessors is represented by the Companions of the Prophet (*al-ṣaḥāba*):

> Kaʿb al-Aḥbār said: "There is none of the Companions of Muḥammad to whom intercession (*al-shafāʿa*) will not be granted on the Day of Resurrection." Then al-Mughīra ibn Nawfal asked Kaʿb to intercede for him (*an yashfaʿ lahu*) on the Day of Resurrection.[602]

In the *al-Shifāʾ* appears for the first time a tradition that, from this time onwards, will often be mentioned in apologetic literature of intermediation and intercession, given the eminence of its protagonist, Imām Mālik (d. 795):

---

598 The author is probably referring to this passage in *Revelation* 2:26–28: "To everyone who conquers and continues to do my works to the end, I will give authority over the nations; to rule them with an iron rod, as when clay pots are shattered, even as I also received authority from my Father. To the one who conquers I will also give the morning star." He therefore interprets this New Testament passage as referring to the prophet Muḥammad.

599 al-Qāḍī ʿIyāḍ al-Yaḥṣubī, *al-Shifāʾ bi-taʿrīf ḥuqūq al-*muṣṭafā, ed. ʿAbduh ʿAlī Kūshak (Dubai: Jāʾizat Dubay al-dawliyya li-l-Qurʾān al-karīm, 2013), 291–293.

600 Ibid., 527.

601 Ibid., 530.

602 Ibid., 539.

> Abū Humayd said: 'Abū Jaʿfar, the Prince of the Believers,[603] had a dispute with Mālik in the Prophet's mosque. Mālik said to him: 'Prince of the Believers, do not raise your voice in this mosque. God has taught mankind how to behave (*addaba qawm*) saying: 'O believers, do not raise your voice above that of the Prophet, and do not raise your voice with him as you raise it when you speak among yourselves, for you would risk making your deeds vain without your knowledge'[604] and He has praised mankind saying: 'Those who lower their voices before the Messenger of God are those whose hearts God has disposed to fear. They will have forgiveness and immense reward'[605] and he disapproved of people saying: 'As for those who call to you from outside your inner chambers, most of them understand nothing.'[606] Respect for him when he is dead is the same as when he was alive.' Abū Jaʿfar was humbled by this, and he asked Mālik: 'Abū ʿAbd Allāh, when you supplicate do you turn towards the direction of Mecca (*qibla*) or do you turn to the Messenger of God?' He replied: 'Why should you turn away from him when he is your intermediary (*wasīla*) and the intermediary of your father Adam towards God on the Day of Resurrection? Approach him and ask him to intercede, and God will fulfil his intercession.'[607]

From these passages, we can infer the relevance of the notion of intercession in the *al-Shifāʾ*, a treatise which, as we have seen, has enjoyed and still enjoys in our day an enormous diffusion throughout the Islamic world. This is further evidence of how the notion of intercession, due to its direct repercussions on the ultimate fate of the believer, has gradually moved from the pen of theologians towards devotional treatises, becoming part of the literature focusing on religious and spiritual practices, as well as strongly characterising these same practices.

With the spread of Sufism organised into brotherhoods (*tarīqa*, pl. *ṭuruq*), starting in the eleventh century, we see the emergence of litanies composed by important personalities of a specific brotherhood, often by the founding eponyms themselves. These litanies may take the name *ḥizb* (pl. *aḥzāb*), meaning "portion," a term also used for the ritual division into sixty parts of the Qurʾān for the purpose of reading.[608] Another term used is *wird* (pl. *awrād*), synonymous with the previous term, which also shares its primary meaning as "portion" of the Qurʾān for the purposes of reading.[609] These are litanies designed to be recited individually or collectively, which may be totally or partially original, often contain-

---

603 Abū Jaʿfar al-Manṣūr, the second caliph of the Abbasid dynasty, who ruled from 754 to 775.
604 Q 49:2.
605 Q 49:3.
606 Q 49:4.
607 al-Qāḍī ʿIyāḍ al-Yaḥṣubī, *al-Shifāʾ bi-taʿrīf ḥuqūq al-*muṣṭafā, ed. ʿAbduh ʿAlī Kūshak (Dubai: Jāʾizat Dubay al-dawliyya li-l-Qurʾān al-karīm, 2013), 520–521.
608 Edward William Lane, "*ḥ-z-b*," *An Arabic-English Lexicon* (London: Williams and Norgate, 1863–93).
609 Ibid., "*w-r-d.*"

ing Qur'anic passages or invocations attributed to the Prophet. These designations may derive precisely from the fact that, at an early stage, the presence of portions of the Qur'ān in these litanies was preponderant, if not exclusive. Sometimes, the term used for such a litany is instead *waẓīfa*, meaning "daily duty" or "assigned duty".[610] Further emphasising the use of these litanies as a daily duty incumbent on the person affiliated with a particular brotherhood. Invocations of blessing on the Prophet (*ṣalā ʿalā al-nabī*) may also be part of the daily duties of a member of a brotherhood, and invocations of this kind often appear in collections of litanies belonging to a particular *ṭarīqa*. Within them, the notion of intercession very often makes its appearance.

Some of the earliest litanies are those attributed to ʿAbd al-Qādir al-Jīlānī (d. 1166), the eponymous founder of the Qādiriyya, one of the earliest, longest-lived and most widespread brotherhoods in the history of Sufism. Among these litanies, one finds many references to intermediation and intercession, but especially to the already mentioned notion of requesting help (*istighātha*), particularly with regard to the figure of the Supreme Helper (*al-ghawth al-aʿẓam*), and for this reason we will return to these litanies in the next chapter. We will also return to a very important litany attributed to ʿAbd al-Salām ibn Mashīsh (d. 1227) since it too is centred on the figure of the Mediator (*al-wāsiṭa*).

Sung poetry (*qaṣīda*, pl. *qaṣāʾid*) is widespread in the context of Sufism and often contain references to intercession. One of the major examples is the poem entitled "The shining stars: praise of the best of creatures" (*al-Kawākib al-durriyya fī madḥ khayr al-bariyya*), composed by Muḥammad al-Būṣīrī (d. 1294).[611] This poem in praise of Muḥammad, the most famous and widespread throughout the Islamic world, is commonly called "The Poem of the Mantle" (*qaṣīdat al-burda*) after an episode, related to intercession, featuring the author himself:

> Al-Buṣīrī had been stricken with hemiplegia, which left him half-paralysed. Therefore he thought of composing his poem (*qaṣīda*) and asking God for intercession through it (*tawassalu bihā ilā Allāh*). Then he fell asleep and saw the Prophet, who caressed his face and threw a cloak (*burda*) over him. At this point he woke up healed, stood up and left the house without informing anyone. He met some sufis (*fuqarāʾ*) and one of them said to him: 'I want you to transmit to me the poem with which you praised the Messenger of God.' Then the sufi said, after reciting its beginning: 'By God, I heard it yesterday when it was recited before the Messenger of God, and I saw him move, take pleasure in it, and throw a cloak over

---

610 Ibid., "*w-ẓ-f.*"

611 Suzanne Pinckney Stetkevych, *The Mantle Odes: Arabic Praise Poems to the Prophet Muhammad* (Bloomington & Indianapolis: Indiana University Press, 2010).

> the one who had sung it.' At that point al-Buṣīrī transmitted the poem to the sufi, and the story became known.[612]

Again, as with the *Shifā'* of the Qāḍī Iyāḍ, there is a close connection between devotion to the Prophet and the quest for intercession and healing, at once material and spiritual. The great diffusion of this poem is indeed due to the fact that it is considered by those who recite it as an instrument, at the same time, of intercession and healing.[613] In particular, the ninth chapter of this poem, verses 140 – 151, is explicitly related to intercession and is entitled "Intermediation and intercession" (*al-tawassul wa-l-tashaffu'*). The author states that he composed this poem in praise of the Prophet to ask forgiveness for his wasted life as a court poet, in which he lost his youth by obeying temptations, selling his life in the Hereafter for the life of this world, and only obtaining a load of sins and regrets. However, he never broke his covenant (*'ahd*) with the Prophet or sever his bond (*ḥabl*) with him. Only the fact that he bears his own name, Muḥammad, provides him with his protection, according to the Prophet's own promise.[614] The author considers himself dependent on the Prophet's major intercession on the Day of Judgement, otherwise he will undoubtedly be destined for Hell. In any case, he states, the Prophet does not reject any Muslim who seeks his benevolence and protection. Since the poet concentrated strongly on his praise, he was consequently able to see the Prophet's resolve for his salvation. The section ends with the poetic image of rain that makes flowers bloom even on hilltops, as a spiritual metaphor for the Prophet's blessing of Muslims who seek his protection.

The Poem of the Mantle is probably, as we have said, the most widespread religious poem in the Islamic world, translated into all the languages of the world and, above all, sung in all latitudes in Arabic, even by people who do not speak this language. We can therefore measure also from this the great diffusion of the Prophet's notion of intercession and protection among Muslim peoples.

The same process can be observed in relation to the invocation of blessing on the Prophet (*ṣalā 'alā al-nabī*), the theological premises of which are present in the

---

612 Sharaf al-Dīn Abī 'Abd Allāh Muḥammad ibn Sa'īd al-Būṣīrī, *Dīwān al-Būṣīrī* (Bayrūt: Dār al-kutub al-'ilmiyya, 2005), 7.

613 Stefan Sperl. "Al-Busiri's Burdah," in *Qasida Poetry in Islamic Asia and Africa, vol. 2, Eulogy's Bounty, Meaning's Abundance: An Anthology*, edited by Stefan Sperl and Christopher Shackle (Leiden: Brill, 1996), 470 – 71.

614 "Whoever is born a son and names him Muḥammad for my sake and to obtain blessings from my name, then he and his son will both go to Paradise," a tradition not contained in the main collections but in 'Alā' al-Dīn 'Alī al-Muttaqī ibn Ḥusām al-Dīn al-Hindī, *Kanz al-'ummāl fī sunan al-aqwāl wa-l-af'āl* (Bayrūt: Mu'assasat al-risāla, 2008), 8:174.

primary sources of Islam, but whose practice gradually spread over the centuries along with devotion to Muḥammad. The crowning achievement of this process is a collection composed by Muḥammad ibn Sulaymān al-Jazūlī (d. 1465), subdivided for each day of the week for regular and constant recitation, entitled "The Indications of the Benefits and the Outpouring of Lights in the Invocation of Blessings on the Chosen Prophet" (*Dalā'il al-khayrāt wa shawāriq al-anwār fī dhikr al-ṣalā ʿāla al-nabī al-mukhtār*). From the late fifteenth century to the present day, this will be the most important and widespread collection of *al-ṣalā ʿāla al-nabī* throughout the Islamic world. From an analysis of the specimens in various manuscript collections in the Arabic and Islamic world, it is possible to conclude that it is one of the most widespread texts, if not the most widespread, after the Qur'ān.[615]

This genre of texts, along with collections of sung poems, is considered secondary to doctrinal Sufi literature or even as emanating from a supposedly "popular" dimension of Sufism. As scholars have already shown, this literature, produced to be recited, sung and often even learnt by heart, does in reality contain and synthesise esoteric knowledge of doctrinal literature. This is certainly the case in the *Dalā'il al-khayrāt*, which shows a great influence of the doctrines expounded by Muḥyiddīn Ibn al-ʿArabī (d. 1240) and some Sufi authors after him.[616] Similarly, the presence of numerous references to intercession reveals the importance of this notion in the domain of religious and spiritual practice experienced by Muslim populations, at least as far as the Sunni world is concerned. Moreover, the treatment of intercession in this text bears evidence of the development of the doctrine of intermediation and intercession within the esoteric literature of Sunni Islam, as we shall see below.

The text is introduced by the list of God's names, followed by the list of the Prophet's names, which contains, as we have already observed with regard to the *Shifā'* of the Qāḍī Iyāḍ, numerous names related to intercession. The text is then divided into chapters, one for each day of the week. Similarly to when the believer, at the end of a ritual reading of the entire Qur'ān, recites the first *sūra* again and the beginning of the second one, thus marking the cyclical nature of the reading, the recitation of the *Dalā'il al-khayrāt* also includes an eighth chapter that returns to Monday.

Therefore, there are many references to intercession in this text, and I will only mention those that seem most interesting and significant to me.

---

615 On the manuscript tradition of the *Dalā'il al-khayrāt*, see D. Beyazit – G. Burak – S. Göloğlu (eds.), *Special Issue: 'From West Africa to Southeast Asia: The History of Muḥammad al-Jazūlī's Dalā'il al-Khayrāt (15th-20th centuries)*, in Journal of Islamic Manuscripts, 12, 3–4 (Nov 2021).

616 Vincent Cornell, *The Realm of the Saint: Power and Authority in Moroccan Sufism* (Austin: University of Texas Press, 1998), 211.

Throughout the sections on the days of the week, the recurring motif is the request to God to grant Muḥammad the spiritual degree that would allow him to exercise intercession. In this text, we find all the terminology seen previously, relating, for example, to mediation (*al-wasīla*), the Station of praise (*al-maqām al-maḥmūd*), the spiritual degree (*al-daraja*) – which is often accompanied by adjectives such as "great" (*kabīra*), "elevated" (*al-rafīʿa*), "superior" (*al-ʿuliyya*) – to proximity (*al-qurba*), to station (*manzila, maqām*). By accessing this degree, the Prophet is able to exercise major intercession (*al-shafāʿa al-kubrā*). In the Tuesday section, we find a series of invocations of blessing upon the Prophet that incorporate within them numerous features of the Prophet's intercessory function, and considering that these are litanies to be recited, it is interesting to note that they proceed according to a poetic rhyme, of which we can show a few examples:

Allāhumma ṣalli ʿalā ṣāḥib al-ḥawḍ al-mawrūd
Allāhumma ṣalli ʿalā ṣāḥib al-maqām al-maḥmūd
Allāhumma ṣalli ʿalā ṣāḥib al-liwāʾ al-maʿqūd
Allāhumma ṣalli ʿalā ṣāḥib al-makān al-mashhūd

O God, send blessings upon the possessor of the heavenly Basin visited
O God, send blessings on the possessor of the Station of praise
O God, send blessings on the possessor of the wielded Banner
O God, send blessings on the possessor of the known Place.

In the Thursday section, we find an evocative passage highlighting the transition between degree, station and intercession:

Allāhumma ijʿalhu akram al-akramīn ʿindaka manzila [...]
wa-unzilhu fī ghurafāt al-firdaws min al-darajāt al-ʿulā allatī lā daraja fawqahā

O God, Thou who art most generous, grant him a station with Thee [...].
And make him dwell in the chambers of Paradise in the highest degrees, above which there is no degree.

Allāhumma ṣalli ʿalā sayyidinā Muḥammad awwal shafīʿ wa-afḍal mushaffaʿ
wa-shaffiʿh fī ummatihi bi-shafāʿa yaghbiṭhu bihā al-awwalūn wa-l-ākhirūn

O God, send blessings upon our Lord Muḥammad, the first intercessor and the best of intercessors, and accept his intercession for his community through the intercession that the first and the last envy him.

In the Saturday section, we find a straightforward intercessory formula, which is of particular importance throughout the *Dalāʾil al-khayrāt*, since it is the only one that is repeated three times in succession throughout the text and in which one of the key terms noted above, "rank" (*jāh*), appears:

Allāhumma innī as'aluka wa-atawajjahu ilayka bi-ḥabībika al-muṣṭafā ʿindaka yā ḥabībinā yā sayyidinā Muḥammad innā natawassalu bika ilā rabbika, fa-shfaʿ lanā ʿinda al-mawlā al-ʿaẓīm yā niʿmat al-rasūl al-ṭāhir, Allāhumma shaffiʿhu fīnā bi-jāhihi ʿindaka

O God, we ask Thee and turn towards Thee, and we ask Thee our Lord for intercession through Thy beloved, the Chosen One with Thee, our beloved and Lord Muḥammad! O blessing of pure Messenger! Intercede for us with the Immense Lord! O God! Grant us intercession through his rank with Thee!

Finally, at the end of the sections, we find a series of final invocations (*khatm*), in which there is again a passage on intercession:

Allāhumma innā nastashfiʿu bihi ilayka, idh huwa awjah al-shufaʿāʾ ilayka wa-nuqsimu bihi ʿalayka, idh huwa aʿẓam man uqsimu bi-ḥaqqihi ʿalayka wa-natawassalu bihi ilayka idh huwa aqrab al-wasāʾil ilayka nashkū ilayka yā rabbī qaswat qulūbinā wa-kathrat dhunūbinā

O God, we ask intercession towards Thee through him, if he is the foremost of intercessors with Thee, and we take covenant with Thee through him, if he is the foremost of those who take covenant through his right with Thee, and we seek intercession towards Thee through him, if he is the closest of mediators towards Thee, we complain to Thee O Lord, of the hardness of our hearts and the great number of our sins!

As can be seen, the notion of intercession plays a fundamental role in one of the most widespread texts throughout the Sunni Islamic world, from the Maghreb to Indonesia, from the fifteenth century to the present day. This is equally the case in all collections of blessings on the Prophet as can be verified by consulting one of the most comprehensive, entitled "The Best Invocation of Blessing on the Master of Masters" (*Afḍal al-ṣalāwāt ʿalā sayyid al-sādāt*), composed by Yūsuf al-Nabahānī (d. 1932).[617] This author compiled a large number of works devoted to the Prophet Muḥammad. Given the large number of *ṣalāwāt* collected by Nabahānī, I will limit myself to reporting only two of them, related to the Prophet's spiritual rank (*al-jāh*), similar to the one previously mentioned in the *Dalāʾil al-khayrat*. The first is attributed by Nabahānī to the mysterious figure of al-Khāḍir,[618] who is said to have transmitted it to the Moroccan Sufi ʿAbd al-ʿAzīz al-Dabbāgh (d. 1719):

617 Yūsuf ibn Ismāʿīl al-Nabahānī, *Afḍal al-ṣalāwāt ʿalā sayyid al-sādāt* (Dimashq: Dār iqrā', 2001). There are two other collections of invocation of blessings on the Prophet composed by the same author. The first is very voluminous: *Saʿādat al-dārayn fī-l-ṣalā ʿalā sayyid al-kawnayn* (Bayrūt: Dār al-Fikr, 1980); the second is entitled *Jāmiʿ al-ṣalawāt wa-majmaʿ al-saʿādāt fī-l-ṣalā ʿalā sayyid al-sādāt* (Bayrūt: Dār al-kutub al-ʿilmiyya, 2005).

618 Al-Khāḍir or al-Khiḍr is a character who, according to some Muslim exegetes, appears in the Qur'ān, without being named, as the guide of Moses (Q 18:65–82). According to legend he is ever living, and represents a mysterious figure between a prophet and a holy initiator who follows the spiritual maturation of prophets and great saints.

> *Allāhumma yā rabbī bi-jāh sayyidinā Muḥammad ibn ʿAbd Allāh ṣallā Allāh ʿalayhi wa-sallam ajmaʿ baynī wa-bayna sayyidinā Muḥammad ibn ʿAbd Allāh fī-l-dunyā qabla al-ākhira*
>
> O God, O Lord, through the spiritual rank of our lord Muḥammad son of ʿAbd ʿAllāh, upon him be blessing and peace, create a bond between me and our lord Muḥammad son of Abd ʿAllāh, in this world and in the Hereafter.[619]

Of the second, however, the benefits are described, but it is mentioned without naming a specific author:

> *Allāhumma ṣalli wa-sallim wa-bārik ʿalā sayyidinā Muḥammad al-nabī al-ummī al-ḥabīb al-ʿālī al-qadr al-ʿaẓīm al-jāh wa-ʿalā ālihi wa-ṣaḥbihi wa-sallim*
>
> O God, bless and send peace and blessing upon our Lord Muḥammad, the unlettered prophet, the beloved of high spiritual rank and immense measure, upon his family and his Companions.[620]

These blessings on the Prophet reaffirm the widespread belief in the very close connection between Muḥammad's spiritual rank (*jāh*) and the exercise of mediation and intercession.

The belief in the Prophet's intermediary function also shows a further reflection on popular devotion through what is considered to be the quintessential sung poem (*qaṣīda*) dedicated to the Prophet, entitled "The full moon has risen upon us" (*Ṭalaʿa-l-badr ʿalaynā*), which has always enjoyed enormous popularity in Islamic societies. Some ancient treatises, such as Bayhaqī's "The Proofs of the Prophecy" (*Dalāʾil al-nubuwwa*), report that the inhabitants of Yathrib, the future Medina, sang it when the Prophet arrived in the oasis on the occasion of the Hegira in 622,[621] or according to other versions, on his return from the Tabūk expedition.[622] What particularly interests us is the opening motif of this *qaṣīda*, which employs the metaphor of the "full moon" (*badr*). This metaphor can be clearly interpreted in the following way: the moon does not emit light of its own, but rather performs an intermediary function, reflecting the light of the sun; the full moon, with respect to the various gradations of the crescent of the moon, thus manifests this possibility of reflection in a full and complete manner. This is particularly the case during the night, when the sunlight is not directly accessible on the shaded part of the earth.

---

619 Yūsuf ibn Ismāʿīl al-Nabahānī, *Afḍal al-ṣalāwāt ʿalā sayyid al-sādāt* (Dimashq: Dār iqrāʾ, 2001), 36.
620 Ibid., 107.
621 Abū Bakr Aḥmad ibn Ḥusayn al-Bayhaqī, *Dalāʾil al-nubuwwa wa-maʿrifat aḥwāl ṣāḥib al-sharīʿa* (Bayrūt: Dār al-kutub al-ʿilmiyya, 1988, 2019), 2:506 – 507; 5:266.
622 Ibn Ḥajar al-ʿAsqalānī, *Fatḥ al-bārī sharḥ ṣaḥīḥ al-Bukhārī* (al-Qāhira: al-Maktaba al-salafiyya, 2015), 7:261 – 262.

The Prophet is thus likened to the "full moon" since he is the one who fulfils the intermediary function connected to the refraction of divine Light: the sun represents God, who emits divine Light, which is reflected in the Prophet in a complete, and not partial, manner. In Jewish, Christian and Islamic sources one can find the doctrine according to which the divine Light is untenable to the human eye and only some prophets, under exceptional conditions, may be able to resist its perception. The most representative episode in this regard concerns the prophet Moses, who, in the Old Testament as well as in Islamic sources, following his direct conversation with God on the mountain, is forced to wear a veil over his face so as not to blind the creatures with the light emanating from his face.[623] According to Islamic tradition, therefore, from a spiritual point of view, man finds himself in the nocturnal condition, in which it is not possible to perceive the light of the sun directly but only through the reflection of the moon, a function that Muḥammad, as well as Moses before him, completely fulfilled as the 'full moon'. This attribute of the Prophet as the one who completely reflects the divine Light is consistent with the doctrine of the Perfect Man (*al-insān al-kāmil*), which we will discuss later, wherein the term kāmil conveys the idea of human perfection and completeness.

To finally conclude this analysis of the presence of intercession in Sunni devotional literature, it is necessary to mention a form of devotion that is both literary and visual, called "ornament" (*ḥilya*). Given the complex issue of the prohibition of the representation of deities as well as human and animal figures in Islamic jurisprudence, Muslim artists over the centuries have experimented with forms of artistic reproduction that religious scholars could also accept. In the Ottoman world, starting in the seventeenth century, to overcome the impossibility of directly reproducing the Prophet's features, artists developed a special calligraphic form from a text describing his physical characteristics.[624] Below the main text, in the lower part of the *ḥilya*, we find the concluding sentence:

> *Allāhumma ṣalli wa-sallim ʿalā nabī al-raḥma wa-shafīʿ al-umma Muḥammad wa-ālihi al-ṭāyyibīn al-ṭāhirīn.*
>
> O God, send blessing and peace upon Muḥammad, prophet of mercy and intercessor of the community, and upon his good and pure family members.

623 *Exodus*, 24:29–35; Muḥammad ibn Jarīr al-Ṭabarī, *The History of Al-Tabari Volume 3: The Children of Israel*, tr. by Franz Rosenthal (Albany: State University of New York Press, 1989), 78.

624 Valerie Behiery, "Hilya," in *Muhammad in History, Thought, and Culture: An Encyclopedia of the Prophet of God*, edited by Coeli Fitzpatrick, Adam Walker (Santa Barbara: ABC-CLIO, 2014), 258–263.

Again, as can be seen, although the information related to the Prophet's devotion is very succinct, the mention of the Prophet's intercessory function is inevitably present.

With regard to Twelver Shiʿism, in the same way as for Sunnism, it is possible to assert that the belief in intercession is not limited to the theological aspect but also finds an equally relevant development in the devotional dimension. In this regard, the most extensive and important text, which gathers together various types of invocations and prayers taken from the *ḥadīth* and previous devotional literature, is called "The Keys to the Gardens [of Paradise]" (*Mafātiḥ al-jinān*) and was composed by the scholar ʿAbbās Qommī (d. 1941). There are multiple references to intercession in this collection, confirming the great relevance of this notion in Twelver Shiʿism up to contemporary times, as well as the centrality of the function of the Imām in it.[625]

625 ʿAbbās al-Qummī, *Mafātiḥ al-jinān* (Bayrūt: Dār al-aḍwāʾ, 2014).

Chapter 9
The Mediator and his station in Islamic esoteric literature

1 The Mediator (*al-wāsiṭa*)

The central doctrine within Islamic theology is, as we have seen, the doctrine of divine Oneness (*tawḥīd*). In the context of the doctrines of Islamic esotericism, *tawḥīd* is interpreted from an esoteric perspective through the well-known doctrine of the oneness of existence or vision (*waḥdat al-wujūd, waḥdat al-shuhūd*).[626] Similarly, the theological doctrine of intermediation and intercession (*shafāʿa, wasīla, tawassul*), as we shall see, is interpreted from an esoteric perspective in the same circles through the doctrine of the Perfect Man (*al-insān al-kāmil*). As Vincent Cornell has affirmed, the idea that the Prophet possesses a universal spiritual dimension makes its way into esoteric literature from the very beginning: in the *Kitāb al-lumaʿ* of Abū Naṣr al-Sarrāj (d. 988), one of the oldest texts of this literature, Muhammad is described as the spiritual archetype of all humanity.[627] Among the esoteric doctrines related to the Prophet's spiritual nature, one of the oldest is that relating to the so-called Muḥammadan Light (*al-nūr al-muḥammadiyya*), which alludes to the belief that Muḥammad's essence is considered to be identical to the divine Light and pre-existent to Adam's creation. This light would have been transmitted to Muḥammad's physical body by his ancestors through procreation and would have been transmitted by him in turn to his progeny. This conception, which shows more than one analogy with the doctrine of the *logos* in other philosophical, religious and esoteric spheres, is described in the Sunnite tradition, as well as in the Shiʿite tradition, through various designations, among which we can cite Muḥammadan Reality (*al-ḥaqīqa al-muḥammadiyya*), Muḥammadan Spirit (*al-rūḥ al-muḥammadī*), as well as Universal Intellect (*al-ʿaql al-kullī*) or Prime Intellect (*al-ʿaql al-awwal*).[628] This culminates in the doctrine, developed in particular in the work of Ibn al-ʿArabī and the authors belonging to his school, according to which the essence of Muḥammad is a perfect Man (*insān*

626 Bakri Aladdin, "Oneness of Being (*waḥdat al-wujūd*). The term and the doctrine," *Journal of the Muhyiddin Ibn Arabi Society* 51 (2012), 3–26.

627 Vincent Cornell, *The Realm of the Saint: Power and Authority in Moroccan Sufism* (Austin: University of Texas Press, 1998), 199–211.

628 Khalil Andani, "Metaphysics of Muhammad. The Nur Muhammad from Imam Ja'far al-Sadiq (d. 148/765) to Nasir al-Din al-Tusi (d. 672/1274)," *Journal of Sufi Studies* 8 (2019), 99–175.

https://doi.org/10.1515/9783111500966-014

kāmil), a synthesis of the Universe, the intermediate bridge between the divine and the human.[629]

This conception, although embodied from an earthly point of view by Muḥammad, the "best of creatures," shows a metaphysical dimension as pure intermediation between the divine and the human. Among some authors of Islamic esotericism, this figure is called of Mediator (*wāsiṭa*), in connection with the Perfect Man. Indeed, this function acquires a universal dimension, not referring explicitly to Muḥammad as a prophet and as a man, but to his cosmological dimension as the perfect Man, as we can observe in a famous poem, disseminated in various Sufi circles, composed by the Moroccan master ʿAbd al-Salām Ibn Mashīsh (d. 1227):

> O my God, bless the one from whom the secrets come and from whom the lights flow,
> he in whom realities ascend and in whom the sciences of Adam were made to descend, so that creatures were made powerless by him,
> and intellects shrink in comparison, so much so that none of us, neither predecessor nor successor, can grasp it;
> the gardens of the *malakūt* are adorned with the flower of its beauty, and the basins (*ḥyāḍ*) of the *jabarūt* overflow from the flow of its lights;
> there is nothing that is not related to him, since, as has been said, without the Mediator (*al-wāsiṭa*) everything that depends on him would disappear![630]

Ibn Mashīsh's poem begins with a prayer formula (*Allāhumma ṣalli ʿalā*), not followed, as is usually the case, by Muḥammad's name, but by the formula "He from whom…" (*man minhu*), and then by a series of characteristics that show the uniqueness and election of the object of divine blessing, the understanding of which is beyond human capabilities. The following verses then describe the cosmological context in which the reality of the object of divine blessing is situated, which includes the higher worlds from the perspective of God as King (*Malik*), seen above, namely the *ʿālam al-malakūt* and the *ʿālam al-jabarūt*. Noteworthy in this passage is the reference to the heavenly Basins (*ḥiyāḍ*) in the plural, since as we have seen, the Prophet's heavenly Basin is usually one, but according to some traditions there would be other basins connected to other prophets. Ibn Mashīsh's vision seems to refer to a higher level in which the various basins are under the jurisdiction of the perfect Man, the archetype of each prophet possessing the basin, in their eschatological function. Each prophet thus leads the chosen believers to drink from his basin, which, in the author's words, overflows with the

629 Ibid., 153–157.
630 ʿAbd al-Ḥalīm Maḥmūd, *al-Quṭb al-shahīd ʿAbd al-Salām ibn Bashīsh* (al-Qāhira: Dār al-Maʿārif, 1976), 37–38; Bashīsh is the Arabic form of the name Mashīsh, which is instead a Maghrebi dialectal form. In this edition, the poem is followed by a commentary by Aḥmad al-Ṣāwī (d. 1825).

flow of divine Light, which, as we have seen in esoteric Islamic doctrine, is often called the "Muḥammadan Light," but which in reality has a universal function.

Finally, the following and final verses of the quotation hint at the central issue: everything is linked (*manūṭ*) to the perfect Man since he represents the very fabric of all creation, and if the Mediator (*al-wāsiṭa*) were to disappear, the very creation that depends on him (*al-mawsūṭ*) would also disappear with him. In the author's vision, as we can see, the Mediator is synonymous with the perfect Man. Indeed, these verses represent a concise description in poetic form of the doctrine of the Perfect Man, which nevertheless contains all the features necessary to describe it according to the doctrines of Islamic esotericism.[631] This doctrine shows clear similarities with the aforementioned doctrine of the *logos* prevalent both in the ancient world and in the other Abrahamic religions. It will later be developed in a more complete and structured manner, as we have seen, by Ibn al-ʿArabī and the main authorities of the school that draws on his teaching. From a historical point of view, we can observe that Ibn Mashīsh lived at about the same time as Ibn al-ʿArabī and, according to hagiographic sources, both indicate as their primary reference the teaching of Abū Madyan Shuʿayb (d. 1198), known as "The Helper" (*al-ghawth*).[632] Considering this doctrine, it is not surprising that Ibn Mashīsh's prominent disciple, Abū-l-Ḥasan al-Shādhilī (d. 1258), founder of the Shādhiliyya brotherhood, is the author of a "Litany of Intercession" (*Ḥizb al-tawassul*), in which, however, the intercessor disappears:

> O God, I seek intercession with You through You (*Allāhumma innī atawassalu bika ilayka*), O God, I swear by You through You (*Allāhumma innī uqsimu bika ʿalayka*), O God, just as You Yourself are the indication that leads me to You, be my intercessor to You (*Allāhumma kamā kunta dalīlī ʿalayka fa-kun shafīʿī ilayka*).[633]

In this litany, intercession is interpreted from an esoteric point of view, and Shādhilī seems to aspire to the removal of all mediation between God and the creature, in order to address God directly.

---

631 Titus Burckhardt, "The Prayer of Ibn Mashīsh," in *Mirror of the Intellect: Essays on Traditional Science and Sacred Art* (Albany: State University of New York Press, 1987), 183–192.

632 Vincent J. Cornell, *The way of Abū Madyan: doctrinal and poetic works of Abū Madyan Shuʿayb ibn al-Ḥusayn al-Anṣārī (c. 509/1115–594/1198), Edited and Translated with Introduction and Notes by Vincent J. Cornell* (Cambridge: The Islamic Texts Society, 1996).

633 Aḥmad ibn Muḥammad ibn ʿAbbad, *al-Mafākhir al-ʿaliyya fī al-maʾāthir al-shādhiliyya* (al-Qāhira: al-Maktaba al-azhariyya li-l-turāth, 2004), 224–225.

Instead, we find the Mediator (*wāsiṭa*) in a passage of an invocation of blessing (*al-ṣalā al-kubrā*) attributed to Ibn al-ʿArabī, where he describes the perfect Man in these words:

> Mediator of the divine descent from the heaven of eternity to the earth of eternity" (*wāsiṭa al-tanazzul al-ilāhī min samāʾ al-azaliyya ilā al-arḍ al-abadiyya*)[634]; "Mediator of that which lies between existence and nothingness" (*wāsiṭa mā bayna al-wujūd wa-bayna al-ʿadam*); " Bond that unites the new with the ancestral" (*wa-rābiṭat taʿalluq al-ḥudūth bi-l-qidam*); "He who ascends to the station of the distance of an arc or even nearer" (*wa-taraqqā ilā manzila qāb qawsayn aw adnā*).[635]

We have already quoted the Qurʾanic verse (53:9) that refers to this terminal station achieved by the Prophet, according to Islamic tradition, during his Ascension (*miʿrāj*).

This spiritual dimension of the Prophet as a perfect Man emerged gradually in Islamic esoteric literature until it became a well-established and widespread theme from the thirteenth century onwards, in the wake of the dissemination of the teachings of Ibn al-ʿArabī. As a result of this, the idea that a certain category of holy men (*awliyāʾ*) can come into contact with the spiritual dimension of the Prophet, either through truthful dreaming or in the waking state, is increasingly developed, and he is progressively perceived as the source of the spiritual magisterium of the masters of Sufism, the one from whom the covenant proper to Islamic initiatory organisations (*bayʿa, mubāyʿa*) originates.[636] Some important personalities of Sufism have claimed to have met the Prophet in the waking state following long recitations of invocations of blessing upon him, and to have entered into an initiatory pact with him, thus rendering their previous Sufi chain of transmission obsolete. This is at the origin of a particular initiatory mode, often called the "Muḥammadan way" (*al-ṭarīqa al-muḥammadiyya*)."[637]

At the same time, if in the formative phase of Sufism, the sources insist on the initiate's attempt to extinguish his human dimension in God (*al-fanāʾ fī Allāh*), in

---

634 ʿAbd al-Ghānī al-Nābulusī, *Sharḥ al-ṣalā al-kubrā li-l-shaykh al-akbar Ibn ʿArabī* (Bayrūt: Books-Publisher, 2012), 32.

635 Ibid., 33.

636 Michel Chodkiewicz, "Le modèle prophétique de la sainteté en Islam," in *Al-Masāq* 7:1 (1994), 201–226; Denis Gril, "Le modèle prophétique du maître spirituel en islam," in *Maestro e discepolo. Temi e problemi della direzione spirituale tra VI secolo a.c. e VII secolo d.c.*, edited by Giovanni Filoramo (Piacenza: Centro di alti studi in scienze religiose di Piacenza, 2002), 345–360.

637 Rachida Chih, "Discussing the Sufism of the Early Modern Period. A New Historiographical Outlook on the *Tariqa Muhammadiyya*," in *Sufism East and West. Mystical Islam and Cross-Cultural Exchange in the Modern World*, edited by Jamal Malik and Saeed Zarrabi-Zadeh (Leiden: Brill, 2019), 104–126.

the next phase, we observe a shift towards the practice of extinction in the Prophet (*al-fanā' fī al-rasūl*) as a method of spiritual realization.[638] This process runs in parallel with the development of the recourse to the Prophet's intermediation and intercession, which, as we have seen, underwent a progressive development over the centuries under consideration. What can be argued, more generally, is that the doctrines and practices related to the Prophet's intermediation and intercession, both religious and esoteric, find a privileged environment in Sufism, which makes possible their development and diffusion at any level of Islamic societies.

2 The Station of praise (*al-maqām al-maḥmūd*) and the Pedestal (*al-kursī*)

Thanks to the considerations introduced in the previous chapter, we have observed how the intermediary function of the Prophet is charged with a marked spiritual dimension in esoteric Islamic literature. In some texts, however, Muḥammad's function of intermediation and intercession as a prophet and his esoteric intermediation coexist and prelude to his universal cosmological function. The function of the Prophet is then complemented by that of the saints (*al-awliyā'*), who inherit the same attributes in terms of intermediation and intercession. This process appears clearly in the work of one of the main precursors of Ibn al-ʿArabī, the aforementioned al-Ḥakīm al-Tirmidhī (d. 869), and in particular in "The Lives of the Saints" (*Sīrat al-awliyā'*), generally known as "The Seal of the Saints" (*Khatm al-awliyā'*).[639] For the first time in Islamic esoteric literature, the spiritual dimension of Muḥammad is systematically embedded in a complex cosmological structure of an esoteric order. Tirmidhī states that the first entity to be brought into existence is Remembrance (*dhikr*), followed by Knowledge (*ʿilm*) and Will (*mashī'a*). The first thing remembered by God is Muḥammad, and in the Knowledge of God appears successively the Knowledge of Muḥammad, and later, in the Will of God, the Will of Muḥammad. He is the first in a series of ancestral events: to be mentioned in the divine decrees (*al-maqādīr*), to be inscribed in the Table (*al-lawḥ* [*al-maḥfūẓ*]) to enter into a covenant with God (*al-mīthāq*). Just as he is the first in this initial cosmogonic sequence, he is also the first in the final eschatological sequence: the

638 Valerie J. Hoffman, "Annihilation in the Messenger of God: The Development of a Sufi Practice," *International Journal of Middle East Studies* 31, 3 (1999), 351–369.

639 al-Ḥakīm al-Tirmidhī, *Thalāthat muṣannafāt li-l-Ḥakīm al-Tirmidhī*, ed. Berndt Radtke (Shtūtgārt et Bayrūt: Dār al-nashr Frānts Shtāynar, 1992–1996); al-Ḥakīm al-Tirmidhī, *The Concept of Sainthood in Early Islamic Mysticism, tr. by Bernd Radtke and John O'Kane* (Richmond Surrey: Curzon Press, 1996).

first for whom the earth will open to restore him to life, the first to whom God will speak, the first to stand before God; the first, finally, to practise intercession (*al-shafāʿa*).[640] This will be made possible because, at the moment when God will stand as a judge on the Day of Judgement addressing mankind from the height of His Rigour (*jalāl*) and Immensity (*ʿaẓama*), no creature will be able to retain his senses and move, except Muḥammad, who will instead advance by a "step of sincerity" (*qadam ṣidq*, Q 10:2), even in comparison to the other prophets. For this reason, God will accept his sincerity and grant him the Station of praise (*maqām maḥmūd*), which, according to Tirmidhī's interpretation, is located at the Pedestal (*ʿinda al-kursī*).[641] We also find the interpretation of the Qur'anic formula "step of sincerity" in relation to the Station of praise in the Qurṭubī commentary. In contrast, in the Ṭabarī commentary, we discover the opinion of some commentators that it is Muḥammad himself who must be identified with the "step of sincerity," since he is the first intercessor, who is granted precedence over other intercessors.[642] When Muḥammad settles in this station, which Tirmidhī defines as the station of the "seal" (*khatm*), God will remove its veil, and the light that will be released will envelop Muḥammad to the extent that praise towards God will flow from his heart to the Prophet's tongue, which will praise God with praise that no human had ever heard before until all the prophets will know that Muḥammad is the most knowledgeable among them. He is the first preacher (*khaṭīb*), the first intercessor (*shafīʿ*), and he will be granted the Standard of praise (*liwāʾ al-ḥamd*) for the monotheists (*al-muwaḥḥḥidūn*) and the keys of munificence (*mafātiḥ al-karam*) for the prophets (*al-anbiyāʾ*). He will intercede for the prophets and the saints (*awliyāʾ*).[643] According to Tirmidhī, God brought together in Muḥammad all the parts that constitute prophethood and, having thus perfected prophethood itself, placed His seal (*khatm*) on it. He highlights the relationship between the prophets' function as a seal and intercession, citing a tradition:

> When they come to Adam and ask him to intercede with his Lord on their behalf, he will answer them: 'If one of you sets aside his possessions during his absence, he will affix a seal (*khatm*) to them. Now, could anyone have access to possessions except through the seal?' Then they shall go to Muḥammad, for he is the seal of the prophets (*khatm al-anbiyāʾ*).[644]

---

640 al-Ḥakīm al-Tirmidhī, *Thalāthat muṣannafāt li-l-Ḥakīm al-Tirmidhī*, ed. Berndt Radtke (Shtūtgārt et Bayrūt: Dār al-nashr Frānts Shtāynar, 1992–1996), 39.
641 Ibid., 40.
642 Ibid., 104–105.
643 Ibid., 40.
644 Ibid., 41–42.

Since the Last Judgement will take place by groups, Muḥammad will lead the first due to his function as a seal, and then will come the group of the saints (*awliyā*ʾ), and they too will have their seal, the "Seal of the saints" (*khatm al-awliyā*ʾ). He will be their leader, he will be first among them as Muḥammad is the first among the prophets, and he will be granted the Station of intercession (*maqām al-shafāʿa*), and he too will praise his Lord with such special praise that the saints will acknowledge that he is the most knowledgeable among them.[645] The Seal of the saints will also be the first among the saints in the same series of ancestral events listed with regard to the Prophet, including the fact that he will be the first among them to exercise intercession. The other friends of God will be behind him, in a less elevated station than him, one rank after another, while the stations of the prophets will be similarly ordered in a mirror-image manner before him.[646]

Tirmidhī, answering the question of who are God's friends or saints (*awliyā*ʾ), states that they are the forty chosen ones who are always present in the world. He adds that they are the People of the House of God (*ahl bayt Allāh*), pointing out, however, that he is not referring to the Prophet's family but rather to the People of the House of Mention (*ahl bayt al-dhikr*), sent to establish the Mention of God (*dhikr*) on earth. Thus, the following *ḥadīth*, according to Tirmidhī, refers to them and not to the Prophet's family:

> The People of my House are the guarantors for the protection of my community. When they die, my community suffers what is destined for it.

These forty friends of God are therefore the guarantee for the protection of the Muslim community. The earth exists through them, and through them people ask for intercession by praying for rain (*istisqā*ʾ).[647]

In a passage from another work, Tirmidhī states that the hallmark of the intermediary and intercessory function of the saints, inherited from that of the Prophet, is that they, too, on the Day of Judgement, will be endowed with a banner (*liwā*ʾ). People will be divided according to their spiritual rank so that all people who will accede to a particular rank can gather under the banner of the related saint. Tirmidhī uses a royal and political metaphor in his vision: there will be ranks for the chiefs in the presence of the king and ranks for the attendants, divided into the various provinces.[648] He then describes the moment when the Proph-

645 Ibid., 44–45.
646 Ibid., 45.
647 Ibid., 45–46.
648 Ibid., 233–234.

et will accede to the intermediary and intercessory function by combining scriptural data and esoteric interpretations in a very original manner:

> When the banners are raised, the banners of God's messengers will be raised. Each envoy has a banner within his community. Under the banner of each envoy are gathered all the other banners that we have described above. Then will come the banner of Muḥammad and all the messengers will be under his banner. And this is the Banner of praise. It is the banner of all those who profess the Oneness of God. The banner of the community is in the hand of the leader of the community and of the one who comes after him, according to the bestowal by God. The banner of Muḥammad comes from the Light of the primordial beginning. When God has finished judging His creatures and judging at the Pedestal of the Throne (*kursī*), Muḥammad will present himself before the Pedestal, and this is the Station of praise (*maqām al-maḥmūd*), from which the Banner of Praise (*liwā' al-ḥamd*) will originate. God will hold it and present the banner of the community to its leader, and His banner held by His leader will be the equivalent of all the banners of the other messengers. When Muḥammad stands before the Pedestal, he will praise his Lord with a praise that no one in the past or present has ever heard. Then his seal (*khatm*) will be removed, so that the place will shine with his light and the light will illuminate the Pedestal and make it clear to all the messengers that Muḥammad is their leader. Then Muḥammad will utter a loud call that will extend throughout the Universe: 'O people of this place, praise be to God, Lord of creation!' Then there will not be a single messenger of the Unity of God who will not respond to him with, 'Praise be to God, Lord of creation!' In the meantime, Iblīs will have mounted a pulpit (*minbar*) of fire that will be placed before the gate of Hell and will shout, 'O people of this place, praise be to God, Lord of creation!' And there will not be a single infidel or polytheist or hypocrite or misguided person who will not respond to him with, 'Praise God, Lord of creation!'[649]

As can be clearly observed, the specificity of the Tirmidhī system consists in merging the religious and esoteric dimensions of Muḥammad's function of intermediation and intercession. His doctrine on this subject will find extensive and accomplished development in the work of Ibn al-ʿArabī and his successors.[650]

One detail indicated by Tirmidhī is particularly relevant to our discussion, as it allows us to reconstruct, from his influential work, a cosmological structure related to the function of intermediation and intercession. Indeed, Tirmidhī repeatedly proposes an identity between the Station of praise (and thus, as we have seen, with the Qur'anic *wasīla*) and the Pedestal (*kursī*). This can be interpreted in two directions. The first is connected to the metaphor of kingship seen above, according to which on the Day of Judgement, Muḥammad's position in relation to God will be analogous to that of a vizier in the presence of the King: God as King will be seated

649 Ibid., 235.

650 Michel Chodkiewicz, "The Banner of Praise," in *Journal of the Muhyiddin Ibn Arabi Society* 21 (1997), 45–58.

on the Throne (*ʿarsh*), and Muḥammad's seat as vizier would instead be, in this sense, the Pedestal (*kursī*). The second interpretation is instead based on esoteric sources since we have seen that Muḥammad's spiritual dimension is that of the Perfect Man (*al-insān al-kāmil*), and thus the Pedestal as a cosmological place would be nothing other than the station of the Perfect Man.

Interestingly, the use of a spatial metaphor is also observed with regard to the Pedestal. In the Pedestal verse, it is stated that it is "as wide as the heavens and the earth" or, according to another interpretation made possible by the different values of the verb, "includes, contains the heavens and the earth."[651] It is therefore a complementary notion of vertical intermediation, of connection between the divine and human worlds. This adds a further dimension to the metaphor seen above, increasing its complexity from a cosmological point of view.

Another previously mentioned Qur'anic metaphor of intermediation, the Rope of God (*ḥabl Allāh*), is equally subject to interpretation in esoteric Islamic literature. Ibn al-ʿArabī, for example, dwells on the Rope of God in the thirty-eighth chapter of the Meccan Illuminations (*al-Futūḥāt al-Makkiyya*), which is dedicated to the divine Name "He Who Elevates to the Highest Levels, Possessor of the Throne" (*Rafīʿ al-darajāt dhī-l-ʿarsh*), which as we have seen concerns the divine action of elevating the spiritual levels of creatures. He discusses the level (*rutba*) of the letter *wāw*, relating it to the "station of the rope of the well" (*manāzil al-rishāʾ*) since, in his words, it is identical to the rope (*ḥabl*) and the rope is a bond (*waṣl*). It is necessary to cling to this rope as if it came from God, and God brings down the rope according to one's station, as indicated in the Qur'anic verse "Hold on to God's rope,"[652] which Ibn al-ʿArabī relates to another verse, which reads: "Hold on to God (*wa-ʿtaṣimū bi-Llāh*)."[653] In the autograph manuscript of the Meccan Illuminations, he adds a curious drawing of the well rope hanging from the bucket in the margin of this passage, reproduced in some printed editions.[654]

In this same direction proceeds the interpretation of the Rope of God in the work of a celebrated successor of Ibn al-ʿArabī, ʿAbd al-Karīm al-Jīlī (d. 1403). In

651 "*wasiʿa kursiyyuhu al-samāwāti wa-l-arḍ*," Q 2:255. Translators of the Qur'ān generally translate "the Pedestal is wider than the heavens and the earth," or "extends beyond," but this possibility does not seem to be contained in the values of the verb.

652 Q 3:103.

653 Q 22:78.

654 Muḥyīddīn Ibn al-ʿArabī, *al-Futūḥāt al-Makkiyya*, ed. Sulṭān Manṣub (Ṣanʿāʾ: ʿĀṣimat al-thaqāfa al-islāmiyya, Wazīrat al-thaqāfa, 2010), 6:182; Ali Karjoo-Ravary, "Illustrating the Forms: Ibn al-ʿArabī's (d. 638/1240) Images in al-Futūḥāt al-Makkiyya," in *Visualizing Sufism: Studies on Graphic Representations in Sufi Literature (13th to 16th Century)*, ed. Giovanni Maria Martini (Leiden: Brill 2023), 67, 100–101.

his treatise entitled "At the Distance of Two Bows" (*Qāb qawsayn*), Jīlī uses the spatial metaphor to interpret the verse on the Ascension seen above, in which the Prophet comes into close contact with the divine. Indeed, he states that the universal Reality (*al-ḥaqīqa*) can be conceived as a single circle divided into two parts, one representsing eternal and uncreated existence, while the other representing created existence. Each half of this circle is like an arc and these two arcs are divided by a string (*watar*). The rope is identified with the Muḥammadan Station (*al-maqām al-muḥammadī*), which is the isthmus (*barzakh*) between realities and represents "the Reality of all realities". Jīlī further adds that the Muḥammadan Station, at the highest stage of the Ascension, was "above" the divine Throne, which is the upper limit of created things: all created things were "below," and only God was "above". According to Jīlī, therefore, the rope, which represents intermediation, is identical to the Muḥammadan Station, which is the esoteric designation for the Station of praise, since it refers to the Perfect Man just as the Station of praise refers to the Prophet.[655]

3 The Supreme Helper (*al-ghawth al-aʿẓam*)

If the perfect Man is thus the heavenly archetype of all forms of prophecy and holiness, a supreme spiritual function also emerges on earth in the doctrinal literature and oral tradition of Islamic esotericism. This is the highest function in the hierarchy of Sunni Islamic esotericism, consistently embodied by one creature who, when he dies, leaves its place to another. This function is usually called "Pole" (*al-quṭb*) or "Helper" (*al-ghawth*). Some texts support the view that there may be several Poles, up to four, which is why the formula "Pole of Poles" (*quṭb al-aqṭāb*) is commonly used to indicate the Supreme Pole. However, there is only one Helper, often referred to as the Supreme Helper (*al-ghawth al-aʿẓam*), and this function is identical to that of the Supreme Pole. According to some specialists, this function bears strong similarities to the supreme function of the Imām in both the Ismaʿili and the Twelver Shiʿa context.[656]

The term Helper is of particular interest here because it indicates that the function of this figure is in close connection with intermediation and intercession, since the helper is the one who responds to requests for help. This may indicate

655 ʿAbd al-Karīm al-Jīlī, *Qāb qawsayn wa-multaqā al-nāmūsayn fī maʿrifat sayyid al-kawnayn* (al-Qāhira: Dār al-āfāq al-ʿarabiyya, 2006), 97.
656 Frederick de Jong, "al-Ḳuṭb – 2. In mysticism." In *EI*^{2}.

that this figure inherits on earth the cosmological function of intermediation of the perfect Man, thus representing his earthly projection.

We dealt in a previous chapter with the meaning of the help and rescue function from the *ḥadīth.* In the context examined here, we observe instead the esoteric transposition of the same notion, since, from the twelfth century onwards, a number of important personalities are given the epithet "Helper" (*ghawth*). The first is ʿAbd al-Qādir al-Jīlānī (d. 1166). Reference to the role of Helper appears several times in some ancient litanies attributed to him, along with technical terms of intermediation and intercession, such as *wasīla, istighātha, wāsiṭa.*[657] In a collection of these litanies, we also find a chapter entitled "The advantage in receiving help through the presence of the Helper" (*fāʾida fī al-istighātha bi-wāsiṭat ḥaḍrat al-ghawth*), which contains precise instructions on which orations to perform, in what ritual state and at what times of the day, in order to obtain the direct help of ʿAbd al-Qādir al-Jīlānī.[658] Finally, the most important litany of the brotherhood is called "The Sung Poem of the Helper" (*al-qaṣīda al-ghawthiyya*), precisely in honour of the epithet given to this master.[659]

Abū Madyan Shuʿayb (d. 1198), as we have seen, was also honoured with the appellation "Helper". Finally, a master who lived later, in the sixteenth century in India, Muḥammad ibn Khaṭīr al-Dīn Gwaliyārī (d. 1562), will also be habitually called Muḥammad Ghawth.[660]

We can also mention another oral practice, namely the request for "help, rescue, assistance" through the term *madad.* This term derives from the root *m-d-d*, with the primary meanings of "pulling, stretching, drawing water from a well with a rope" and can also indicate the rising of water.[661] It is used in particular as a request for the Prophet's spiritual help and assistance (*madad yā rasūl Allāh*) or of ʿAlī in the Shiʿa context.[662] In the Sufi context, this term is also used to evoke the material and spiritual help of the saints (*awliyāʾ*).[663] The underlying

657 Ismāʿīl ibn Muḥammad Saʿīd al-Qādirī, *al-Fuyūḍāt al-rabbāniyya fī-l-maʾāthir wa-al-awrād al-qādiriyya* (al-Qāhira: Maktabat Muṣṭafa al-Bāb al-Ḥalabī, 1934).

658 Ibid., 63.

659 Ibid., 102.

660 Carl William Ernst, *Sufism and Yoga according to Muhammad Ghawth*, in *Refractions of Islam in India: Situating Sufism and Yoga* (New Delhi: Sage-Yodapress, 2016), 149–160.

661 Edward William Lane, "*m-d-d*," *An Arabic-English Lexicon* (London: Williams and Norgate, 1863–93).

662 Ali Sultaan Asani, *Devotional Practices*, in Farhad Daftary, Amyn Sajoo, Shainool Jiwa (eds.), *The Shiʿi World: Pathways in Tradition and Modernity* (London – New York: I.B. Tauris, 2015), 160–161.

663 Valerie J. Hoffman-Ladd, "Devotion to the Prophet and His Family in Egyptian Sufism," in *International Journal of Middle East Studies* 24, 4 (1992), 626.

idea, encouraged by the root value, seems to be a spiritual connection, stretched like a ray or a rope, from the divine world to the human world.

4 The intercession of the saints (*awliyāʾ Allāh*)

Among the categories of intercessors, as we have seen, we also find God's friends or saints (*awliyāʾ Allāh*). Some *ḥadith* grant certain men an intercessory role similar to the prophetic one, even with regard to the request for rain:

> In my community there will remain seven who whenever they will plead with God, He will answer and through whom will be given victory and rain.[664]
>
> The people of Syria were mentioned in the presence of ʿAlī when he was in Iraq. They said to him: 'Curse them'. He replied: 'I will not, because I heard the Prophet say: 'The Substitutes (*al-abdāl*), they are in Syria. They are forty men and every time one of them dies he is replaced by another. Thanks to them you are given rain, you defeat your enemies, and affliction is averted from the people of Syria.'[665]

In the history of Islamic societies, saints inherit the role of the Prophet not only from a religious and political point of view but also from an esoteric one. If the Prophet, as we have seen, is expected to be elevated to a supreme station, where his function finally takes on a spiritual and cosmological dimension, some saints can be elevated to the Station of proximity (*maqām al-qurba, manzil al-qurba*).[666] In addition to its characteristics, this station seems to have, at the same time, a connection with the special intercession attributed to some among them, both as assistance for those following the spiritual path and as help and succour for believers. It is no coincidence that among the meanings of the term *walī* (pl. *awliyāʾ*), there is also the sense of "protection," in the same way as the appellation "patron" (from the Latin *patronus*, "protector") often appears alongside the term saint in some Western languages.[667]

For this reason, although the term *shafāʿa*, as we have seen, is mainly used in relation to the intercession of the prophet Muḥammad, it is possible to mention some famous examples in which it is also used to denote the intercession of a particular saint with similar characteristics to prophetic intercession. The earliest

664 ʿAbd al-Razzāq ibn Hammām al-Ṣanʿānī, *al-Muṣannaf*, 11:250.

665 Ibn Ḥanbal, *Musnad*, 2:231.

666 Muḥyīddīn Ibn al-ʿArabī, *Kitāb al-qurba*, in *Rasāʾil Ibn ʿArabī*, ed. Maḥmūd Ghurāb (Bayrūt: Dār ṣādir, 1977), 88–95.

667 Eva Riad, "Šafāʿa dans le Coran," in *Orientalia Suecana* XXX (1981), 53.

mentioned in the sources is Uways al-Qaranī (d. 656), a contemporary of the Prophet. According to some traditions, one day Gabriel descended upon the Prophet near the Kaʿba in an unfamiliar guise, and told him:

> Your Lord sends you His greeting and tells you that there will come out of your community a man who will be an intercessor. [...] If you live long enough and meet him, ask him to intercede for your community.[668]

According to the legends that have grown up around this character, Uways wanted to emigrate to join the Prophet's community but preferred to stay in his place of origin, Yemen, to care for his elderly and ill mother.[669] Some *ḥadīth* resume the narrative at a later time, when the second caliph, ʿUmar ibn al-Khaṭṭāb, who had received instructions from the Prophet in this regard, questioned the military auxiliaries arriving from Yemen to find out whether there was a man among them called Uways al-Qaranī with all the characteristics the Prophet had foretold. Uways was recognised, and ʿUmar begged him to ask divine forgiveness for him, which he did.[670] From these narratives, the Sufi tradition in particular, celebrated the figure of Uways, claiming that he was in spiritual contact with the Prophet without ever having met him personally, having nevertheless received his cloak (*burda*) as a gift from him. In the Sufi hagiographies, the narrative concerning his power of intercession has thus been transmitted, for instance in Farīd al-Dīn ʿAṭṭār's (d. 1221) famous "Memorial of the Saints" (*Tadhkirat al-awliyāʾ*).[671]

There are other later saints whose intercession is often evoked through the term *shafāʿa*. These are the famous Four Poles (*al-aqṭāb al-arbaʿa*): ʿAbd al-Qādr Jīlānī (d. 1166), Aḥmad al-Rifāʿī (d. 1183), Aḥmad al-Badawī (d. 1276) and Ibrāhīm al-Dusūqī (d. 1296). In the Egyptian area, it is in particular the *shafāʿa* of Aḥmad al-Badawī, as well as his succour (*istighātha*), that is invoked by the population on the occasion of individual and collective hardships and calamities.[672]

---

668 Katia Zakharia, "Uways al-Qaranī, Visages d'une légende," in *Arabica* XLVI, 2 (1999), 238 (tr. by the author).

669 Abū Nuʿaym al-Iṣfahānī, *Ḥilyat al-awliyāʾ wa-ṭabaqāt al-aṣfiyāʾ* (Bayrūt: Dār al-kutub al-ʿilmiyya, 1997) 2:79–87.

670 Muslim, *Ṣaḥīḥ Muslim*, 6:401–403.

671 Farīd al-Dīn al-ʿAṭṭār, *Takhkirat al-awliyāʾ* (Dimashq: Dār al-maktabī, 2009), 41–49.

672 Catherine Mayeur, "L'intercession des saints en Islam égyptien: autour de Sayyid al-Badawī," in *Annales Islamologiques* 25 (1991), 363–388.

Chapter 10
Opposition to the Notions of Intermediation and Intercession by Islamic Reformation Movements

As we have seen, recourse to intermediation and intercession is a practice perfectly integrated into the religious system of Sunnism and Twelver Shiʿism. However, as early as the thirteenth/ fourteenth century, in Sunni circles, some religious scholars disapproved of the resort to intermediation and severely limited the scope of the notion of intercession. From the nineteenth century onwards, then, some Islamic Reformation movements inaugurated a veritable theological conflict against intermediation and intercession, culminating, as we shall see, in the destruction of the sacred places associated with them.

1 Ibn Taymiyya and the birth of polemical literature against intermediation and intercession

The first to systematically challenge the Sunnite formulation concerning intercession was the famous ḥanbalite scholar Aḥmad Ibn Taymiyya (d. 1328), who was born and lived in Damascus.[673] His impressive work represented the first structured proposal for reform in Sunnite Islam throughout its history.

An essential point of his doctrine is precisely the refutation of the Sunni notion of intercession: he accepts the intercession of the Prophet and other prophets and devout believers only on the Day of Judgement. From this postulate derives his polemic against visiting graves. Starting with some *ḥadīth,* he advocated a ban on constructing buildings on tombs, even disapproving of the construction of the dome on the Prophet's tomb in Medina. He also states that visiting the tomb of the Prophet should be forbidden, and a fortiori visiting any other tomb. This is because in his thought, which strongly insists on divine Unity (*tawḥīd*) and the transcendence of God, the believer must always and only turn towards his Creator. Any quest for intercession, even that of the Prophet, amounts to an attestation of polytheism (*shirk*) and must therefore be severely sanctioned. His polemic rages, in particular, against the veneration of saints and the system of pilgrimages to the shrines of the founding masters of the Sufi orders.[674] He also harshly criticised

---

673 Jon Hoover, *Ibn Taymiyya, Makers of the Muslim World* (London: Oneworld Academic, 2019).
674 Muhammad Umar Memon, *Ibn Taymiyya's Struggle against Popular Religion,* (The Hague – Paris: Mouton 1976).

https://doi.org/10.1515/9783111500966-015

the veneration of the Prophet's relics, going so far as to attempt to destroy a footprint attributed to Muḥammad in Jerusalem and then having to escape a lynching after being caught in the act.[675] This provoked a vehement reaction from the Sunnite scholars of his time, who accused him of placing himself outside the majority consensus (*ijmāʿ*) by opposing accepted and established beliefs.

In his work, Ibn Taymiyya returns several times to the issue of intermediation and intercession. In the "Creed of Wasīṭ" (*al-ʿAqīda al-wasīṭiyya*), which is the answer to a question put to him by the judge (*qāḍī*) of the Iraqi city of Wasīṭ, Ibn Taymiyya limits himself to a brief mention of intercession. He states that, on the Day of Judgement, there will be three types of intercession (*shafāʿa*). The first two will be reserved for the Prophet alone: the first will be exercised towards the believers awaiting the Judgement after the Resurrection (*ahl al-mawqif*), while with the second, he will authorise the believers' entry into Paradise. With the third, finally, the Prophet will intercede for those destined for Hell for a while or eternally, who can be saved not only through his intercession but also through that of other prophets, pious men and other categories of intercessors (*al-nabiyyīn al-siddiqīn wa-ghayrihim*). Finally, God will deliver some people from Hell without the need for intercession, but only through His mercy.[676] He also introduces into his creed the belief in the heavenly Basin, but without connecting it with intercession.[677]

In another work, entitled "The Epistle of Ṣafad" (*al-Risāla al-ṣafadiyya*), Ibn Taymiyya summarises the three main views on intercession among the believers of the Abrahamic religions and movements within Islam in this way:

> Unbelievers, Christians and innovators, such as those who exaggerate with their masters (*shuyūkh*) and others, consider that the intercession with God of those whom they worship has the same characteristics as the intercession we see in this lower world (*dunyā*). The Muʿtazilites and Kharijite , on the other hand, deny that our prophet Muḥammad intercedes for those who have committed grave sins. The Sunnis (*ahl al-sunna wa-l-jamāʿa*), finally, claim that our Prophet will intercede for those who have committed grave sins, and others will intercede as well, but no one will intercede until God gives him permission and sets a limit for his intercession.[678]

675 Muhammad Umar Memon, *Ibn Taymiyya's Struggle against Popular Religion*, (The Hague – Paris: Mouton 1976), 362, f. 301.

676 Aḥmad Ibn Taymiyya, *al-ʿAqīda al-wasīṭiyya* (al-Riyāḍ: Maktaba aḍwāʾ al-salaf, 1999), 100–101.

677 Ibid., 99.

678 Aḥmad Ibn Taymiyya, *al-Risāla al-ṣafadiyya, qāʿida fī taḥqīq al-risāla wa-bṭāl sawl ahl al-zaygh wa-l-ḍalāla* (al-Riyāḍ: Aḍwāʾ al-salaf, 2002), 2:290–291.

In his voluminous collection of legal answers (*fatāwā*), we find a detailed treatment in relation to the issue of intermediation, republished in recent times as an excerpt in various editions under the title "Epistle on the Intermediation between Creation and God" (*Risālat al-wāsiṭa bayna al-khalq wa-l-ḥaqq*). The treatise is a theological refutation of those who claim that an intermediary (*wāsiṭa*) is necessary to reach God. The Damascene scholar responds by stating that if this is meant as an intermediary for the transmission of the divine Order, this is indeed the case, and on this issue, there is also agreement among the believers of the other Abrahamic religions, Jews and Christians. If, on the other hand, one understands by intermediary an entity whose task it is to provide sustenance, guidance and victory for men, one then moves into the territory of the grave sin of association (*shirk*). To support his argument, Ibn Taymiyya quotes the Qur'anic verses, seen above, that tend to deny intercession on the Day of Judgement. Next, he addresses the central issue of God's kingship, showing that he thoroughly understands its theological implications, although he vehemently opposes its application as a metaphor for human intercession. Some, says the Damascene theologian, believe that there are intermediaries between God and his creatures, with the task of getting their requests to God, just as viziers or chamberlains (*ḥājib*) stand between the king and his subjects. Creatures would address their requests to these intermediaries, and these intermediaries would bring them back to God, just as intermediaries bring back requests for people to the king because of their proximity to him. Moreover, people would address their queries to the intermediaries because compliance with etiquette (*adab*) would prevent them from addressing the king directly. To these arguments, Ibn Taymiyya responds by stating that anyone who claims that such intermediaries exist between God and mankind must be considered an unbeliever and an associationist, and must be urged to repent, otherwise, he must be put to death. He introduces some rationalistic arguments to support his position: the King's intermediaries sometimes inform him about matters of which he has no knowledge, whereas God is aware of everything that takes place in the heavens and on earth. The King's informers are thus associated with him in kingship, whereas God has no associates in His kingship.[679]

679 Aḥmad Ibn Taymiyya, *Majmūʿ fatāwa shaykh al-islām Aḥmad Ibn Taymiyya*, ed. ʿAbd al-Raḥmān ibn Muḥammad ibn Qāsim (Madīnat al-munawwara: Wizārat al-shu'ūn al-islāmiyya wa-l-daʿwa wa-l-irshād al-saʿūdiyya, Mujammaʿ al-Malik Fahd li-ṭibāʿat al-muṣḥaf al-sharīf, 2004), 1:121–136; Aḥmad Ibn Taymiyya, *Les intermédiaires entre Dieu et l'homme* (Risālat al-wāsiṭa bayna al-khalq wa al-ḥaqq), *traduction française suivie de Le Shaykh de l'Islam Ibn Taymiyya : chronique d'une vie de théologien militant, par Yahyā Michot, Numéro hors-série de la revue Le Musulman éditée par l'Association des Étudiants Islamiques en France* (Paris: A.E.I.F. Éditions, 1996).

In his legal answers (*fatāwa*), Ibn Taymiyya also discusses the meaning of the terms *wasīla* and *tawassul*. He states that, in primary sources, the unclear context in which they are sometimes used may lead some people to misinterpret them. The first meaning of the Qur'anic term *wasīla* is simply approaching God through the obligatory and optional acts, thus following what the Prophet transmitted, and nothing more. In the language of the Companions, according to him, the formula *tawassul bi-l-nabī* meant "approaching God through the prayer (*al-duʿāʾ*) and intercession (*shafāʿa*) of the Prophet". Instead, in the language of many later scholars, *tawassul* came to mean "to call upon God on behalf of the prophets and pious men" or those they considered as such. Ibn Taymiyya mentions and interprets here the episode of the asking for rain by ʿUmar ibn al-Khaṭṭāb through ʿAbbās, seen earlier. He states that, on this occasion, ʿUmar does indeed claim to have asked for the Prophet's intercession in the past, but through his prayer and not through himself. Moreover, according to him, ʿUmar considers that asking for the Prophet's intercession is no longer possible after his departure, and therefore, he asks for intercession through the prayer of ʿAbbās, the most eminent member of the Prophet's family who is still alive. This kind of *tawassul* is no longer possible since the Prophet died and will not be possible again until the Day of Judgement, whereas "ordinary" *tawassul* is always possible through obedience to the Prophet. Asking and praying to God in the Prophet's name, according to Ibn Taymiyya, is instead a practice that none of the Companions ever performed, either during the Prophet's lifetime or after his death, and all the *ḥadīth* that refers to the latter kind of intercession are not authentic.[680]

In another *fatwā*, Ibn Taymiyya states that although the Muslim community is unanimous in affirming the Prophet's high rank (*jāh*) in the presence of God, his prayer or intercession, like those of the other prophets, should not be equated with faith in his message and observance of the rules he transmitted. Only the latter ensure deliverance from punishment and salvation in the Hereafter, while his prayer and intercession cannot benefit those who do not fulfil certain conditions. They cannot, for example, save someone from hell if that person does not have faith in the Prophet's message and the rules he transmitted. However, they can lessen the suffering of some people who have faith in the Prophet, as was the case with his uncle Abū Ṭālib. As for the Prophet's request for forgiveness for his mother, God did not accept it since she was a member of the associators (*mushrikūn*) in her time, while God accepted that the Prophet visit her grave. The Proph-

680 Aḥmad Ibn Taymiyya, *Majmūʿ fatāwa shaykh al-islām Aḥmad Ibn Taymiyya*, ed. ʿAbd al-Raḥmān ibn Muḥammad ibn Qāsim. (Madīnat al-munawwara: Wizārat al-shuʾūn al-islāmiyya wa-l-daʿwa wa-l-irshād al-saʿūdiyya, Mujammaʿ al-Malik Fahd li-ṭibāʿat al-muṣḥaf al-sharīf, 2004), 1:199–203, 222–223.

et's intercession and prayer will benefit the believers, adding to their merits and raising their spiritual rank on the Day of Judgement. Sinners among the followers of any prophet will certainly benefit from that prophet's intercession: there is total consensus among the community of Muslims on this point. The intercession that the Qur'an rejects, on the other hand, is that on behalf of those guilty of association against God (*shirk*) among the People of the Book and believers who think that there may be men with a position of honour with God who can intercede with Him on their behalf without His permission, implicitly referring to the adherents of Sufism.[681]

Ibn Taymiyya dedicates other treatises to the question of intermediation and intercession, showing the importance, in the context of his work, of the refutation of their broader understanding. In these texts, however, he does not add much to what is already expressed in his *Fatāwā.* Among these works, we can mention "The Important Principle on Intercession and Intermediation" (*Qāʿida jalīla fī al-tawassul wa-l-wasīla*),[682] and "The Call for Help, on the Refutation of al-Bakrī" (*al-Istighātha fī-l-radd ʿalā al-Bakrī*).[683] In these two works, Ibn Taymiyya's polemic is mainly directed against Sufi brotherhoods and their practice of seeking the intercession and help of the spiritual master (*shaykh*). He claims that when a disciple seeks the supernatural help of the master, invoking his name and protection, the devils take advantage of this to mock him, appearing in the form of that master. Those who seek help and succour from absent, or even worse deceased, masters, fall into the category of idol worshippers: the devil himself is deceiving and misleading them as he has deceived and misled idol worshippers. Demons can take the form of those who are asked for help and offer predictions about the future, mixing truth and deception. These demons can fulfil some of their requests and, in this way, the disciples will believe that it is the work of their master, who possesses extraordinary powers. The same occurs when fortune-tellers believe they are communicating with the spirit of the deceased, and it has happened and continues to happen with those who turn to idols, to whom demons respond instead.[684]

---

681 Ibid., 1:145–152.

682 Aḥmad Ibn Taymiyya, *Qāʿida jalīla fī al-tawassul wa-l-wasīla* (al-Riyāḍ: Riʾasat idārat al-buḥūth al-ʿalamiyya wa-l-iftāʾ al-ʿāmma li-l-ṭabʿ, 1999).

683 Aḥmad Ibn Taymiyya, *al-Istighātha fī-lradd ʿalā al-Bakrī* (al-Riyāḍ: Maktabat dār al-minhaj, 2005).

684 Ibid., 246.

2 The Sunni apologetic response: al-Subkī

Ibn Taymiyya had little impact on the Sunni majority milieu of his time and the following centuries until the seventeenth and eighteenth centuries. His manuscript works did not circulate outside the cities of Damascus and Cairo, where they were nonetheless read by some of his disciples who were part of the circle of the most rigorous ḥanbalites, first and foremost Ibn Qayyim al-Jawziyya (d. 1350).[685] The Sunni apologetic reaction to different theses elaborated by Ibn Taymiyya dates back to this period, first elaborated by the Shafiʿite chief judge of Damascus, Taqī al-Dīn al-Subkī (d. 1355). One of the main theses was that travelling to visit the tomb of the Prophet was an innovation (*bidʿa*) and should be prohibited. Subkī composed a long treatise against this opinion, entitled "The Healing of Sickness, on the Ritual Visit to the Best of Men" (*Shifāʾ al siqām fī ziyārat khayr al-anām*). Much of this text is devoted to the legitimacy and recommendation of the visit to the Prophet's tomb and the associated rules of good behaviour (*ādāb*) through primary sources and the interpretations of Sunni scholars. Great attention is also paid to the question, analysed above, of whether prophets, saints and pious men should be considered alive in their graves and whether one can, therefore, turn to them for intercession or requests for help. After a detailed analysis, Subkī provides an affirmative answer to this question. Finally, several chapters are specifically dedicated to the refutation of Ibn Taymiyya's position in relation to intercession:

> Know that it is lawful and appropriate to practise intermediation (*tawassul*), request for succour (*istighātha*) and intercession (*tashaffuʿ*) through the Prophet, towards his Lord. The permissibility and appropriateness of this is known to all religious people, and is well known from the actions of the prophets and envoys and the behaviour of the pious ancestors (*al-salaf al-ṣāliḥūn*), the scholars and the common Muslims. No one among the believers of the various religions denied this, nor was it heard of at any time until the arrival of Ibn Taymiyya. He spoke of this in words that would deceive the weak and inexperienced, and he innovated in matters that no one in previous eras had advocated. This is why he attacked the episode we have already mentioned concerning Imām Mālik, which contains his statement to al-Manṣūr: "Seek intercession through him," and we have already clarified its authenticity.[686] This is the reason why we have also mentioned the request for succour (*istighātha*) in this book, because of the attack against it and against the visit [to the Prophet's tomb], and it should be sufficient for you that Ibn Taymiyya's denunciation against the request for succour

685 Jon Hoover, *Ibn Taymiyya, Makers of the Muslim World* (London: Oneworld Academic, 2019), 143–144.

686 See above, 135-136.

and intercession is a statement that no scholar before him had uttered, and with which he created dissension among the people of Islam.[687]

He then continues with the following words:

Intermediation (*tawassul*) through the Prophet is permissible in every situation, both before his creation and after it, during the time of his life in this world, as well as after his death in the intermediate period (*barzakh*), and after the Resurrection in the Judgment and Paradise.

There are three types of intermediation (*tawassul*).

The first is that a person seeks intermediation (*tawassul*) through him, which means that the one who seeks the satisfaction of his need asks God through him or his rank or his blessing (*bihi aw bi-jāhi aw bi-barakātihi*). This is permissible in all three situations and for all of them there are authentic traditions [in support].[688]

The second type consists of seeking his mediation (*tawassul*) through him by asking him for a supplication (*du'ā'*).[689]

The third type of intermediation (*tawassul*) consists of asking the Prophet for information on the desired topic, in the sense that he can be an intermediary in this (*bi-annahu qādir 'alā al-tasabbub fīhi*), asking his Lord and through his intercession with Him (*shafā'atihi ilayhi*). This leads us back to the second type in meaning, although the expression is different. [...]

So if these types [of intermediation] and the situations concerning the one who asks the Prophet have become clear and the meaning has become apparent, then you should not care what you call it: whether it is *tawassul, tashaffu'*, *istighātha, tajawwuh* or *tawajjuh*,[690] because the meaning of all these [terms] is the same.[691]

Subkī also refutes Ibn Taymiyya's criticism in detail in other passages:

If the accuser says: 'I do not reject intermediation (*tawassul*) and intercession (*tashaffu'*) because of the narratives and evidence you have cited, but rather I reject the use of intercession through rank (*tajawwuh*) and request for help (*istighātha*), because they may give the impression that the one through whom help is sought is superior to the One from whom help is sought.' To this we reply: 'No Muslim believes this and the formulas *tajawwuh* and *istighātha* indicate this. This is because *tajawwuh is* derived from *jāh* and *wajāhah* and its meaning is high measure and position (*'uluww al-qadr wa-l-manzila*). *Tawassul* may be demanded by a possessor of rank (*jāh*) from one who possesses a higher rank than his own. *Istighātha* is the seeking of help, and the one who seeks help asks the one from whom help is sought to obtain it from another, even if that other is higher than him. Hence *tawassul, tashaffu'*, *tajaw-*

687 Taqī al-Dīn al-Subkī, *Shifā' al-siqām fī ziyārat khayr al-anām* (Bayrūt: Dār al-kutub al-'ilmiyya, 2008), 357.
688 Ibid., 358.
689 Ibid., 372.
690 The *tawajjuh* conveys the idea of spiritually orienting oneself towards God (*wajh*, direction), in this specific context through an intercessor.
691 Taqī al-Dīn al-Subkī, *Shifā' al siqām fī ziyārat khayr al-anām* (Bayrūt: Dār al-kutub al-'ilmiyya, 2008), 382–383.

> *wuh* and *istighātha* through the Prophet and the rest of the prophets (*anbiyā'*) and the righteous (*ṣāliḥūn*) have no other meaning in the hearts of Muslims than this, and none of them intends [to obtain] through them anything beyond this. [...] The One whose help is sought is actually God the Most High, and the Prophet is an intermediary (*wāsiṭa*) between Him and the one seeking help.'[692]

This marked the beginning of a harsh confrontation between opponents and supporters of Ibn Taymiyya's theses, which continued over the following centuries, without, however, leaving the sphere of theologians and experts in Islamic jurisprudence. Among the main themes, intermediation and intercession are always strongly represented in the literature produced in the wake of these polemics, which, although it will be plentiful, will not offer radical innovations compared to the original polemic engaged in by Ibn Taymiyya and Subkī. It is only from the seventeenth century onwards, as we shall see, that Ibn Taymiyya's theses will manage to find not only an intellectual, but also, and above all, a political support.

3 Qāḍīzādeli, Wahhabism and Salafism

In the Ottoman intellectual and political milieu, by then strongly consolidated during the fifteenth century as Sunni of māturidite and ḥanafite tendency, and in particular very much imbued with Sufism at all levels of society, a movement developed during the seventeenth century that took up, without citing the source, certain theses of Ibn Taymiyya. This movement, known as the Qāḍīzādeli, was inspired by a certain moralism that transpired in the works of the ḥanafite and Sufi scholar Muḥammad Birgīvī (d. 1573), who lived in the immediately preceding era. The movement was named after Qāḍīzāde Meḥmed Efendi (d. 1635), a religious scholar with an important career as a preacher, going so far as to be in charge of sermons at the famous mosque and former cathedral of St. Sophia in Constantinople. He succeeded in exerting some influence on the Ottoman Sultan Murād IV (r. 1623–1640), pushing him towards a moralising action against everything perceived by Qāḍīzāde as innovation (*bid'a*) and bad custom. For instance, all the cafés in the Empire were closed down, and numerous people were put to death on charges of having consumed illegal substances, such as coffee and tobacco. One of the main targets against which Qāḍīzāde and the members of his movement raged was the doctrinal Sufism of Ibn al-ʿArabī and the Sufi brotherhoods of the Empire, particularly the Khalwatiyya. The opposition between Qāḍīzāde

---

692 Ibid., 378–379.

and the master of this brotherhood at the time, Sivasi Efendi (d. 1639), soon became a personal matter, with very violent polemical peaks. In this regard, one of the main controversies raised by the Qāḍīzādeli is precisely the practice of intermediation (*tawassul*) and asking for help (*istighāta*), particularly in the context of Sufi brotherhoods.[693]

At this stage, another very influential figure among the Qāḍīzādeli is Aḥmad Rūmī Aqḥḥiṣārī (d. 1632), who composed several works that represent the theoretical foundation of the movement, and which show the explicit influence of the work of Ibn al-Qayyim al-Jawziyya (d. 1350), and even more so the unspoken influence of the work of the latter's master, Ibn Taymiyya.[694]

With the death of Qāḍīzāde Meḥmed Efendi, the movement came under the leadership of Üstüwānī Meḥmed Efendi (d. 1661), who was even more determined than his predecessor to reform Ottoman society, pushing it towards a "return to the roots," with regard to Islamic religious practice. With the growth of the movement, its activists embraced the use of violence, beginning to enter mosques, Sufi brotherhood lodges and cafes to punish those who contravened their view of Islamic orthodoxy. Despite this, the movement failed to influence the religious environment of the Ottoman Empire, which was not receptive to the reforming influence of the theses of Ibn Taymiyya and his successors, and was deeply involved in the life of Sufi brotherhoods. Because of this, the influence of the Qāḍīzādeli gradually declined until it disappeared.

Two centuries later, in a very marginal area of the Ottoman Empire, the central region of the Arabian desert called the Najd, and in a totally different intellectual context, another movement revived and consolidated the polemics against intermediation and intercession. This movement developed from the preaching of the ḥanbalite theologian Muḥammad Ibn ʿAbd al- Wahhāb (d. 1792), and took the teachings of Ibn Taymiyya to their extreme consequences. This movement, which would be called "Wahhabism" by its adversaries after the name of its eponymous founder, thanks to its religious and political alliance with the Saʿūd dynasty, took control of the Arabian Peninsula over the following centuries until its final conquest in 1932 with the creation of modern-day Saudi Arabia. Again, one of the major polemical targets is the doctrinal Sufism of Ibn al-ʿArabī and the world of Sufi brotherhoods. Particularly vehement is the opposition to practices related to intermediation and intercession. Indeed, Wahhabism inherits the activism of Ibn Taymiyya, and from the very beginning is distinguished by a certain

693 Mustapha Sheikh, *Ottoman Puritanism and its Discontents: Aḥmad al-Rūmī al-Āqḥiṣārī and the Qāḍīzādelis* (Oxford: Oxford University Press, 2016), 102–103, 107, 139–140.
694 Ibid., 42.

tendency to put its beliefs into practice. While Ibn ʿAbd al-Wahhāb's work does not contain much criticism of intermediation and intercession, the real change is that he, and especially the Wahhabi scholars who would come after him, obtained permission from the ruling dynasty to destroy the main places where intercession could be practiced.

Theological controversies on intercession would continue in the centuries to come; numerous polemical or apologetic works would be published, and this is a trend that does not cease to the present day. Among the most relevant works of this literature, we can point to the text "The Proofs of Truth, on Seeking Help through the Lord of Creation" (*Shawāhid al-ḥaqq fī istighātha bi-sayyid al-khalq*), composed by the scholar and Sufi Yūsuf al-Nabahānī (d. 1932).[695] This text is a refutation of the Wahhabi and Salafist school contemporary with him, and in particular of the theses on intermediation and intercession by Maḥmūd Shukrī al-Ālūsī (d. 1924), who in turn responded with two treatises against Nabahānī.[696]

Another well-known controversy on intercession is the one between the Moroccan *ḥadīth* scholar and Sufi Aḥmad al-Ghumarī (d. 1961) and the influential Syrian Salafist traditionalist of Albanian origin Muḥammad Naṣīr al-Dīn al-Albānī (d. 1999). The latter dedicates a treatise to the subject entitled "Intermediation: types and rules" (*al-Tawassul: anwāʿuhu wa-aḥkāmu-hu*), in which he resumes Ibn Taymiyya's theses, refining his method and rejecting a number of *ḥadīth* often used by Sunni scholars to endorse intercession but considered by him to be non-authentic. In the second part, Albānī instead directly attacks the theses of the Syrian scholar and Sufi Muḥammad Saʿīd Ramaḍān al-Būṭī (d. 2013).[697] In the same period, ʿAbd Allāh al-Ghumarī (m. 1993), son of Aḥmad al-Ghumarī and also an important scholar and Sufi, published refutations of Albānī's theses, some of which are dedicated to intermediation and intercession. The most important is entitled "The Gift of the Discerning through the Lawfulness of Intermediation through Prophets and Saints" (*Itḥāf al-adhkiyāʾ bi-jawāz al-tawassul bi-l-anbiyāʾ wa-l-awliyāʾ*).[698]

As far as the Twelver Shiʿi context is concerned, as we have seen, not even the most rigid of the *Akhbārī* scholars, Majlisī (d. 1699), who also strongly raged against

---

695 Yūsuf ibn Ismāʿīl al-Nabahānī, *Shawāhid al-ḥaqq fī istighātha bi-sayyid al-khalq* (Bayrūt: Dār al-kutub al-ʿilmiyya, 2007).

696 Maḥmūd Shukrī al-Ālūsī, *Āyat al-kubrā ʿalā ḍalāl al-Nabahānī fī rāʾiyatihi al-ṣughrā* (al-Riyāḍ: Dār al-miʿrāj al-duwalīya li-l-nashr, 2002); Maḥmūd Shukrī al-Ālūsī, *Ghāyat al-amānī fī al-radd ʿalā al-Nabahānī*, (al-Riyāḍ: Maktabat al-rushd, 2005).

697 Muḥammad Naṣīr al-Dīn al-Albānī, *al-Tawassul anwāʿu-hu wa aḥkāmu-hu* (al-Riyāḍ: Maktabat al-maʿārif, 2001).

698 ʿAbd Allāh al-Ghumarī, *Itḥāf al-adhkiyāʾ bi-jawāz al-tawassul bi-l-anbiyāʾ wa-l-awliyāʾ* (al-Qāhira: Maktabat al-Qāhira, 2012).

Sufi brotherhoods, opposed practices related to intermediation and intercession. This situation does not change throughout the history of modern Twelver Shiʿism, with one notable exception, represented by the work and preaching of the reformist theologian Sharīʿat Sangelajī (d. 1891). In his work, he so vehemently opposes the practice of intermediation and intercession that his contemporaries labelled him a "Wahhabite," comparing him to Ibn Taymiyya and Muḥammad ibn ʿAbd al-Wahhāb. However, specialists believe there are more differences than similarities between the Iranian polemicist and the two celebrated authorities of the Islamic Reformation.[699]

4 The destruction of places of intercession: tombs and shrines

The opposition of the various movements of the Islamic Reformation to intermediation and intercession had a very significant consequence. We have mentioned Ibn Taymiyya's early efforts to destroy relics in order to prevent their veneration materially. We then observed attempts by Qāḍīzādeli activists to physically block Sufi gatherings and close down the headquarters of the brotherhoods. However, it was not until the nineteenth century that successful attempts were made to eliminate the places where intercession could be practised, namely tombs and shrines. This would take place during the campaign of conquest of the Arabian Peninsula, then under the control of the Ottoman Empire, by militias led by the Saʿūd dynasty, allied with supporters of the doctrines of Muḥammad ibn ʿAbd al-Wahhāb.

This campaign took place in two distinct phases. In the first phase, in 1802, an army of 12,000 soldiers from the Najd region stormed the Shiʿite holy city of Karbalāʾ in Iraq and killed about 5,000 people before seizing a large booty and destroying every holy site in the city, especially the shrine of al-Ḥusayn. The following year, the same army stormed the region of Ḥijāz, managing to enter Mecca for the first time, where they engaged in the first wave of destruction of shrines, tombs and relics before being subsequently defeated and repulsed in Najd by the Egyptian army under the orders of the Ottoman Empire.[700]

In the second phase, between 1913 and 1927, a division of the Saudi army, the *Ikhwān* (the brothers), a radical Wahhabi militia, took control of the Ḥijāz region and completed the work begun in the previous century, razing all the shrines and

699 Ali Rahnema, *Shi'i Reformation in Iran. The Life and Theology of Shari'at Sangelaji* (Oxon-New York: Routledge, 2016).
700 Alexei Vassiliev, *The History of Saudi Arabia* (London: Saqi Books, 2013), 188–200.

tombs that had been rebuilt by the Ottoman rulers, and eradicating in particular some Sufi brotherhoods that had played a role in the management of the shrines, which until then had been under the protection of the Empire.[701] Although the exact details and extent of the destruction are unknown, the result was certainly devastating when one compares the religious landscape of the contemporary Ḥijāz region with that of the rest of the Islamic world. An example of a sacred site razed to the ground at this stage is the so-called Tomb of Eve in Jeddah. Historians of the late nineteenth century described the tomb as more than 120 metres long and only 3.3 metres wide. It was destroyed in 1928, while in 1975, the ground nearby was sealed with cement to prevent pilgrims from praying there.[702]

This effort of purification from all that does not adhere to the theological thought of the Islamic Reformation movements still resonates and progressively expands to all vestiges of the past, to the most important sites of the sacred geography of the Ḥijāz and in particular to those connected to the life of the prophet Muḥammad. In the contemporary Ḥijāz region, the only ancient and medieval vestiges that have survived are the Kaʿba in Mecca and the green dome above the shrine of the prophet Muḥammad in Medina, which also protects the shrines of the caliphs Abū Bakr and ʿUmar, although in the recent past several calls have been made for its destruction, including by the Saudi Ministry of Religious Affairs.[703] All cemetery buildings and gravestones have been destroyed, particularly in the ancient cemeteries of Medina and Uḥud, where the Prophet's most important family members and Companions are buried. Today, their graves are indicated by simple stones.[704] The dome that is said to have protected the teeth that the Prophet lost during the battle of Uḥud was razed to the ground, and the relic is now lost, like all the relics that the Ottoman rulers failed to transfer to Constantinople before the Saʿūd dynasty came to power.[705] The tomb of the Prophet's mother, Amīna bint Wahb, located in the village of al-Abwāʾ, was also demolished in 1998, while in 2002, the mosque and shrine of Jaʿfar al-Ṣādiq, located near Medina,

701 David Commins, *The Wahhabi mission and Saudi Arabia* (London-New York: I.B. Tauris, 2006), 80–92.

702 Simon Ross, *Force and fanaticism: Wahhabism in Saudi Arabia and beyond* (London: Hurst & Company, 2015), 175–190.

703 Ondřej Beránek and Pavel Ťupek, *The Temptation of Graves in Salafi Islam. Iconoclasm, Destruction and Idolatry* (Edinburgh: Edinburgh University Press, 2018), 101–102.

704 Werner Ende, "Baqīʿ al-Gharqad," in *EI3*; Ondřej Beránek and Pavel Ťupek, *The Temptation of Graves in Salafi Islam. Iconoclasm, Destruction and Idolatry* (Edinburgh: Edinburgh University Press, 2018), 108–109.

705 Simon Ross, *Force and fanaticism: Wahhabism in Saudi Arabia and beyond* (London: Hurst & Company, 2015), 188.

was blown up with explosives.[706] Finally, in Mecca, the house of Khadīja, the Prophet's first wife, was recently destroyed to be replaced by public toilets.[707]

What drove the Saudi power, under the leadership of the Wahhabi religious authorities, to undertake these destructions? Their main reason is that the believer should focus only on God and not turn his worship towards human buildings and objects.[708] Some sayings of the Prophet forbid building over graves, to prevent the veneration of the deceased from turning into idolatry over time. Nevertheless, Sunni scholars maintain that this applies to the graves of ordinary mortals, which should not be monumental, while the graves of prophets and saints should be built and solid, out of respect for them, to remember where they are buried and to protect the place. In any case, building a height difference on all types of tombs is useful to allow them to be recognised and to prevent people from praying or walking on them.[709]

However, these are the places where intermediation and intercession are practised, and therefore their destruction represents an opportunity for the authorities of some Islamic Reformation movements to counter what they see as innovations and abominable practices of associationism (*shirk*).

In recent years, new destructions have been carried out by radical reformist, Salafist and Wahhabi groups. The most significant of these began in the period following the so-called "Arab Springs' of 2011, during the temporary rise to power of political parties linked to the The Society of the Muslim Brothers. During this phase, some radical groups carried out a large number of demolitions of holy sites. The governments led by the The Society of the Muslim Brothers (Egypt and Tunisia) did not take any measures to stop the destruction, allowing the groups to act, and it was only with their downfall, in 2013, that the situation came back under control.[710]

At the same time, radical Salafist and Wahhabist militias engaged in armed conflicts in Libya and Syria, and the militias of the ephemeral "Islamic State" in Syria and Iraq launched a new wave of destruction. They used heavy vehicles, jackhammers, automatic weapons, and explosives to achieve their goal. Their main tar-

---

706 Ondřej Beránek and Pavel Ťupek, *The Temptation of Graves in Salafi Islam. Iconoclasm, Destruction and Idolatry* (Edinburgh: Edinburgh University Press, 2018), 186–187.
707 Ziauddin Sardar, *Mecca the Sacred City* (London: Bloomsbury, 2014), 343–364.
708 ʿAbd al-ʿAzīz Ibn Bāz et al, *al-Bidaʿ wa-l-muḥaddathāt wa mā lā aṣla lahu* (al-Riyāḍ: Dār Ibn Khuzayma, 1998) 294.
709 Ondřej Beránek and Pavel Ťupek, *The Temptation of Graves in Salafi Islam. Iconoclasm, Destruction and Idolatry* (Edinburgh: Edinburgh University Press, 2018), 18–40.
710 Jon B. Alterman (ed.), *Religious Radicalism after the Arab Uprisings* (Lanham, Boulder, New York, London: Center for Strategic & International Studies, Rowman & Littlefield, 2015), 122–143.

gets were buildings built on tombs, Sufi shrines, Shiʿa shrines, non-Islamic religious sites, archaeological remains and some statues.[711] Again, with the end of hostilities, the situation normalised, and there have been no such cases of destruction in recent years. However, these episodes show how a purely theological issue can manage to reverberate on the course of historical events and leave deep traces, as happened in sixteenth and seventeenth century Europe when the Calvinists, in particular, destroyed a large number of Catholic churches and relics throughout Europe. Similarly, Islamic Reformation activists sought to enforce their theological theses by destroying religious monuments, leaving a very strong imprint on the urban and architectural religious landscape of the contemporary Islamic world.

711 Luca Patrizi, "A New Wave of Iconoclasm? The Destruction of Sacred Places in the Contemporary Islamic world," in *Constructing and Contesting Holy Places in Medieval Islam and Beyond*, edited by Andreas Görke and Mattia Guidetti. (Leiden: Brill, 2023), 434–465.

Conclusion

The primary concern underlying this study is to contribute to the revitalisation and promotion of the field of Islamic theology which, as we have already had occasion to say, has not received adequate attention from specialists in Islamic studies to date. Moreover, in this context, the topic of intermediation and intercession has been almost totally, and unjustly, neglected, as I believe has become even more evident by the end of this survey.

Indeed, an in-depth analysis of the notion of intermediation and intercession has allowed the emergence of a primary issue that characterises this belief in both Sunni and Twelver Shiʿism, and which I will now attempt to discuss: the relationship between God and the creation. The position of Sunnism and Twelver Shiʿism postulates the existence of a connection between God and creation, which can be identified precisely in the notion of intermediation analysed so far. In the first part of this study, I dealt with the entities that act as intermediaries between God and creation. The main one is the Spirit (*al-rūḥ*) and its forms, among which we can mention the archangel Gabriel (Jibrīl) and other angelic creatures, the sacred texts (*kutub*) and in particular the Qurʾān. Another dimension of the descent of the Spirit analysed here is the prophetic function itself, as a complement to the descent of Revelation through the holy books, and in particular the conclusive and all-encompassing prophetic function embodied in the Revelation descended upon Muḥammad.

Does the Spirit, when descending, represent a veritable spiritual connection between God and creation? This is perhaps the biggest problem Islamic theology has faced throughout its history, in the form of the controversy over the created or uncreated Qurʾān, which shows undeniable similarities to the controversy over the nature of the Word in early Christianity.

The opponents of the doctrine of the uncreated Qurʾān, represented in particular by the Muʿtazilite theologians, feared in this doctrine a danger to their belief in the absolute transcendence of God with respect to creation and, therefore, rejected it with great vehemence and even resorting, in a political phase favourable to them, to the persecution of opponents through an inquisitorial tribunal (*miḥna*). Sunni theologians sought to overcome this problem through a compromise that would not endanger the doctrine of divine Unity (*tawḥīd*). The view they held was therefore that the Qurʾān was uncreated in its essence but created in its material supports such as the letters of which it is composed and the paper on which it is transcribed. However, according to this doctrine, the Qurʾān that is "in the hearts" of the believers, the one memorised and recited, remains uncreated in

https://doi.org/10.1515/9783111500966-016

its intimate nature. This indicates that, ultimately, according to Sunni doctrine, the divine can "dwell" in creation, albeit in a recondite spiritual dimension.

The question concerning the nature of prophecy is also part of this issue. Starting from the theological elaboration of one of the most influential Muslim scholars ever, Muḥammad al-Shāfiʿī (d. 820), Sunnism considers the Prophet's teaching and behaviour (*sunna*) as an integral part of Revelation, as a complement to the descent of the Qur'ān. Moreover, from this conviction Shāfiʿī elaborates the definition of Sunnism, which is thus the religious position of those who regard the Prophet's sunna, like the Qur'ān, as divine Revelation. The Qur'ān and the sunna thus represent a connection with the divine, but what happens when the Revelation of the Qur'ān ceases and the Prophet himself takes leave of this world? In Sunni theology, this gap is filled by recourse to the normative value of majority consensus (*ijmāʿ*) on a given theological and legal issue. This conception is, as we have seen, the basis of the very denomination of Sunnism as "People of the sunna and the community" (*ahl al-sunna wa-l-jamāʿa*). This formula can be understood as follows: Sunnis are those who derive the foundations of their religion from the Qur'ān, which is not mentioned in it because its authority is accepted indiscriminately by all those who call themselves Muslims; from the sunna of the Prophet, as a complement to the Qur'anic Revelation; and finally, from the recognition that Revelation can also endure through recourse to the majority opinion of the community – implied, of its scholars – (*ijmāʿ*). If, on the other hand, one considers the position of Twelver Shiʿism, one realises that while the first two sources of Revelation, though not made explicit, are the same, Revelation endures after the Prophet's death through the Imāms, who are his heirs. They are in constant contact with creation even after their major Occultation (*ghayba*), following which they dwell in the unseen world (*al-ghayb*), and there is no need to resort to the majority consensus of scholars. However, the contemporary doctrine of the "guardianship (or political power) of the jurisprudent" (*wilāyat al-faqīh*) represents a solution to this problem close to that of the Sunni *ijmāʿ*. What is ultimately interesting for this specific discussion is that both the Sunnite and the Twelver Shiʿa positions envisage the possibility of the permanence of a connection between God and creation even after the Prophet's death.

In addition to this, esoteric doctrines have emerged in both contexts, which, as we have observed, also grant men, and not only prophets, the possibility of rising to spiritual degrees close to God, and thus being able to represent a constant connection between God and creation, even after their death. The figures analysed in the two contexts, respectively the Pole Helper (*al-Quṭb al-ghawth*) and the Imām, are the highest example of this possibility, and below them, as far as the Sufi Sunni context is concerned, we find the friends of God or saints (*awliyāʾ*).

The doctrine of Sunni and Twelver Shiʿa intermediation and intercession represents another singular modality of this connection, allowing the prophetic function to continue even after Muḥammad's death. The possibility for believers to have recourse to the Prophet's function of intermediation and intercession at every moment of their lives creates, in this respect, a constant connection between God and creation.

An antithetical position to this is that represented by the muʿtazilite doctrine, according to which there is no possibility of a connection between God and creation through the earthly Qurʾān, which is created as the creation itself, nor through recourse to intermediation and intercession, which as we have seen are dismissed as being at odds with divine omnipotence and transcendence.

The position of the various movements of the Islamic Reformation in relation to intermediation and intercession also contrasts with the Sunni and Twelver Shiʿa view, severely restricting the possibility of a connection between God and creation through the rejection of the possibility of recourse to the Prophet after his death and before the Day of Judgement. The opposition is even greater with regard to the possibility of a connection between God and creation represented by the doctrine of the Twelver Shiʿa Imām and the doctrine of holiness in Sufism.

The rejection of intermediation and intercession was accompanied in the reformist milieu by the conviction that, despite the belief in the total transcendence of God with respect to creation, it is possible to address Him directly for every request and invocation without resorting to the prophets or other creatures, depending on their degree of closeness to God. However, as we have observed, this conviction, on the part of Islamic Reformation movements, is not limited to theological speculations, but, at least since the nineteenth century, and more intensely in recent decades, has emerged forcefully within the history of contemporary Islamic societies, managing to imprint deep traces even in the urban and architectural religious landscape, through the destructions recalled in the last chapter of this study.

This long journey, in conclusion, has led us through the origin and development of a theological doctrine that is apparently secondary and neglected by specialists in contemporary Islamic studies, a doctrine whose importance we have tried, on the contrary, to highlight. The concern of this study has not, however, been only of a theological and doctrinal nature, as in-depth references have constantly been provided in relation to how these doctrines have spread in the common feeling of different Muslim populations, and what religious and esoteric practices they have helped to shape and spread.

Bibliography

Primary sources

ʿAbd al-Ḥalīm Maḥmūd. *al-Quṭb al-shahīd ʿAbd al-Salām ibn Bashīsh.* al-Qāhira: Dār al-Maʿārif, 1976.

Abū Ḥanīfa al-Nuʿmān. *Imām Abū Ḥanīfa's Al-Fiqh al-Akbar Explained by Abū ʿl-Muntahā al-Maghnīsāwī with Selections from ʿAlī al-Qārī's Commentary, including Abū Ḥanīfa's Kitāb al-Waṣiyya.* London-Santa Barbara: White Thread Press, 2014.

Abū Ḥanīfa al-Nuʿmān. *Waṣiyya al-imām Abū Ḥanīfa al-Nuʿmān.* Bayrūt: Dār Ibn Ḥazm, 1997.

Ajurrī (al-), Abū Bakr. *Kitāb al-sharīʿa.* al-Riyāḍ: Dār al-waṭan, 1997.

al-Shaykh al-Mufīd, Muḥammad ibn Muḥammad al-Nuʿmān. *Awāʾil al-maqālāt fi al-madhāhib al-mukhtārāt.* Bayrūt: Dār al-kitāb al-islāmī, 1983.

al-Shaykh al-Mufīd, Muḥammad ibn Muḥammad al-Nuʿmān. *The Emendation of A Shiʿite Creed, a translation of Taṣḥīḥu ʿl-Iʿtiqād of Abū ʿAbdillāh Muḥammad ibn Muḥammad ibn Nuʿmān, Known ash-Shaykh al-Mufīd (336/948 or 338/950–413/1022),* tr. by ʿIrfān ʿAbdu ʿl-Ḥamīd, 2 Vols. Tehran: World Organisation for Islamic Services (WOFIS), 2006.

Albānī (al-), Muḥammad Naṣīr al-Dīn. *al-Tawassul anwāʿu-hu wa aḥkāmu-hu.* al-Riyāḍ: Maktabat al-maʿārif, 2001.

Ālūsī (al-), Maḥmūd Shukrī. *Āyat al-kubrā ʿalā ḍalāl al-Nabahānī fī rāʾiyatihi al-ṣughrā.* al-Riyāḍ: Dār al-miʿrāj al-duwalīya li-l-nashr, 2002.

Ālūsī (al-), Maḥmūd Shukrī. *Ghāyat al-amānī fī al-radd ʿalā al-Nabahānī*, 2 vols. al-Riyāḍ: Maktabat al-rushd, 2005.

Ashʿarī (al-), Abū al-Ḥasan. *Maqālāt al-Islāmiyyīn wa-ikhtilāf al-muṣallīn*, edited by Helmut Ritter. Wiesbaden: Franz Steiner, 1963.

ʿAṭṭār (al-), Farīd al-Dīn. *Takhkirat al-awliyāʾ*. Dimashq: Dār al-maktabī, 2009.

Azraqī (al-), Abū al-Walīd Muḥammad ibn ʿAbd Allāh ibn Aḥmad. *Akhbār Makka wa-mā jāʾ fīhā min al-āthār.* Makkat al-mukarrama: Maktabat al-asadī, 2003.

Bayḍāwī (al-), ʿAbd Allāh Ibn ʿUmar; Iṣfahānī, Maḥmūd ibn ʿAbd al-Raḥmān. *Nature, Man and God in Medieval Islam Abd Allah Baydawi's Text, Tawaliʿ al-Anwar Min Mataliʿ al-Anzar, Along with Mahmud Isfahani's commentary Mataliʿ al-Anzar, Sharh Tawaliʿ al-Anwar, ed. and tr. by Edwin Elliott Calverley and James W. Pollock*, Volume One. Leiden: Brill, 2002.

Bayḍāwī (al-), ʿAbd Allāh Ibn ʿUmar. *The Lights of Revelation and the Secrets of Interpretation. Hizb I of the Commentary on the Qurʾān by al-Bayḍāwī, Arabic Edition & English Translation with Introduction and notes by Gibril Fouad Haddad.* Manchester: Beacon Books, 2016.

Bayhaqī (al-), Abū Bakr Aḥmad ibn Ḥusayn. *Dalāʾil al-nubuwwa wa-maʿrifat aḥwāl ṣāḥib al-sharīʿa*, 7 vols. Bayrūt: Dār al-kutub al-ʿilmiyya, 1988, 2019.

Bayhaqī (al-), Abū Bakr Aḥmad ibn Ḥusayn. *Ḥayāt al-anbiyāʾ ṣalawāt Allāh ʿalayhim baʿd wafātihim.* al-Madīna al-munawwara: Maktaba al-ʿulūm wa al-ḥikma, 1993.

Bayhaqī (al-), Abū Bakr Aḥmad ibn Ḥusayn. *The Creed of Imam Bayhaqī, An Abridged Translation of al-Iʿtiqād wa-l-hidāya ilā sabīl al-rashād*, tr. by Nasir Abdussalam. London: Turath Publishing, 2017.

Būṣīrī (al-), Sharaf al-Dīn Abī ʿAbd Allāh Muḥammad ibn Saʿīd. *Dīwān al-Būṣīrī*, Bayrūt: Dār al-kutub al-ʿilmiyya, 2005.

Dhahabī (al-), Shams al-Dīn. *Ithbāt al-shafāʿa.* al-Riyāḍ: Maktaba aḍwaʾ al-salaf, 2000.

Fīrūzābādī (al-), Majīd al-Dīn Muḥammad ibn Yaʿqūb. *al-Ṣilāt wa al-bushr fī al-ṣalāt ʿalā khayr al-bashar.* Dimashq: Dār al-Qurʾān, 1966.

https://doi.org/10.1515/9783111500966-017

Fyzee, Asaf Ali Asghar. A *Shi'ite Creed, A translation of Risālatu'l-I'tiqādāt of Muḥammad b. 'Alī Ibn Bābawayhi al-Qummī known as Shaykh Ṣadūq*. Oxford: Oxford University Press, 1942.

Ghazālī (al-), Abū Ḥāmid. *al-Maḍnūn bihi 'alā ghayr ahlihi*. In *Majmū'at rasā'il al-imām al-Ghazālī*, ed. Ibrāhīm Āmīn Muḥammad. al-Qāhira: al-Maktaba al-tawfīqiyya, 2002.

Ghazālī (al-), Abū Ḥāmid. *Iḥyā' 'ulūm al-dīn*, 9 vols. Jadda: Dār al-minhaj, 2011.

Ghazālī (al-), Abū Ḥāmid. *The Remembrance of Death and the Afterlife – Kitāb Dhikr al-mawt wa-mā ba'dahu – Book XL of the Revival of the Religious Sciences – Iḥyā' 'ulūm al-dīn, tr. with an Introduction and notes by T.J. Winter.* Cambridge: Islamic Texts Society, 2015.

Ghumarī (al-), 'Abd Allāh. *Itḥāf al-adhkiyā' bi-jawāz al-tawassul bi-l-anbiyā' wa-l-awliyā'*. al-Qāhira: Maktabat al-Qāhira, 2012.

Ḥalabī (al-), 'Alī ibn Burhān al-Dīn. *Insān al-'uyūn fī sīrat al-amīn al-ma'mūn*. Bayrūt: Dār al-kutub al-'ilmiyya, 2013.

Hindī (al-), 'Alā' al-Dīn 'Alī al-Muttaqī ibn Ḥusām al-Dīn. *Kanz al-'ummāl fī sunan al-aqwāl wa-l-af'āl*. Bayrūt: Mu'assasat al-risāla, 2008.

Ibn Abī Dāwūd, Abū Bakr. *al-Ba'th wa-l-nushūr: al-ḥayā ba'd al-mawt*. al-Qāhira: Maktabat al-turāth al-islāmī, 1986.

Ibn Abī Ya'lā. *Ṭabaqāt al-ḥanābila*. al-Qāhira: Maṭba'at al-sunnat al-muḥammadiyya, 2016.

Ibn al-'Arabī, Muḥyīddīn. *al-Futūḥāt al-Makkiyya*, 13 vols., ed. Sulṭān Manṣub. Ṣan'ā': 'Āṣimat al-thaqāfa al-islāmiyya, Wazīrat al-thaqāfa, 2010.

Ibn al-'Arabī, Muḥyīddīn. *Kitāb al-qurba*. In *Rasā'il Ibn 'Arabī*, ed. Mahmūd Ghurāb. Bayrūt: Dār ṣādir, 1977.

Ibn Bāz, 'Abd al-'Azīz et al. *al-Bida' wa al-muḥaddathāt wa-mā lā aṣla lahu*. al-Riyāḍ: Dār Ibn Khuzayma, 1998.

Ibn Ḥajar al-'Asqalānī. *Fatḥ al-bārī sharḥ ṣaḥīḥ al-Bukhārī*, 13 vols. al-Qāhira: al-Maktaba al-salafiyya, 2015.

Ibn Ḥazm al-Ẓāhiri al-Andalusī. *al-Faṣl fī al-milal wa-l-ahwā' wa-l-niḥal*, 5 vols. al-Qāhira: Maktabat al-salām al-'āliyya, 1929.

Ibn Isḥāq. *The Life of Muhammad, A Translation of Ibn Isḥāq's Sīrat rasūl Allāḥ, with introduction and notes by A. Guillaume*. Oxford: Oxford University Press, 1955.

Ibn Khallikān. *Wafayāt al-a'yān wa-anbā' abnā' al-zamān*, 8 vols. Bayrūt: Dār ṣādir, 1978.

Ibn Manẓūr. *Lisān al-'arab*, 6 vols. Bayrūt: Dār al-ma'ārif, 1984–1986.

Ibn Sīda al-Mursī. *al-Muḥkam wa-l-muḥīṭ al-a'ẓam*, 11 vols. Bayrūt: Dār al-kutub al-'ilmiyya, 2000.

Ibn Taymiyya, Aḥmad. *al-Istighātha fī-lradd 'alā al-Bakrī*. al-Riyāḍ: Maktabat dār al-minhaj, 2005.

Ibn Taymiyya, Aḥmad. *al-Risāla al-ṣafadiyya, qā'ida fī taḥqīq al-risāla wa-bṭāl sawl ahl al-zaygh wa-l-ḍalāla*. al-Riyāḍ: Aḍwā' al-salaf, 2002.

Ibn Taymiyya, Aḥmad. *al-'Aqīda al-wasīṭiyya*. al-Riyāḍ: Maktaba aḍwā' al-salaf, 1999.

Ibn Taymiyya, Aḥmad. *Les intermédiaires entre Dieu et l'homme (*Risālat al-wāsiṭa bayna al-khalq wa al-ḥaqq*), traduction française suivie de Le Shaykh de l'Islam Ibn Taymiyya : chronique d'une vie de théologien militant, par Yahyā Michot, Numéro hors-série de la revue Le Musulman éditée par l'Association des Étudiants Islamiques en France.* Paris: A.E.I.F. Éditions, 1996.

Ibn Taymiyya, Aḥmad. *Majmū' fatāwa shaykh al-islām Aḥmad Ibn Taymiyya*, 37 vols, ed. 'Abd al-Raḥmān ibn Muḥammad ibn Qāsim. Madīnat al-munawwara: Wizārat al-shu'ūn al-islāmiyya wa-l-da'wa wa-l-irshād al-sa'ūdiyya, Mujamma' al-Malik Fahd li-ṭibā'at al-muṣḥaf al-sharīf, 2004.

Ibn Taymiyya, Aḥmad. *Qā'ida jalīla fī al-tawassul wa-l-wasīla*. al-Riyāḍ: Ri'asat idārat al-buḥūth al-'alamiyya wa-l-iftā' al-'āmma li-l-ṭab', 1999.

Ibn 'Abbad, Aḥmad ibn Muḥammad. *al-Mafākhir al-'aliyya fī al-ma'āthir al-shādhiliyya*. al-Qāhira: al-Maktaba al-azhariyya li-l-turāth, 2004.

Ibn 'Abbās, 'Abd Allāh. *Tanwīr al-miqbās min tafsīr Ibn 'Abbās*. Bayrūt: Dār al-kutub al-'ilmiyya, 1992.

Ibn ʿAsākir. *Tārīkh madīnat Dimashq*, 80 vols. Bayrūt: Dār al-Fikr, 1997.

Iṣfahānī (al-), Abū Nuʿaym. *Ḥilyat al-awliyāʾ wa-ṭabaqāt al-aṣfiyāʾ*, 10 vols. Bayrūt: Dār al-kutub al-ʿilmiyya, 1997.

Jīlī (al-), ʿAbd al-Karīm. *Qāb qawsayn wa-multaqā al-nāmūsayn fī maʿrifat sayyid al-kawnayn*. al-Qāhira: Dār al-āfāq al-ʿarabiyya, 2006.

Kharkūshī (al-), Abū Saʿd ʿAbd al-Mālik ibn Abū ʿUthmān Muḥammad. *Manāḥil al-shifāʾ wa-manāhil al-ṣafā bi-taḥqīq kitāb sharaf al-muṣṭafā*, 6 vols. Makkat al-mukarrama: Dār al-bashāʾir al-islāmiyya, 2003.

Lālakāʾī (al-), Abū al-Qāsim. *Sharḥ uṣūl iʿtiqād ahl al-sunna wa-l-jamāʿa min al-kitāb wa-l-sunna wa-ijmāʿ al-ṣaḥāba*. Iskandariyya: Maktabat dār al-baṣīra, 2001.

Majlisī (al-), Muḥammad Bāqir. *Biḥār al-anwār al-jāmiʿa li-durar akhbār al-aʾimma al-aṭhār*, 110 vols. Bayrūt: Dār al-iḥyāʾ al-turāth al-ʿarabī, 1983.

Mānkdīm, Aḥmad ibn al-Ḥusayn ibn Abī Hāshim (incorrect attribution to ʿAbd al-Jabbār ibn Aḥmad). *Sharḥ uṣūl al-khamsa*, edited by ʿAbd al-Karīm ʿUthmān. al-Qāhira: Maktabat wahba, 1965.

Nabahānī (al-), Yūsuf ibn Ismāʿīl. *Afḍal al-ṣalāwāt ʿalā sayyid al-sādāt*. Dimashq: Dār iqrāʾ, 2001.

Nabahānī (al-), Yūsuf ibn Ismāʿīl. *Jāmiʿ al-ṣalawāt wa-majmaʿ al-saʿādāt fī-l-ṣalā ʿalā sayyid al-sādāt*. Bayrūt: Dār al-kutub al-ʿilmiyya, 2005.

Nabahānī (al-), Yūsuf ibn Ismāʿīl. *Saʿādat al-dārayn fī-l-ṣalā ʿalā sayyid al-kawnayn*. Bayrūt: Dār al-Fikr, 1980.

Nabahānī (al-), Yūsuf ibn Ismāʿīl. *Shawāhid al-ḥaqq fī istighātha bi-sayyid al-khalq*. Bayrūt: Dār al-kutub al-ʿilmiyya, 2007.

Nābulusī (al-), ʿAbd al-Ghānī. *Sharḥ al-ṣalā al-kubrā li-l-shaykh al-akbar Ibn ʿArabī*. Bayrūt: Books-Publisher, 2012.

Numayrī (al-), Muḥammad ibn ʿAbd al-Raḥmān. *Kitāb al-iʿlām bi-faḍl al-ṣalāt ʿalā al-nabī wa-l-salām*. Bayrūt: Dār al-kutub al-ʿilmiyya, 2009.

Qāḍī ʿIyāḍ (al-), al-Yaḥṣubī. *al-Shifāʾ bi-taʿrīf ḥuqūq al-*muṣṭafā, ed. ʿAbduh ʿAlī Kūshak. Dubai: Jāʾizat Dubay al-dawliyya li-l-Qurʾān al-karīm, 2013.

Qādirī (al-), Ismāʿīl ibn Muḥammad Saʿīd. *al-Fuyūḍāt al-rabbaniyya fī-l-māthur wa-wird al-qādiriyya*. al-Qāhira: Maktabat Muṣṭafa al-Bāb al-Ḥalabī, 1934.

Qaṣrī (al-), Abū Muḥammad ʿAbd al-Jalīl ibn Mūsā ibn ʿAbd al-Jalīl al-Andalūsī. *Shuʿab al-īmān*. Bayrūt: Dār al-kutub al-ʿilmiyya, 1995.

Qummī (al-), ʿAbbās. *Mafātiḥ al-jinān*. Bayrūt: Dār al-aḍwāʾ, 2014.

Qurṭubī (al-), Abū ʿAbd Allāh. *al-Jāmiʿ li-aḥkām al-Qurʾān wa-l-mubayyin li-mā taḍammanahu min al-sunna wa-āyyi-l-furqān*, 24 vols. Bayrūt: Muʾassasat al-risāla, 2006.

Qurṭubī (al-), Abū ʿAbd Allāh. *Kitāb al-tadhkira bi-aḥwāl al-mawtā wa-umūr al-ākhira*, 3 vols., al-Riyāḍ: Maktabat dār al-minhāj, 2004.

Rāzī (al-), Fakhr al-Dīn. *al-Shafāʿa al-uẓmā fī yawm al-qiyāma*. al-Qāhira: al-Maktaba al-azhariyya li-l-turāth, 1988.

Sakhāwī (al-), Muḥammad ibn ʿAbd al-Raḥmān. *al-Qawl al-badīʿ fī al-ṣalā ʿalā al-ḥabīb al-shafīʿ*. al-Madīna al-munawwara: Muʾassasat al-rayyān, 2002.

Shaʿrānī (al-), ʿAbd al-Wahhāb. *Lawāqiḥ al-anwār al-qudsīyya fī bayān al-ʿuhūd al-muḥammadiyya*. Bayrūt: Dār al-kutub al-ʿilmiyya, 2005.

Subkī (al-), Taqī al-Dīn. *Shifāʾ al siqām fī ziyārat khayr al-anām*. Bayrūt: Dār al-kutub al-ʿilmiyya, 2008.

Sulamī (al-), ʿAbd al-Raḥmān. *Ḥaqāʾiq al-tafsīr. Tafsīr al-Qurʾān al-ʿazīz*, 2 vols. Bayrūt: Dār al-kutub al-ʿilmiyya, 2001.

Suyūṭī (al-), Jalāl al-Dīn; Maḥallī (al-), Jalāl al-Dīn. *Tafsīr al-Jalālayn*. al-Qāhira:Dār al-ḥadīth, 2001.

Suyūṭī (al-), Jalāl al-Dīn. *Taʾrīkh al-khulafāʾ*. Bayrūt: Muʾassasat ʿIzz al-Dīn, 1992.

Ṭabarī (al-), Muḥammad Ibn Jarīr. *Tafsir Ṭabarī: Jāmiʿ al-bayān ʿan taʾwīl āyy al-Qurʾān*, 25 vols. Jīza: Hajr li-l-ṭibāʿa wa-l-nashr, 2008.
Ṭabarī (al-), Muḥammad ibn Jarīr. *The History of Al-Tabari Volume 3: The Children of Israel*, tr. by Franz Rosenthal. Albany: State University of New York Press, 1989.
Ṭaḥāwī (al-), Aḥmad. *The Creed of Imam al-Ṭaḥāwī. Translated, Introduced, And Annotated by Hamza Yusuf.* Berkeley: Zaytuna Institute, 2008.
Tirmidhī (al-), al-Ḥakīm. *Naṣṣ risāla budūwwu sha'n Abī ʿAbd Allāh Muḥammad al-Ḥakīm al-Tirmidhī*, in *Kitāb khatm al-awliyāʾ*, ed. ʿUthmān Ismāʿīl Yaḥyā. Bayrūt: al-Maṭbuʿat al-kāthūliyya, 1965.
Tirmidhī (al-), al-Ḥakīm. *Thalāthat muṣannafāt li-l-Ḥakīm al-Tirmidhī*, ed. Berndt Radtke. Shtūtgārt et Bayrūt: Dār al-nashr Frānts Shtāynar, 1992–1996.
Tirmidhī (al-), al-Ḥakīm. *The Concept of Sainthood in Early Islamic Mysticism, tr. by Bernd Radtke and John O'Kane.* Richmond Surrey: Curzon Press, 1996.
Wāqidī (al-). *Kitāb al-maghāzī*, 3 vols., edited by Marsden Jones. London: Oxford University Press, 1966.
Zabīdī (al-), Murtaḍā al-Ḥusaynī. *Tāj al-ʿarūs min jawāhir al-qāmūs*, 40 vols. al-Kuwayt: Muʾassasat al-kuwayt li-l-taqaddum al-ʿilmī, 2001.

Secondary sources

Abdulsater, Hussein Ali. *Shiʿi Doctrine, Muʿtazili Theology: Al-Sharīf al-Murtaḍā and Imami Discourse.* Edinburgh: Edinburgh University Press, 2017.
Abrams, Daniel. "The Evolution of the Intention of Prayer to the 'Special Cherub': From the Earliest Works to a Late Unknown Treatise." *Frankfurter Judaistische Beiträge* 22 (1995): 1–26.
Afifi Al-Akiti, Muhammad. "The Good, the Bad, and the Ugly of Falsafa: Al-Ghazālī's *Maḍnūn*, *Tahāfut*, and *Maqāṣid*, with Particular Attention to their Falsafī Treatments of God's Knowledge of Temporal Events." In *Avicenna and his Legacy: A Golden Age of Science and Philosophy*, edited by Yitzhak Tzvi Langermann. Turnhout: Brepols, 2010, 51–100.
Afsaruddin, Asma. "Shafāʿa." In *The Qurʾan: An Encyclopaedia*, edited by Oliver Leaman. London: Routledge, 2006, 582–583.
Ahmed, Shahab. *Before Orthodoxy: The Satanic Verses in Early Islam.* Cambridge, Massachusetts: Harvard University Press, 2017.
Aladdin, Bakri. "Oneness of Being (*waḥdat al-wujūd*). The term and the doctrine." *Journal of the Muhyiddin Ibn Arabi Society* 51 (2012): 3–26.
Albarrán Iruela, Javier. "Intercession." In *Islam. A Worldwide Encyclopedia*, edited by Cenap Cakmak. Santa Barbara: ABC-CLIO, 2017, 725–728.
Alterman, Jon B., ed. *Religious Radicalism after the Arab Uprisings.* Lanham, Boulder, New York, London: Center for Strategic & International Studies, Rowman & Littlefield, 2015.
Álvarez Millán, Cristina. "Bloodletting and cupping." In *EI*^{3}.
Andani, Khalil. "Metaphysics of Muhammad. The Nur Muhammad from Imam Ja'far al-Sadiq (d. 148/765) to Nasir al-Din al-Tusi (d. 672/1274)." *Journal of Sufi Studies* 8 (2019): 99–175.
Andræ, Tor, *Die person Muhammeds in lehre und glauben seiner gemeinde.* Stockholm: Norstedt & Toner, 1917.
Asani, Ali Sultaan. "Devotional Practices." In *The Shiʿi World: Pathways in Tradition and Modernity*, edited by Farhad Daftary, Amyn Sajoo, Shainool Jiwa. London – New York: I.B. Tauris, 2015.
Ayoub, Mahmoud. "Arbaʿīn." In *EIr.*

Ayoub, Mahmoud. *Redemptive Suffering in Islam. A Study of the Devotional Aspects of ʿĀshūrāʾ in Twelver Shīʿism.* The Hague-Paris-New York: Mouton Publishers, 1978.
Balserak Jon et al. "Intercession, Intercessory Prayer." In *Encyclopedia of the Bible and its Reception (EBR), Vol. 13, Integrity – Jesuit Order,* edited by Dale Clifford Allison et al. Berlin: De Gruyter, 2016, 2–32.
Bashier, Salman H. *Ibn al-'Arabi's Barzakh: The Concept of the Limit and the Relationship between God and the World.* Albany: SUNY Press, 2012.
Batut, Jean-Pierre. *Pantocrator: "Dieu le Père tout-puissant" dans la théologie prénicéenne.* Paris: Institut des Études Augustiniennes, 2009.
Begley, Wayne Edison. "The Myth of the Taj Mahal and a New Theory of Its Symbolic Meaning." *The Art Bulletin* 61, 1 (1979): 7–37.
Behiery, Valerie. "Hilya." In *Muhammad in History, Thought, and Culture: An Encyclopedia of the Prophet of God,* edited by Coeli Fitzpatrick, Adam Walker. Santa Barbara: ABC-CLIO, 2014, 258–263.
Bellver, José. "Ascetics and Sufis." In *The Routledge handbook of Muslim Iberia,* edited by Maribel Fierro. Abingdon, Oxon – New York: Routledge, 2020, 318–343.
Benkheira, Mohammed Hocine. "Intercession." In *Dictionnaire du Quran,* edited by Mohammad Ali Amir-Moezzi. Paris: Robert Laffont, 2007.
Beránek, Ondřej and Ťupek, Pavel. *The Temptation of Graves in Salafi Islam. Iconoclasm, Destruction and Idolatry.* Edinburgh: Edinburgh University Press, 2018.
Beyazit, Deniz, et al, eds. "From West Africa to Southeast Asia: The History of Muḥammad al-Jazūlī's Dalāʾil al-Khayrāt (15th–20th centuries)," *Journal of Islamic Manuscripts* 12, 3–4 (2021): 231–34.
Bloom, Jonathan M. et al., eds. *The Minbar from the Kutubiyya Mosque.* New York: The Metropolitan Museum of Art; Madrid: Ediciones El Viso, S.A.; Rabat: Ministère des Affaires Culturelles, Royaume du Maroc, 1998.
Bowker, John Westerdale. "Intercession in The Qur'an and the Jewish Tradition." *Journal of Semitic Studies* XI, 1 (1966): 69–82.
Box, George Herbert. "The Idea of Intermediation in Jewish Theology. A Note on Memra and Shekinah." *The Jewish Quarterly Review* 23, 2 (1932): 103–119.
Boyce, Mary. "Gāh, i. Place." In *EIr.*
Brutti, Maria. "The Topic of Intercession in Second Temple Judaism: Between 2 Maccabees and 4 Ezra." In *Understanding Texts in Early Judaism. Studies on Biblical, Qumranic, Deuterocanonical and Cognate Literature in Memory of Géza Xeravits,* edited by Jozsef Zsengellér. Berlin: De Gruyter, 2022, 189–206.
Burckhardt, Titus. "The Prayer of Ibn Mashīsh." In *Mirror of the Intellect: Essays on Traditional Science and Sacred Art.* Albany: State University of New York Press, 1987, 183–192.
Burge. Stephen R. *Angels in Islam: Jalāl al-Dīn al-Suyūṭī's* al-Habāʾik fī akhbār al-malāʾik, Abingdon, Oxon: Routledge, 2012.
Bursi, Adam. *Traces of the Prophets: Relics and Sacred Spaces in Early Islam.* Edinburgh: Edinburgh University Press, 2024.
Burton-Page, John et al. "Minbar." In *EI²*.
Calvin, Jean. *Institutes of the Christian Religion,* edited by John T. McNeil, 2 vols. Louisville: Westminster John Knox Press, 2006.
Caspar, Robert. *Traité de théologie musulmane, t. I, Histoire de la pensée religieuse musulmane.* Rome: Pontificio Istituto di Studi Arabi e d'Islamistica, 1987.

Castiñeiras, Manuel. "The Baldachin-Ciborium. The shifting meanings of a restricted liturgical furnishing in Romanesque art." In *The Regional and Transregional in Romanesque Europe*, edited by J. McNeill and R. Plant, London: Routledge, 2021, 47–67.

Chapman, Marc E. "A Lutheran Response to the Theme of the Virgin Mary as Mother of God, Icon of the Church and Spiritual Mother of Intercession." In *Marian Studies* 48 (1997): 124–125.

Cheddadi, Abdesselam. "Le système du pouvoir en Islam d'après Ibn Khaldûn." In *Annales. Economies, sociétés, civilisations* 3–4 (1980): 534–550.

Chiabotti, Francesco. "Intercession." In *Muhammad in History, Thought, and Culture: An Encyclopedia of the Prophet of God*, edited by Coeli Fitzpatrick, Adam Walker. Santa Barbara: ABC-CLIO, 2014, 299–302.

Chih, Rachida, "Discussing the Sufism of the Early Modern Period. A New Historiographical Outlook on the Tariqa Muhammadiyya." In *Sufism East and West. Mystical Islam and Cross-Cultural Exchange in the Modern World*, edited by Jamal Malik and Saeed Zarrabi-Zadeh. Leiden: Brill, 2019, 104–126.

Chikhaoui, Naima, "The Minbar: Symbol of Verticality and Elevation." In *Sacred Web: A Journal of Tradition and Modernity* 14 (2004): 91–107.

Chodkiewicz, Michel. "Le modèle prophétique de la sainteté en Islam." In *Al-Masāq* 7:1 (1994): 201–226.

Chodkiewicz, Michel. "The Banner of Praise." In *Journal of the Muhyiddin Ibn Arabi Society* 21 (1997): 45–58.

Colby, Frederick S. *Narrating Muḥammad's Night Journey. Tracing the Development of the Ibn 'Abbās Ascension Discourse*, Albany: State University of New York Press, 2008.

Commins, David. *The Wahhabi mission and Saudi Arabia*, London-New York: I.B. Tauris, 2006.

Copsidas, Marina. *Le Christ Pantocrator. Présence et rencontre.* Paris: Cerf, 2009.

Cornell, Vincent J. *The Realm of the Saint: Power and Authority in Moroccan Sufism.* Austin: University of Texas Press, 1998.

Cornell, Vincent J. *The way of Abū Madyan: doctrinal and poetic works of Abū Madyan Shu'ayb ibn al-Ḥusayn al-Anṣārī (c. 509/1115–594/1198), Edited and Translated with Introduction and Notes by Vincent J. Cornell.* Cambridge: The Islamic Texts Society, 1996.

Crump, David. *Jesus the Intercessor: Prayer and Christology in Luke-Acts.* Tübingen J.C.B. Mohr (Paul Siebeck), 1992.

Dakake, Maria Massi. *The Charismatic Community: Shi'ite Identity in Early Islam.* Albany: State University of New York Press, 2007.

De La Puente, Cristina. "The Prayer Upon the Prophet Muhammad (Tasliya): a Manifestation of Islamic Religiosity." In *Medieval Encounters* 5, 1 (1999): 121–129.

Dillon, John. "Ganymede as the Logos: Traces of a Forgotten Allegorization in Philo?" In *The Classical Quarterly*, New Series, 31, 1 (1981):183–185.

Ducène, Jean-Charles. "Rites religieux et crue du Nil en Égypte Médiévale." In *Acta orientalia belgica* 23 (2010) 63–76.

Dujardin, Philippe. "Du rapport aux images religieuses à l'époque moderne : images, médiateurs et médiations." In *Bulletin du Centre de recherche du château de Versailles, Le promeneur de Versailles* (2018, http://journals.openedition.org/crcv/14787).

El-Rouayheb, Khaled. "From Ibn Hajar al-Haytami (d. 1566) to Khayr al-Din al-Alusi (d. 1899): Changing Views of Ibn Taymiyya Amongst Non-Hanbali Sunni Scholars." In *Ibn Taymiyya and His Times*, edited by Yossef Rapoport and Shahab Ahmed. Oxford: Oxford University Press, 2010, 278–279.

Elias, Jamal. "Throne of God." In *EQ*.

Ende, Werner. "Baqīʿ al-Gharqad." In *EI*³.

Ernst, Carl William. "Muhammad as the pole of existence." In *The Cambridge Companion to Muhammad*, edited by Jonathan E. Brockopp. New York: Cambridge University Press, 2010, 123–138.

Ernst, Carl William. "Sufism and Yoga according to Muhammad Ghawth." In *Refractions of Islam in India: Situating Sufism and Yoga*, New Delhi: Sage-Yodapress, 2016, 149–160.

Ernst, Carl William. *Following Muhammad: Rethinking Islam in the Contemporary World.* Chapel Hill & London: The University of North Carolina Press, 2003.

Ernst, Carl William. *Sufism. An Introduction to the Mystical Tradition of Islam.* Boulder: Shambhala, 2016.

Ess (van), Josef. *Theology and Society in the Second and Third Centuries of the Hijra, Tr. from German by John O'Kane*, 4 vols. Leiden-Boston: Brill, 2019.

Firestone, Reuven. "Shekhinah." In *EQ*.

Gardet, Louis et Anawati, Marie-Marcel (Georges Chehata). *Introduction à la théologie musulmane: Essai de théologie comparée.* Paris: Librarie Philosophique J. Vrin, 1948.

Gardet, Louis. "*2. ʿālam al-d̲j̲abarūt, ʿālam al-malakūt, ʿālam al-mit̲h̲āl.*" In Tjitze de Boer and Louis Gardet, *ʿĀlam*, *EI*².

Gardet, Louis. *Dieu et la destinée de l'homme*, Paris: Librairie Philosophique J. Vrin, 1967.

Gilliot, Claude. *Exégèse, langue et théologie en islam: L'exégèse coranique de Tabari.* Paris: Librarie Philosophique J. Vrin, 1990.

Gilsdorf, Sean. *The Favor of Friends: Intercession and Aristocratic Politics in Carolingian and Ottonian Europe.* Leiden: Brill, 2014.

Ginzberg, Louis, *Legends of The Jews, Translated from the German Manuscript by Henrietta Szold and Paul Radin*, 7 vols. Philadelphia: The Jewish Publication Society, 2003.

Goldziher, Ignaz. *Die Richtungen der islamischen Koranauslegung, An der Universität Uppsala gehaltene Olaus-Petri-Vorlesungen.* Leiden: Brill, 1920.

Goldziher, Ignaz. *Muhammedanische Studien*, 2 vols. Halle: M. Niemeyer, 1889–1890; engl. tr. *Muslim Studies*, 2 vols. Chicago: Aldine Publishing Company, 1966–1971.

Goldziher, Ignaz. *Vorlesungen über den Islam. Von Dr. Ignaz Goldziher. Zweite, umgearbeitete Auflage von Dr. Franz Babinger.* Heidelberg: Carl Winter's Universitätsbuchhandlung, 1925; engl. tr. *Introduction to Islamic Theology and Law.* Princeton: Princeton University Press, 1981.

Green, Arthur. "Shekhinah, the Virgin Mary, and the Song of Songs: Reflections on a Kabbalistic Symbol in Its Historical Context." In *Association for Jewish Studies Review* 26:1 (2002): 1–52.

Griffith, Sidney H. *Holy Spirit.* In *EQ*.

Gril, Denis. "Le corps du Prophète." In *Revue des mondes musulmans et de la Méditerranée* 113–114 (2006): 37–57.

Gril, Denis. "Le modèle prophétique du maître spirituel en islam." In *Maestro e discepolo. Temi e problemi della direzione spirituale tra VI secolo a.c. e VII secolo d.c.*, edited by Giovanni Filoramo. Piacenza: Centro di alti studi in scienze religiose di Piacenza, 2002, 345–360.

Gruber, Christiane. "Images." In *Muhammad in History, Thought, and Culture: An Encyclopedia of the Prophet of God*, edited by Coeli Fitzpatrick, Adam Walker. Santa Barbara: ABC-CLIO, 2014, 286–294.

Hamza, Feras. "Temporary Hellfire Punishment and the Making of Sunni Orthodoxy." In *Roads to Paradise: Eschatology and Concepts of the Hereafter in Islam*, Vol. 1, edited by Sebastian Günther and Todd Lawson. Leiden: Brill, 2017, 371–406.

Hamza, Feras. *To Hell and back: a study of the concepts of Hell and intercession in early Islam, PhD Thesis.* Oxford: Wolfson College, University of Oxford, 2002.

Heck, Paul L. "An Early Response to Wahhabism from Morocco: The Politics of Intercession." In *Studia Islamica* 107, 2 (2012): 235–254.

Hillar, Marian. *From Logos to Trinity: The Evolution of Religious Beliefs from Pythagoras to Tertullian.* Cambridge: Cambridge University Press, 2012.

Hoffman-Ladd, Valerie J. "Devotion to the Prophet and His Family in Egyptian Sufism." In *International Journal of Middle East Studies* 24, 4 (1992): 615–637.

Hoffman, Valerie J. "Annihilation in the Messenger of God: The Development of a Sufi Practice." *International Journal of Middle East Studies* 31, 3 (1999): 351–369.

Hoffman, Valerie J. "Intercession." In *EQ.*

Hoffman, Valerie J. *The Essentials of Ibāḍī Islam*, Syracuse-New York: Syracuse University Press, 2012.

Holmes Katz, Marion. "The Prophet Muhammad in Ritual." In *The Cambridge Companion to Muhammad*, edited by Jonathan E. Brockopp. New York: Cambridge University Press, 2010, 139–157.

Holtzman, Livnat. "al-Lālakāʾī, Abū al-Qāsim." In *EI*[3].

Hoover, Jon. *Ibn Taymiyya, Makers of the Muslim World.* London: Oneworld Academic, 2019.

Horten, Max. *Die religiöse Gedankenwelt des Volkes im heutigen Islam.* Halle: Verlag Von Max Niemeyer, 1917.

Huitema, Taede. *De voorspraak (*Shafāʿa*) in den Islam.* Leiden: Brill, 1936.

Ibrahim, Lupti. "The Place of Intercession in the Theology of al-Zamakhsharī and al-Bayḍāwī." In *Bulletin of Christian Institutes of Islamic Studies* 4 (1981): 27–35.

Iwanski, Dariusz. *The Dynamics Of Job's Intercession.* Rome: Pontifical Biblical Institute, 2006.

Jong (de), Frederick. "al-Ḳuṭb – 2. In mysticism." In *EI*[2].

Karjoo-Ravary, Ali. "Illustrating the Forms: Ibn al-ʿArabī's (d. 638/1240) Images in al-Futūḥāt al-Makkiyya." In *Visualizing Sufism: Studies on Graphic Representations in Sufi Literature (13th to 16th Century)*, ed. Giovanni Maria Martini. Leiden: Brill 2023, 51–124.

Kenna, Margaret E. "Icons in Theory and Practice: An Orthodox Christian Example." In *History of Religions* 24, 4 (1985): 345–368.

Kepnes, Steven ed. The Cambridge Companion to Jewish Theology. Cambridge: Cambridge University Press, 2020.

Kister, Meir Jacob. "Maqām Ibrāhīm: A Stone with an Inscription." *Le Muséon* 84 (1971): 477–491.

Kohler, Kaufmann and Ginzberg, Louis. "Ascension." In *Jewish Encyclopedia* 2:164–165.

Lacey (de), D.R. "Jesus as Mediator." In *Journal for the Study of the New Testament* 29 (1987): 101–121.

Lambertini, Renzo. "Sull'origine e la natura dell'intercessio tribunizia." In *Tradizione romanistica e Costituzione*, edited by Luigi Labruna. Naples: Edizioni Scientifiche Italiane, 2006, 613–632.

Lane, Andrew J. *A Traditional Muʿtazilite Qurʾān Commentary: the Kashshāf of Jār Allāh al-Zamakhsharī.* Leiden: Brill, 2006.

Lane, Edward William. *An Arabic-English Lexicon*, 8 Vols. London: Williams and Norgate, 1863–93.

Lange, Christian. "Barzakh." In *EI*[3].

Le Déaut, Roger. "Aspects de l'intercession dans le Judaïsme ancient." In *Journal for the study of Judaism* 1, 1 (1970): 35–57.

Lebreton, Jules. "The Logos." In *The Catholic Encyclopedia*, Vol. 9. New York: Robert Appleton Company, 1910 (http://www.newadvent.org/cathen/09328a.htm).

Lizzini, Olga and Pagani, Samuela, eds. "Islam." In *Angeli: Ebraismo Cristianesimo Islam*, edited by Giorgio Agamben and Emanuele Coccia. Milan: Neri Pozza Editore, 2009, 1573–2197.

Loynes, Simon P. *Revelation in the Qur'an. A Semantic Study of the Roots n-z-l and w-ḥ-y.* Leiden: Brill, 2021.

MacDonald, Duncan Black and Gardet, Louis. "al-Gh̲ayb." In *EI²*.

Madelung, Wilferd, "ʿAbd al-Jabbār B. Aḥmad." In *EIr.*

Majeed, Tehnyat. "The Chār Muḥammad Inscription, *Shafāʿa*, and the Mamluk Qubbat al-Manṣūriyya." In *Roads to Paradise: Eschatology and Concepts of the Hereafter in Islam*, edited by Sebastian Günther and Todd Lawson. Leiden: Brill, 2017, 1:1010–1032.

Marcotte, Roxanne D. "Night of Power." In *EQ.*

Marmon, Shaun E. "The Quality of Mercy: Intercession in Mamluk Society." *Studia Islamica* 87 (1998): 125–139.

Martin, Richard C. "Createdness of the Qur'ān." In *EQ.*

Mayeur-Jaouen, Catherine. "'There Is Matter for Thought': The Episode of the Night Journey and the Heavenly Ascension in the *Sīra ḥalabiyya*, at the Beginning of the Seventeenth Century." In *The Presence of the Prophet in Early Modern and Contemporary Islam: Volume 1, The Prophet Between Doctrine, Literature and Arts: Historical Legacies and Their Unfolding*, edited by Denis Gril, Stefan Reichmuth and Dilek Sarmis. Leiden: Brill, 2022, 115–150.

Mayeur[-Jaouen], Catherine. "L'intercession des saints en Islam égyptien: autour de Sayyid al-Badawī." *Annales Islamologiques* 25 (1991): 363–388.

McDermott, Martin J. *The Theology of al-Shaikh al-Mufid (d. 413–1022).* Beirut: Dar al-Mashreq, 1978.

Memon, Muhammad Umar. *Ibn Taymiyya's Struggle against Popular Religion.* The Hague – Paris: Mouton 1976.

Meri, Josef W. "Aspects of Baraka (Blessings) and Ritual Devotion among Medieval Muslims and Jews." *Medieval Encounters* 5 (1999): 46–69.

Meri, Josef W. *The Cult of Saints among Muslims and Jews in Medieval Syria.* Oxford-New York: Oxford University Press, 2002.

Milwright, Marcus. *The Dome of the Rock and its Umayyad Mosaic Inscriptions.* Edinburgh: Edinburgh University Press, 2016.

Moffitt, David M. "Jesus as Interceding High Priest and Sacrifice in Hebrews: A Response to Nicholas Moore." In *Journal for the Study of the New Testament* 42, 4 (2020): 542–552.

Moore, George Foot. "Intermediaries in Jewish Theology: Memra, Shekinah, Metatron." In *The Harvard Theological Review* 15, 1 (1922): 41–85.

Mostafa, Heba. "The Early Mosque Revisited: Introduction of the *Minbar* and *Maqṣūra.*" In *Muqarnas: An Annual on the Visual Cultures of the Islamic World* 33 (2016):1–16.

Munt, Harry. *The Holy City of Medina: Sacred Space in Early Islamic Arabia.* New York: Cambridge University Press, 2014.

Nagel, Tilman. *The History of Islamic Theology. From Muhammad to the Present.* Princeton: Markus Wiener Publishers, 2000.

O'Carroll, Michael. "Intercession, Mary's." In *Theotokos: A Theological Encyclopedia of the Blessed Virgin Mary*, edited by Michael O'Carroll. Eugene – Oregon: Wipf and Stock Publishers, 2000, 186–189.

Padwick, Constance E. *Muslim Devotions: A Study of Prayer-Manuals in Common Use*, London: S.P.C.K, 1961.

Pagani, Samuela. "Roi ou serviteur? La tentation du Prophète, ou le choix d'un modèle." In *Archives de sciences sociales des religions*, 178 (2017): 43–68.

Palmer, Paul F. "Mary in Protestant Theology and Worship." In *Theological Studies* 15, 4 (1954): 519–540.

Patrizi, Luca. "A New Wave of Iconoclasm? The Destruction of Sacred Places in the Contemporary Islamic world." In *Constructing and Contesting Holy Places in Medieval Islam and Beyond*, edited by Andreas Görke and Mattia Guidetti. Leiden: Brill, 2023, 434–465.

Patrizi, Luca. "La vénération des reliques du prophète Muḥammad en Islam entre dévotion et fondement du pouvoir." In *The Presence of the Prophet in Early Modern and Contemporary Islam, Volume 3, Prophetic Piety in Islam: History and Anthropology*, edited by Nelly Amri, Rachida Chih and Stefan Reichmuth. Leiden: Brill, 2023, 223–249.

Patrizi, Luca. "The Metaphor of the Divine Banquet and the Origin of the Notion of *Adab.*" In *Knowledge and Education in Classical Islam. Religious Learning between Continuity and Change*, edited by Sebastian Günther. Leiden: Brill, 2020, 1:539–568.

Petersen, Andrew. "Minbar." In *Dictionary of Islamic architecture*, edited by Andrew Petersen. London and New York: Routledge, 1996, 191–192.

Petrone, Michele. "'Special Features of the Prophet' (*Khaṣā'iṣ nabawiyya*) From Jurisprudence to Devotion." In *The Presence of the Prophet in Early Modern and Contemporary Islam, Volume 1, The Prophet Between Doctrine, Literature and Arts: Historical Legacies and Their Unfolding*, edited by Denis Gril, Stefan Reichmuth and Dilek Sarmis. Leiden: Brill, 2021, 197–228.

Petrone, Michele. "Prayer on the Prophet between Devotion and Scholarship." In *Oriente moderno* 102 (2022): 1–35.

Picotin, Nadège and Déléry, Claire. "Fragments d'histoire du *minbar* de Kairouan." In *The Aghlabids and their Neighbours. Art and Material Culture in Ninth-Century North Africa*, edited by Glaire D. Anderson, Corisande Fenwick, and Mariam Rosser-Owen. Leiden: Brill, 2018, 207–227.

Pinckney Stetkevych, Suzanne. *The Mantle Odes: Arabic Praise Poems to the Prophet Muhammad.* Bloomington & Indianapolis: Indiana University Press, 2010.

Plessner, Martin. "Ramaḍān." In *EI²*.

Polak, Frank H. "Theophany and Mediator: The Unfolding of a Theme in the Book of Exodus." In *The Book of Exodus*, edited by Marc Vervenne. Leuven: Leuven University Press and Peeters, 1996, 113–147.

Rahnema, Ali. *Shi'i Reformation in Iran. The Life and Theology of Shari'at Sangelaji.* Oxon-New York: Routledge, 2016.

Reynolds, Gabriel Said. "The Rise and Fall of Qadi ʿAbd al-Jabbar." In *International Journal of Middle East Studies* 37, 1 (2005), 3–18.

Riad, Eva. "Šafāʿa dans le Coran." In *Orientalia Suecana* XXX (1981): 37–62.

Rippin, Andrew. "Taṣliya." In *EI²*.

Ross Valentine, Simon. *Force and fanaticism: Wahhabism in Saudi Arabia and beyond.* London: Hurst & Company, 2015.

Rossier, François. *L'intercession entre les hommes dans la Bible hébraïque : l'intercession entre les hommes aux origines de l'intercession auprès des Dieu.* Göttingen: Universitätsverlag Freiburg Schweiz/Vandenhoeck & Ruprecht, 1996.

Rudolph, Ulrich. *Al-Māturīdī and the Development of Sunnī Theology in Samarqand.* Leiden: Brill, 2015.

Sajid, Mehdi. "Spiritual Legacy, Sufi Identity, and Mystical Knowledge in Taṣliya formulae." In *Die Welt des Islams* (2022): 1–30.

Sardar, Ziauddin. *Mecca the Sacred City.* London: Bloomsbury, 2014.

Sauvaget, Jean. *La Mosquée Omeyyade de Médine: Étude sur les origines architecturales de la mosquée et de la basilique.* Paris: Vanoest, 1947.

Scannell, Thomas. "Intercession (Mediation)." In *The Catholic Encyclopedia*, Vol. 8. New York: Robert Appleton Company, 1910 (http://www.newadvent.org/cathen/08070a.htm).

Schaff, Philip. *The Creeds of Christendom, with a History and Critical Notes: Volume III, The Evangelical Protestant Creeds, with Translations.* New York: Harper & Brothers, 1919.
Schiffman, Lawrence Harvey. "Temple, Sacrifice and Priesthood in the Epistle to the Hebrews and the Dead Sea Scrolls." In *Echoes from the Caves: Qumran and the New Testament*, edited by Florentino García Martínez. Leiden: Brill, 2009, 165–176.
Schimmel, Annemarie. *Und Muḥammad Ist Sein Prophet.* Dusseldorf/Koln: Eugen Diederichs Verlag, 1981; eng. tr. *And Muhammad Is His Messenger. The Veneration of the Prophet in Islamic Piety.* Chapel Hill and London: The University of North Carolina Press, 1985.
Schmidtke, Sabine, ed. *The Oxford Handbook of Islamic Theology.* Oxford: Oxford University Press, 2016.
Schrieke Bertram et al. "Miʿrād̲j̲." In *EI²*.
Sells, Michael. "Spirit." In *EQ.*
Shapiro, Marc B. "Maimonides' Thirteen Principles: The Last Word in Jewish Theology?" *The Torah* U-Madda *Journal* 4 (1993): 187–242.
Shboul, Ahmad. "Greek destinies among Arabs: Rumi Muslims in Arab-Islamic civilization." In *Modern Greek Studies (Australia & New Zealand)* 14 (2010): 287–304.
Sheikh, Mustapha. *Ottoman Puritanism and its Discontents: Aḥmad al-Rūmī al-Āqḥiṣārī and the Qāḍīzādelis.* Oxford: Oxford University Press, 2016.
Shoemaker, Stephen J. "The Ancient Dormition Apocrypha and the Origins of Marian Piety. Early Evidence of Marian Intercession from Late Ancient Palestine." In *Presbeia Theotokou: The Intercessory Role of Mary across Times and Places in Byzantium (4th-9th Century)*, edited by Leena Mari Peltomaa, Andreas Külzer and Pauline Allen. Wien: Verlag der Österreichische Akademie der Wissenschaften, 2015, 23–39.
Sperl, Stefan. "Al-Busiri's Burdah." In *Qasida Poetry in Islamic Asia and Africa, vol. 2, Eulogy's Bounty, Meaning's Abundance: An Anthology*, edited by Stefan Sperl and Christopher Shackle. Leiden: Brill, 1996, 388–411.
Steingass, Francis Joseph. *A comprehensive Persian-English dictionary, including the Arabic words and phrases to be met with in Persian literature, being Johnson and Richardson's Persian, Arabic, and English dictionary revised, enlarged, and entirely reconstructed.* London: Routledge & Kegan Paul Limited, 1892.
Takim, Liyakat. "Saul." In *EQ.*
Thomas Aquinas. *The Summa Theologica*, 2 vols. Chicago: William Benton Publisher, 1923.
Tor Andrae, *Die person Muhammeds in lehre und glauben seiner gemeinde*, Stockholm: Norstedt & Toner, 1917.
Tornero, Emilio. "Šafā'a. La cohesión de una sociedad." *Al-Qanṭara* XI 2 (2019): 431–454.
Tornero, Emilio. "*Sakina:* contribución a su estudio." *Al-Qanṭara* XXXIV 1 (2013): 65–87.
Tottoli, Roberto. "Origin and Use of the Term *Isrāʾīliyyāt in Muslim Literature.*" *Arabica* 46 (1999): 193–209.
Ullah, Kifayat. *Al-Kashshāf. Al-Zamakhsharī's Muʿtazilite Exegesis of the Qurʾān.* Berlin/Boston: De Gruyter, 2017.
Unterman, Alan et al. "Shekhinah." In *Encyclopaedia Judaica*, 18:440–444.
Vassiliev, Alexei. *The History of Saudi Arabia.* London: Saqi Books, 2013.
Verdier, Philippe. *Le Couronnement de la Vierge. Les origines et les premiers développements d'un thème iconographique.* Paris: Librarie Philosophique J. Vrin, 1980.
Vimercati Sanseverino, Ruggero. "Theology of Veneration of the Prophet Muḥammad. Knowledge and love in the *Shifāʾ* of al-Qāḍī ʿIyāḍ (d. 544/1149) between *ḥadīth*, philosophy and

spirituality." In *The Presence of the Prophet in Early Modern and Contemporary Islam, Volume 1, The Prophet Between Doctrine, Literature and Arts: Historical Legacies and Their Unfolding*, edited by Denis Gril, Stefan Reichmuth and Dilek Sarmis. Leiden: Brill, 2021, 153 – 196.

Watt, William Montgomery. *The Formative Period of Islamic Thought.* Edinburgh: Edinburgh University Press, 1973.

Wensinck, Arent Jan; Gimaret, Daniel; Schimmel, Annemarie. "SHAFĀʿA", in *EI*[2].

Wensinck, Arent Jan. "Ḳurbān." In *EI*[2].

Wensinck, Arent Jan. "Shafāʿa." In *The Encyclopaedia of Islam. A Dictionary of the Geography, Ethnography and Biography of the Muhammadan Peoples, edited by M. Th. Houtsma, A. J. Wensinck, H.A.R. Gibb, W. Heffening and Lévi-Provençal.* London: E.J. Brill, Leiden – Luzac & Co, 1934, Vol. IV (S-Z), 250 – 251.

Wensinck, Arent Jan. *The Muslim Creed. Its Genesis and Historical Development.* New York: Barnes & Noble, 1932.

Wheeler, Brannon. *Mecca and Eden: ritual, relics, and territory in Islam.* Chicago and London: The University of Chicago Press, 2006.

Widmer, Michael. *Moses, God, and the Dynamics of Intercessory Prayer: A Study of Exodus 32 – 34 and Numbers 13 – 14.* Tübingen: Mohr Siebeck, 2004.

Winter, Tim, ed. *The Cambridge Companion to Classical Islamic Theology.* Cambridge: Cambridge University Press, 2008.

Wolfson, Harry Austryn. *Philo: Foundations of Religious Philosophy in Judaism, Christianity, and Islam*, 2 vols. Cambridge, Massachusetts: Harvard University Press, 1962.

Wright, William. *A Grammar of the Arabic Language, translated from the German of Caspari and edited with numerous additions and corrections by W. Wright.* Cambridge: Cambridge University Press, 2009.

Zakharia, Katia. "Uways al-Qaranī, Visages d'une légende." In *Arabica* XLVI, 2 (1999): 230 – 258.

Index of Names

https://doi.org/10.1515/9783111500966-018

Index of Places

https://doi.org/10.1515/9783111500966-019

Index of Terms

https://doi.org/10.1515/9783111500966-020